The Performance of Pleasure in English
Renaissance Drama

The Performance of Pleasure in English Renaissance Drama

Ronald Huebert

Dalhousie University
and the University of King's College
Halifax, Nova Scotia

First published 2003 by
PALGRAVE MACMILLAN
Houndmills, Basingstoke, Hampshire RG21 6XS and
175 Fifth Avenue, New York, N.Y. 10010
Companies and representatives throughout the world

PALGRAVE MACMILLAN is the global academic imprint of the Palgrave Macmillan division of St. Martin's Press, LLC and of Palgrave Macmillan Ltd. Macmillan® is a registered trademark in the United States, United Kingdom and other countries. Palgrave is a registered trademark in the European Union and other countries.

ISBN 0–333–99557–0

This book is printed on paper suitable for recycling and made from fully managed and sustained forest sources.

A catalogue record for this book is available from the British Library.

Library of Congress Cataloging in Publication Data
Huebert, Ronald.
    The performance of pleasure in English Renaissance drama / by Ronald Huebert.
        p.   cm.
    Includes bibliographical references and index.
    Contents: Interpreting pleasure—Tobacco and boys : Christopher Marlowe—A shrew yet honest : Ben Jonson—The adverse body : John Marston—One wench between them : Thomas Heywood, Francis Beaumont, and John Fletcher—Impossible desire : John Webster—An art that has no name : Thomas Middleton—Endless dreams : John Ford.
    ISBN 0–333–99557–0 (hardback)
    1. English drama—Early modern and Elizabethan, 1500–1600—History and criticism.   2. English drama—17th century—History and criticism.   3. Pleasure in literature.   4. Aesthetics, Modern—16th century.   5. Aesthetics, Modern—17th century.   6. Renaissance—England.   7. Aesthetics, British.   8. Sex in literature.   I. Title.

    PR658.P57H84 2003
    822'.309353—dc21

                                                                  2003043145

10 9 8 7 6 5 4 3 2 1
12 11 10 09 08 07 06 05 04 03

Printed and bound in Great Britain by
Antony Rowe Ltd, Chippenham and Eastbourne

To Elizabeth

Contents

Bibliographical Note

The editions used for citations from English Renaissance plays are identified only once, in a separate list of *Drama Texts* at the beginning of the Bibliography. In quotations from old-spelling texts, usage of i/j, u/v, and long s is silently modernized, and a few archaic contractions are silently expanded. Extended passages of italic type – such as songs within plays – are silently altered to roman, but in all other cases italics in quotations are reproduced from the sources quoted.

Preface

This book has travelled with me for a long time. It was nourished on two separate periods of sabbatical leave, during which I was a visiting scholar at the University of California, Berkeley, and then a visiting member of Darwin College, Cambridge. Both of these homes away from home were extremely generous in providing the kinds of resources that scholarship depends on: access to vast collections of books and articles, opportunities to confer with learned and curious people from many parts of the world, and the numerous benefits of encountering intellectual and cultural practices a little different from one's own. Still, most of the support for my work has come from Dalhousie University, and from the University of King's College, where almost everything in these pages has been ventured in one way or another, in my teaching, in presentations at departmental seminars, or simply in conversation with colleagues and students. Dalhousie has also contributed in practical ways; my sojourns elsewhere have been made possible by sabbatical leave provisions, and in some cases have been supported by the university's Research Development Fund. In addition I have been the recipient of awards from the Social Sciences and Humanities Research Council of Canada; both the Leave Fellowships Programme and the Research Grants Programme have given material assistance that enabled me to explore, to think, and to write. I am grateful to all of these institutions for generously sustaining my work.

Portions of Chapter 2 and Chapter 7 have been printed previously as 'Tobacco and Boys and Marlowe', *The Sewanee Review* 92 (1984): 206–24 and 'Middleton's Nameless Art', *The Sewanee Review* 95 (1987): 591–609. An earlier version of Chapter 3 appeared as 'A Shrew Yet Honest: Manliness in Jonson', *Renaissance Drama* 15 (1984): 31–68, published by Northwestern University Press. I am grateful to the editors for permission to reprint my work here.

Friends, colleagues, and students have contributed in countless ways, at least some of which I am able to specify. For reading portions of my text as it evolved, for commenting on it, and for improving it with insight of various kinds, I would like to thank Leonard Barkan, Jennifer Brady, George Core, John Fraser, Edward Pechter, and Roy Wolper. Jonas Barish's name belongs at the head of this list, but his death has prevented me from offering appropriate thanks. John Baxter and Christina Luckyj have offered helpful commentary on segments of my work, have enriched my knowledge of what is at stake in the interpretation of Renaissance drama, have argued about questions that matter to all three of us, and have preserved our friendship over many years of working together. Ingrid Hotz-Davies read the entire text at a time when it most needed another's appraisal, and allowed me to profit from her generous critical intelligence. For many other kinds of intellectual or professional support I am grateful to Alan Andrews, Elizabeth Archibald, Melissa Furrow, Bruce Greenfield, Victor Li, Robert M. Martin, David McNeil, Brian Parker, Trevor Ross, Rowland Smith, Gary Wihl, Daniel Woolf, and Sheldon Zitner. Peter O. Clarke and Mike Malloch have given me ready access to their wit, intelligence, and healthy scepticism about merely academic writing; their conversation has been both a joy and a constant source of perspective. The former student whose hypothesis about *The Duchess of Malfi* is cited in this book (page 116) is Dorothy de Krom Kisiell. She is one of many former graduate students who have contributed to my work largely by their willingness to argue inventively about questions that bear on the interpretation of Renaissance drama. I am grateful to every student in this large group, but I can mention only a few: Roberta Barker, Rick Bowers, Christine Cornell, Marcella Bungay Stanier, Ian McAdam, Rebecca Million, Mavis Reimer, David Sullivan, and Tonny van den Broek. For expert guidance and cheerful assistance in the various stages of the publication process, I am grateful to Eleanor Birne, Paula Kennedy, Becky Mashayekh, Emily Rosser, and Barbara Slater.

The person who has given more to this project than I could ever have dared to ask is Elizabeth Edwards, my wife. This book is, as the dedication implies, profoundly and always hers.

RH

1
Interpreting Pleasure

This is a book about pleasures of many different kinds. First, and most obviously, it is about pleasure and the pursuit of pleasure as represented in the drama of some of the most interesting playwrights of the English Renaissance. Pleasure occupied a different and much more prominent place in the agenda of these playwrights than it had in the medieval drama. In the morality play, for example, the pleasures of carnal indulgence are likely to appear only under the sign of allegorical disapproval, personified as Voluptas or Wantonness. Some of this rhetoric does carry forward into the drama from Marlowe to Ford, but on the whole the register in which pleasures are represented is vastly expanded: it has obviously become possible to think of pleasure, even erotic pleasure, as something quite different from sin. Or, to pick up the same idea at the opposite end, the concept of sinfulness was no longer sufficient to describe authoritatively the diversity of pleasures known to the playwrights and their audience. The more conservative wing of the puritan movement was eager to denounce the new interest in pleasure as inherently sinful, but its spokesmen weren't the voices most listened to at the Globe, the Swan, and the Blackfriars playhouse.

As I've already implied, pleasure in Renaissance drama is represented most conspicuously and most persuasively as erotic pleasure. This appears at first glance to be a narrowing of the field of possibility, but even here the readiness to explore a wide and expanding range of experience is what makes these playwrights remarkable. There are numerous instances of fairly conventional erotic attraction, of course – erotic attraction of the kind that can be or ought to be sanctioned by marriage if the obstacles to such a resolution were to be overcome. But there are many far more problematic instances of erotic pleasure arising from socially proscribed or at least ambivalent situations: homosexual attraction, adultery, voyeurism, and incest. And there is a further willingness to explore the bodily and social pleasures associated with sexual experience: the pleasures of eating and drinking, of disguise and masquerade, of licentious poetry and enticing speech. What stands out in all of this is a new attitude towards pleasure

1

among Renaissance playwrights: an attitude that strongly endorses the notion of choice. In many cases, the first step towards ensuring that an experience will be a pleasure rather than just another obligation is to guarantee the right of participants to enter and exit as they choose. This model is of course too crude to apply to all of Renaissance drama; in the chapters that follow it will become quickly apparent that playwrights were fond of dramatizing stories and devising scenarios that would render the experience of pleasure, and the spectators' response to it, deeply perplexing and problematic. But I hope to argue that the question of choice (or consent) tends to emerge as important in even the most complicated representations of pleasure. And I believe that the value invested in the act of choosing is both a distinctive feature of Renaissance drama and one of the reasons why these plays can still matter to us as readers after the intervening four hundred years.

In commenting on sexual pleasure as represented in these texts I do make allowances for changes in social and cultural circumstances. As every reader conversant with social history, or with Shakespeare for that matter, is in some sense aware, families in 1600 were not precisely what they are today; the legal and medical professions offered advice that would not be tolerated now; religious and political institutions were built on a structure of beliefs and a system of conduct that have subsequently been discarded. For these reasons it's necessary to imagine, when reading about sex in a sixteenth or seventeenth-century context, a world with very little privacy, no reliable contraception, no divorce, and no prevailing assumptions about equality. These are striking differences, and I think they help to account for what might seem like artificial behaviour in some of the characters represented in Renaissance drama. But even after such allowances have been made, much of the semiology of sexual interaction remains quite readable four hundred years later. People tried to escape from frustrating marriages by entering into affairs that led nowhere, then as now; men exploited opportunities for extorting sexual favours from women, then as now; members of both sexes had to juggle the claims of spontaneous attraction and long-term prudence when they thought about marriage, then as now; and since so much of the great mating dance was (and is) profoundly irrational, the people who looked like the ideal couple at the outset might be hurling legal weapons and public abuse at one another in a few years' time, while the hopelessly thwarted couple who persisted might end up with an enduring relationship that nobody would have predicted. The experience of erotic pleasure is historically inflected, but there's a fundamental humanity in a great deal of Renaissance drama that allows these plays to speak to us in language that hardly seems dated and seldom needs antiquarian glosses. There's a sense in which responding to a past culture which continues to live requires genuine historical imagination, and it is this kind of negotiation with the past that my critical practice aspires to.

Although I am not constructing a work of literary history, I should point out that there is a chronological sequence along which the various plays and playwrights can be arranged. This isn't a mechanically rigid sequence, but there is an observable line of change between Marlowe (in the 1590s) and Ford (in the 1630s). Chapters 2, 3, and 4 concentrate on three versions of masculinity: homoerotic temptation/seduction in Marlowe, assertively self-contained manliness in Jonson, and satiric loathing of the (female) body in Marston. Chapters 6, 7, and 8, by contrast, offer a series of three female responses to the kinds of masculine sexual aggression or dismissiveness implied in the earlier chapters. These three responses might be described as the recognition of female nobility in Webster, the clearing of a space for female assertiveness and initiative in Middleton, and the creation of symbolic identity between female and male (most strikingly through the device of incest) in Ford. The central chapter (5) is not based on the work of a single playwright, but is rather the place where the masculine aggressions of the previous three chapters and the female responses of the next three collide in the most drastic ways: in short, it is a chapter about violence against women in two particularly revealing texts. The point of creating this structure is in part to suggest how, in the few brief decades which separate Marlowe from Ford, theatrical representation of pleasure is modified, inflected, complicated, and pushed to the limit of what most readers or spectators might want to recognize as pleasure. So although my interests are principally in critical elucidation of dramatic texts, there are inferences about historical change to be drawn from the analyses I offer; this indeed is a question which I hope to address in more detail in my Conclusion.

In appealing repeatedly to the experience of readers and spectators I have been alluding to a second kind of pleasure, namely aesthetic pleasure: not the pleasure being represented in the dramatic text, but the pleasure implicit in and arising from the representation. This kind of pleasure is a recurring theme in the chapters that follow insofar as they are concerned with the question: what is there in the artistic practice of these playwrights that provokes a pleasurable response? I should mention at once that for me aesthetic pleasure covers a disparate range of experiences, that it's perhaps more prudent to speak of aesthetic pleasures in the plural, but that it's also necessary to think of this idea in the singular for purposes of clarity and definition. In order to situate the notion of aesthetic pleasure, it might be helpful as a first step to refer to Immanuel Kant's description of aesthetic judgement:

> When the form of an object (as opposed to the matter of its representation, as sensation) is, in the mere act of reflecting upon it, without regard to any concept to be obtained from it, estimated as the ground of a pleasure

in the representation of such an Object, then this pleasure is also judged
to be combined necessarily with the representation of it....The object is
then called beautiful; and the faculty of judging by means of such a
pleasure...is called taste.[1]

Kant is here engaged in establishing what he takes to be the *disinterested*
nature of aesthetic pleasure. In order to do so he distinguishes between
aesthetic pleasure and (1) delight in the agreeable on the one hand, (2) delight
in the good on the other. Both the sensory pleasure prompted by an agreeable
glass of wine, for example, and the moral pleasure called into being by one's
admiration for an altruistic action, are 'invariably coupled with an interest in
their object' (48). You don't derive pleasure from a wine you could never
afford to drink, or from the actions (however self-sacrificing) of a person
whose objectives you find deplorable. Aesthetic pleasure, Kant argues, is not
subject to interest in either of these ways, and if he is right, then this could be
part of the explanation for the peculiar pleasures of reading and watching
Renaissance drama.

From Kant's elevated theoretical viewpoint it is much easier to tell what
aesthetic pleasure is not than what it is: the beautiful is not the agreeable, nor
the good; aesthetic pleasure, which arises from reflection on the beautiful, is
not subject to or directed by interest. In what follows I will take a far more
practical approach to the question, because for me the aesthetic pleasures of
Renaissance drama are manifold, plural, multiple, and therefore doubtless
impure in various ways. The sequence of pleasures I am about to name is
provisional, but I offer it as a point of departure. The aesthetic pleasures
I associate with Renaissance drama are the pleasure of mimesis, the pleasure
of pathos, the pleasure of discovery, the pleasure of recognition, and the
pleasure of escape.

The notion of mimesis (most often translated as imitation or representation) has a very long history. Aristotle begins the *Poetics* by underlining this
idea: 'Epic and tragic poetry, comedy too, dithyrambic poetry, and most
music composed for the flute and the lyre, can all be described in general
terms as forms of imitation or representation.' And his famous definition of
tragedy takes mimesis as a first principle: 'Tragedy, then, is a representation
of an action...'.[2] If on the surface mimesis appears to be a valuable activity
in Aristotle, this is certainly not true in Plato, where the exclusion of
poets from the ideal commonwealth hinges on suspicion of the imitative.
The real world for Plato is of course the world of the Forms, and the world
as we experience it is only an imitation of the Forms. To borrow one of
his own examples from the *Republic*, the highest level of reality for the
object we call a table is the Form of the table; any table constructed by a
carpenter, however wonderful, is but an imitation of the Form of the table;
and the image of a table created by a painter, using the carpenter's table as
his model, would be an imitation of an imitation. By analogy, what is true

of painters of tables is true of other artists as well: 'those who attempt tragic poetry', for example, 'are all altogether imitators'; and 'this business of imitation is concerned with the third remove from truth'.[3] The likelihood that truth will be distorted by the various levels of imitation is what leads Plato to expel the poets as purveyors of misleading doctrine. Subsequent treatments of the mimetic properties of art tend to require, at least implicitly, that art be truthful. Hamlet advises the players 'to hold, as 'twere, the mirror up to nature' (3.2.20–1); his metaphor implies that dramatic art, when well performed, will represent something in a truthful and accurate way.

My interest in mimesis has less to do with the requirement (however important) that art be truthful, and more with the requirement that it be pleasurable.[4] For this reason I propose a different analogy: the analogy of the game. Suppose that Renaissance drama were a game played with words, voices, bodies, stage properties, gestures, sound effects, and so on. The conventions of the various genres would then amount to the rules of the game, and its principal activities would be those of encoding and decoding, of performance and interpretation. The reader or spectator would then have an active role as a participant (on the decoding end) of the game, and the pleasure experienced would be an inevitable by-product of the activity of playing (at least if one played well). Such a model of aesthetic pleasure seems to me strikingly true for a great deal of Renaissance comedy, where the spectator is typically engaged in a contest of wit just as surely as the tricksters and gulls who populate the stage. Furthermore, the analogy of the game seems to have been part of mimetic thinking from the beginning. Plato uses it dismissively: 'imitation is a form of play, not to be taken seriously' (827). For the reader of Renaissance drama this observation combines a fundamental truth with a piece of very bad advice. Imitation is indeed a form of play that offers its yield of pleasure only to readers and spectators who are willing to play the game in earnest.

The pleasure of pathos is called into being by the scenes of cruelty, torture, and lingering death to be found everywhere in Renaissance tragedy. If we encountered such events directly, or even as mediated by news reporting, we would describe them as actions of genocide, corruption, ethnic hatred, or barbarism, and they would be merely repulsive (though of course fascinating nonetheless). But the buffer of aesthetic distance allows us to reconfigure such experience as in some sense dignified, and therefore worthy of an emotional investment that includes a special kind of pleasure.[5] When we listen to the dying words of the tragic hero, we are drawn into a structure of feeling which includes admiration for the human capacity to endure suffering; there is a pleasure that emerges even from the spectacle of degradation. Often this is a mixed pleasure, because it is mediated to us by actions of cruelty and vindictiveness we have reason to find loathsome; indeed, Aristotle's location of the effect of tragedy in a combination of 'pity and fear' (39) would seem to recognize as much. But no matter how mixed the pleasure of pathos, it is still a pleasure – all the more powerful, I believe, when it includes pity even for the damaged or demented perpetrators of the tortures we have (vicariously) been made to endure.

The pleasure of discovery is what happens when we gain access to an unfamiliar or exotic world. In a word, it is the pleasure of surprise. This may in part be an historical pleasure, in the sense that we may be surprised by the behaviours and beliefs of characters governed by convictions and conventions that we don't encounter in our own culture. But it is also an aesthetic pleasure, in the sense that our surprise is typically the answer to the 'what if' proposition offered by the playwright. Within Renaissance drama we are offered access to a world of limitless ambition: not literally the world of Renaissance expansion into hitherto unknown frontiers, but the world of absolute conquest that might follow from the assumptions on which Renaissance ambitions were based. We are able to enter a world in which female chastity is genuinely felt to be an absolute, and to imagine the consequences (for both genders) of living in such a world. Less portentously, we are invited to explore a world of carnival and appetite as expressed in language particular to the urban culture of London in the early seventeenth century. What I am calling the pleasure of discovery has an effect similar to that of the process of 'defamiliarization' as described in Russian formalist criticism. According to Victor Shklovsky, the purpose of art is to disrupt perceptions that have become virtually automatic because of habit and repetition. 'The technique of art is to make objects "unfamiliar", to make forms difficult, to increase the difficulty and length of perception because the process of perception is an aesthetic end in itself and must be prolonged.'[6] The exotic and unfamiliar elements within Renaissance drama have of course not been implanted there for the purpose of prolonging the enjoyments of twenty-first-century readers. But aesthetically they can act upon us in precisely this way; a perception that may not have been unusual in 1603 may nonetheless be a discovery and a surprise when we encounter it today.

If the pleasure of discovery is created by difference, the pleasure of recognition happens when difference is overcome. My interest here is in recognition on the part of readers and spectators, not recognition on the part of characters in the drama. There are luminous moments when, despite the historical and aesthetic distance which separates us from a particular text, we feel intuitively that it speaks a language we understand. Perhaps the effect I am describing occurs only because various preliminary and preparatory steps have been taken: readers have become familiar enough with the conventions of early modern courtship, for example, and with the hierarchical assumptions of seventeenth-century culture, and with the sometimes cryptic blank verse of a particular playwright to recognize that the characters he now brings on stage are quite genuinely in love. The intuitive leap I am postulating is easier to take in the theatre than in the study for the obvious reason that the spectator gets ample and sometimes wonderful assistance in making it from the actors and other members of the theatrical company. I am aware that some critics will find the value I place on the pleasure of recognition naive; historicists of various kinds may with some justice accuse me of treating characters in a playscript (that is, impersonations by actors based on signs recorded in a manuscript) as if they were real people with emotional lives of their own. This would be a telling critique if it could be used to show that the interpretations I offer are incompatible with (or indeed uninformed by) an awareness of how early modern culture would inflect the behaviour of the characters in question. But insofar as this line of criticism merely prohibits reference to dramatic impersonations 'as if they were real people', I am indeed guilty and happy to be. Without the 'as if' we could not read literature at all, or at least we couldn't read it with the playfulness of mind appropriate to its aesthetic dimension. The intuitive connections we find between our own lived experience and that represented in Renaissance drama may be and should be the result, not of inadequate scholarship, but of imaginative reading and creative interaction with the past.

The current mantra of the Arts and Entertainment channel on American television, 'escape the ordinary', isn't the most scholarly of sources, but it does suggest something real about aesthetic experience: one of the great aesthetic pleasures is the pleasure of escape. Here Freud's theory of jokes is of special value, because it can be read, with very little modification, as a theory of art. Indeed Freud himself suggests that joke theory and aesthetic theory are based on similar principles, though he adds, in a modest disclaimer, 'I understand too little of aesthetics to try to enlarge on this statement.'[7] In his discussion of tendentious jokes – which he subdivides into the hostile and the obscene – Freud argues that 'the joke *will evade restrictions and open sources of pleasure that have been inaccessible*' (8: 103). The joke is therefore one of the principal answers we give to the lifelong work of repression: it 'represents a rebellion against authority, a liberation from its pressure' (8: 105). The same terms would hold for a great deal of comic writing by Renaissance playwrights, insofar as it offers readers and spectators a series of often equivocal strategies for evading the stifling codes of sexual conduct implicit in much early modern writing about sex. Even satiric drama comes close to being a joke in the sense that it offers liberation from the standards of civility and courtesy; if we are all implicated in a confidence game, for example, then we are free to enjoy playing it as long as it lasts. Tragic drama, while certainly not a joke, is nonetheless an escape from the restrictions of the ordinary and therefore the source of otherwise inaccessible pleasures. In Renaissance tragedy we are often drawn into a world of erotic danger; the pleasure of watching the events of the drama unfold is then a kind of voyeurism, but a voyeurism without shame. It is a voyeurism we need to indulge, as a counterweight to authority, repression, banality. In the game played by the tragic protagonists, there is no escape from the consequences of one's actions. But in the game of mimesis, where all is provisional and our interest is by definition not at stake, we come as close as we can to the pleasure of being free.

Up to this point I have been drawing a firm distinction between pleasure as represented in Renaissance drama (erotic pleasure and its complements) and the pleasure implicit in the mode of representation (aesthetic pleasure in its various forms). In doing so I have been following in the tradition authorized by Kant and supported in various ways by subsequent modernist theory. Stephen Dedalus argues, for example, that aesthetic emotion is 'static', and quite unlike the 'kinetic' feelings, such as desire and loathing, which are brought into being by the 'pornographical or didactic' and 'therefore improper arts'. To this careful act of discrimination Stephen's companion Lynch has a ready reply: 'You say that art must not excite desire, said Lynch. I told you one day I wrote my name in pencil on the backside to the Venus of Praxiteles in the Museum. Was that not desire?'[8] The point Lynch is making here is that the borderline between the aesthetic and the erotic is in practice permeable and easy to transgress. That doesn't mean, of course, that the boundary is meaningless, though it does imply that erotic pleasure may have an influence on aesthetic pleasure, and vice versa.

I draw attention to this question because, in the chapters that follow, the erotic and the aesthetic will not be as rigidly separated as the theoretical distinction between them might imply. Indeed, I am particularly interested in the interweaving of these two strands of pleasure – in the give and take between the two that frequently arises from the interpretation of Renaissance drama. This interweaving is greatly fostered, I believe, by the theatrical environment itself, where both erotic and aesthetic pleasures are very much on display. The fact that women's parts on the English stage were played by male actors in drag doesn't refute this assumption, and may indeed augment it. In the English Renaissance theatre, erotic pleasure was necessarily a performance, and therefore called attention to itself by means of various self-conscious strategies that wouldn't be appropriate under more 'realistic' or 'naturalistic' conditions. If the attacks on the theatre by its many puritan opponents are evidence of anything beyond their own hostility, then they would suggest that the theatre was a highly eroticized zone of experience, and that boy actors contributed to this cultural effect.[9]

So the boundary between erotic pleasure and aesthetic pleasure needn't be thought of as absolute, and in Renaissance drama the distinction may be especially precarious. Yes, the drama represents sexual pleasure, but one of the conditions for the completion of this process is the ability of the spectator to experience sexual pleasure in the first place. My argument doesn't require that *direct* sexual communication (such as arousal) be going on in the theatre; this will seldom be the case, and it will never be the whole point. But my argument does presuppose that Renaissance drama is often addressing itself to the sexual awareness of the spectators, and is thus including receptivity to sexual pleasure as part of the representational (and hence aesthetic) experience. Indeed, I will be implicitly arguing throughout this book that without erotic pleasure and its many inflexions, the experience of reading or watching a great many Renaissance plays would be virtually empty.

Two questions might be expected at this point. First, why pleasure as a critical idea? Secondly, why not include Shakespeare in a study of Renaissance drama? Since these are quite separate questions, I will answer them one at a time. But I bring them together here because my answers to both of them will help to situate my own critical practice in relation to the dominant formations within Renaissance studies during the past two decades.

Arguments about pleasure tend to polarize rather decisively into two opposing positions: the hedonistic and the moralistic. The first of these is characterized by the view that pleasure is the good; the second by the view that the good is something over and above pleasure (virtue, justice, and so on) against which the value of pleasure must be assessed. Both positions are already present in Plato, though the second is gradually given more authority at the expense of the first.[10] In the *Phaedrus* Plato has Socrates distinguish as follows between 'two sorts of ruling or guiding principle' for human behaviour: 'One is an innate desire for pleasure, the other an acquired judgment that aims at what is best' (485). A severe separation then emerges between two kinds of pleasure: that of the senses, often referred to as *mere* pleasure, and said to be indistinguishable from the pleasure experienced by animals; and that of the soul, true spiritual joy, that in moments of transcendence can be apprehended as 'a pleasure that is sweet beyond compare' (498). This division was easily adapted by Christian teaching, in which the pleasures of this world are held to be illusory, and well worth renouncing in favour of the far greater bliss of eternal union with God. In the parable of the Sower, for example, the seed which fell among thorns alludes to 'they, which, when they have heard, go forth, and are choked with cares and riches and pleasures of this life' (Luke 8.14) and are therefore unable to wait for the genuine reward which comes only to those who 'keep' the word and 'bring forth fruit with patience' (8.15). In both classical and Christian teaching there is powerful resistance to pleasure in itself in the name of some higher good.

The distinction between hedonism and moralism is, according to Steven Connor, just as pronounced in articulations of aesthetic theory since Kant; these tend to be 'strictly bifurcated', Connor argues, 'between the disapproval of pleasure on the one hand and the assertion that pleasure is all on the other'.[11] In practice this bifurcation too turns out to be less than absolute, as

Connor's analysis shows, because moralists are likely to condemn immediate gratification in the name of some delayed reward which is held to yield pleasure of a higher kind, and hedonists are likely to associate what they believe to be genuine pleasures with the good while dismissing lower levels of gratification as unworthy. Both positions are therefore caught in the same bind as the classical and Christian precedents they have inherited. I mention this problem because it seems to me of great intellectual interest, and because I want to situate my own position in relation to it. My objective is to be neither a hedonist nor a moralist. I do not believe that pleasure is *the* good, nor do I believe that pleasure is worthless. I do believe that pleasure is *a* good, and that a wise interpretation of pleasure in literary texts and in other fields of human endeavour will resist the temptation to translate pleasure into some other, more easily negotiated currency. Furthermore, I believe that pleasure is a *constitutive* good: that without access to pleasure, human beings are less capable of working towards other desirable ends (such as generosity, for example, or justice or truth) than they can be if their experience includes and is open to pleasure. Human culture is in many ways dependent upon pleasure, and that in itself is a powerful argument for attempting an interpretation of how and why it affects us.

What I've just declared about my own position will help to explain why I don't find the treatment of pleasure in contemporary critical discourse at all satisfactory. I'm referring in particular to the critical orientations known as new historicism and cultural materialism, represented in the discussion which follows by Stephen Greenblatt and Catherine Belsey.

To read Stephen Greenblatt's books is to be dazzled by the performance of a virtuoso: the breadth of his scholarship, the subtlety of his critical intelligence, the lucidity of his writing, and the originality of his thinking have attracted widespread and well-deserved praise. But Greenblatt's agenda – the exposure of the ways in which power is embedded in early modern literature and discourse – has been developed and maintained at a price. Feminist scholars have noted, for example, that the treatment of gender in new historicist writing has tended to reproduce 'the same old master plot' in which 'talented middle-class men'[12] seek affirmation within an articulated structure that always leads to a patriarchal authority figure: the patron, the monarch, or God. Women, if they enter this paradigm at all, are consigned pretty securely to the margins.

The men in Greenblatt's texts are preoccupied with travel, conquest, religion, language, status, and politics. If they think about sex at all, it is in a supplementary way. The most obvious exception to this rule is 'Friction and Fiction', the essay in which Greenblatt sets out to explore the sexual energies implicit in Shakespearean comedy. Even here, it seems to me, the thickly layered scholarship helps him avoid rather than confront his proposed subject. Having raised the question of sexual pleasure, for example, Greenblatt makes it at once into a scholarly exercise: 'There is an elaborate medical literature on the purpose of erotic pleasure – as that which enables men to overcome their natural revulsion at the defectiveness of women; that which enables women to overcome their natural reluctance to endure the pain and put their lives at risk in childbearing; that which compensates for the Fall of Man.'[13] The account which follows is, as always in Greenblatt, ingenious and witty. But the intellectual yield in this case strikes me as remarkably impoverished. The governing metaphor of this essay, in which sexual interaction is rendered as friction, seems to me yet another strategy for minimizing the claim that pleasure might make on our critical attention.

Catherine Belsey's reading of Renaissance culture could with some justice be taken as a feminist corrective to Greenblatt's. Belsey too is interested in showing the degree to which texts, including the most canonical and most literary texts of the Renaissance, are imbricated within structures of authority. But she is insistently concerned with the placement of women within these structures. *The Subject of Tragedy*, for example, is divided into two nearly symmetrical movements, Part I: Man, and Part II: Woman. Belsey is clearly redressing an imbalance, and in the process of doing so she gives special attention to those textual and historical moments in which women offer resistance of various kinds to the patriarchal ideology which seeks to enlist their acquiescence. To Joan Kelly-Gadol's famous question – Did women have a Renaissance?[14] – Belsey is offering a guardedly optimistic reply. They weren't going on voyages of discovery, they weren't acting in Shakespeare's plays, but the textual traces that survive suggest that women were the beneficiaries of an emergent subjectivity: 'Loving partners, specialists in domesticity, nurturing, caring mothers, they progressively became autonomous, unified, knowing authors of their own choices.'[15] The persuasiveness of Belsey's argument depends, in large measure, on her practice of listening to women's voices of resistance and protest. It would be fair to say that her critical procedures are unrelentingly adversarial, and that the relations between the sexes, in her narrative, are therefore largely hostile. She may catch a flicker of mutual pleasure in the 'intimate, affectionate and playful' behaviour of lovers (198). But such moments are of no value in the long run, in Belsey's critique, because they merely serve the interests of an emergent liberal humanism; thus, 'the affective ideal which is so glowingly defined' in scenes of erotic pleasure 'collapses into the sad history of collaboration between liberalism and sexism which defines the western family from the seventeenth century to the present' (199–200). Beware of sexual pleasure, especially if you're a woman, because it will only lead to a servitude which is no less degrading because it appears to be voluntary.

Belsey's more recent books, *Desire* and *Shakespeare and the Loss of Eden*, are also works of dissatisfaction, though the object of her aversion is no longer liberal humanism itself so much as its cultural residues, specifically true love and the nuclear family. 'Desire' is most certainly a good thing in Belsey's critical agenda, but only if it is sharply distinguished from pleasure: 'Desire is thrilling, terrifying, euphoric, but it has no necessary connection with pleasure.' Indeed, Belsey positions desire as something very close to the locus of transcendent meaning: 'Desire subsists both within and beyond the realm of the pleasure principle; it cannot be contained by the stable, institutional, public *legality* which is marriage. On the contrary, desire, which is absolute, *knows no law*.'[16] The paradigm of desire to which Belsey offers her allegiance has little room for pleasure, either erotic or aesthetic. In the wordplay of Shakespeare's comedies she does find enjoyment; *Love's Labour's Lost*, for example, 'teases and tantalizes, offering its audience an experience that in some ways resembles the pleasure of seduction itself'.[17] But this is an uncharacteristic admission, and it is quickly subordinated to the larger purpose of discovering the shaky foundations on which the nuclear family is built. The sexual tensions and anxieties of *Cymbeline*, for Belsey, demonstrate that 'prohibition, sin and suffering turn out to inhabit a world of pleasure and delight' (68). This is a far more typical moment in Belsey's criticism; ultimately hers is a moralistic take on pleasure: a negative evaluation based on the assumed complicity of pleasure in the 'sad history' of bourgeois liberalism, and the failure of pleasure to measure up to the 'absolute' she claims to have found in desire.

The dismissive attitude towards pleasure in these two highly influential critics is traceable, in part, to the teachings of their acknowledged mentors: Michel Foucault in the case of Greenblatt, Jacques Lacan in the case of Belsey.[18] In *The History of Sexuality* Foucault offers a series of metaphors which purport to explain the ways in which pleasure and power can be seen to collaborate in the discursive practices of European society since the seventeenth century. He speaks of the pleasure derived from the regime of sexual surveillance, both by the agents of control and by its fugitives. He speaks of 'the power that lets itself be invaded by the pleasure it is pursuing; and opposite it, power asserting itself in the pleasure of showing off, scandalizing, or resisting'. These complementary tensions, he claims, 'have traced around bodies and sexes, not boundaries to be crossed, but *perpetual spirals of power and pleasure*'.[19] The metaphor of the spiral would seem to suggest an equivalence of power and pleasure in Foucault's scheme, but I do not think such a conclusion would be consistent either with the rhetoric of this passage or with the direction of Foucault's thinking as a whole. Notice that, even when blended into a spiral, power is the aggressor and pleasure is the object of pursuit. Power 'lets itself be invaded by' pleasure; and pleasure, as soon as it begins 'asserting itself', becomes a form of power. The point is that, in the game as Foucault sets it up, and as it resurfaces in new historicist thinking, power is always going to win.[20] That's why Greenblatt's reference to erotic pleasure signals an immediate concern with the discourses that managed such pleasure and converted it to various ideological uses. When power is what really matters in any context, pleasure is going to be no more than a useful illusion.

If pleasure enters the field of vision only under the sign of power in Foucault's thinking, in Lacan it enters only under the sign of pathology. Perhaps this is inevitable in psychoanalytic theory; it's only fair to point out that Freud's most comprehensive treatment of the subject is called *Beyond the Pleasure Principle*, and that what he finds in this beyond is the death instinct. Still, Freud is an eloquent exponent of 'the dominance of the pleasure principle in mental life' (18: 9), he maintains the importance of the pleasure principle even in its accommodations to the reality principle, and he recognizes the special role of the pleasure principle in artistic production.[21]

In Lacan's system pleasure plays a far less conspicuous and indeed much diminished role: 'Pleasure limits the scope of human possibility – the pleasure principle is a principle of homeostasis. Desire, on the other hand, finds its boundary, its strict relation, its limit, and it is in the relation to this limit that it is sustained as such, crossing the threshold imposed by the pleasure principle.'[22] This may look at first blush like a careful distinction between pleasure and desire, but I think it is more than that: it is a relegation of pleasure and a promotion of desire. Pleasure in Lacan sounds like merely passive contentment, while it is desire that motivates the strivings of humankind. The same objective of demoting pleasure seems to lie behind Lacan's investment in '*jouissance*', a word tirelessly glossed by translators as untranslatable because it refers (in French) both to joy and to orgasm. If pleasure is no more than contented stasis, then it is necessary to invent a category which rises above it, and this Lacan does by announcing that 'there is a *jouissance* beyond the pleasure principle' (184). Lacan's system is of course far more complicated than this, but my purpose here is only to point out that one of the many ways in which he takes his distance from *his* great mentor, Freud, is in the relegation of pleasure to a much lower order of significance.

This relegation is then echoed in the passages by Belsey which I quoted earlier. It is attached directly to *her* mentor in assertions such as this one: 'Lacan has nothing but contempt for the view that true love leading to happy marriage is the project of desire.'[23] Yes, it is true that desire is a comprehensive principle of lack in the Lacanian structure, and hence a signifier of the insatiable. But the contempt I hear is in Belsey's voice, at least as much as in Lacan's. It is a contempt that makes her a powerful polemical adversary, but at a price I think we should be reluctant to pay.

I have selected Greenblatt and Belsey as exemplars of recent critical practice partly because their work has been widely acclaimed and extremely influential. But similar objections might be legitimately raised about the work of many scholars who align themselves either with new historicism or with cultural materialism or with both. Typically there is very little acknowledgement of pleasure in these texts, and such acknowledgement as there is happens virtually under erasure. I offer one further example of this pattern, namely Jean E. Howard's admirable study of theatrical and antitheatrical rhetoric, *The Stage and Social Struggle in Early Modern England*. Howard sees 'the Renaissance public theater as a vehicle for ideological contestation and social change',[24] a view that all readers of the drama are likely to share in varying degrees. But in her eagerness to discover and interpret the ideological assumptions being played out, she very nearly forgets what brought the spectators into the theatre to begin with. Very nearly, but not quite: 'those who came to the theaters did so as spectators and auditors, not as readers; they took their theatrical pleasure in huge public buildings, not in solitary chambers' (13). Here is Howard's first reference to the pleasure of playgoing, but the pleasure itself is not what interests her. Early modern spectators apparently 'took' their pleasure in much the same way as they might have taken tobacco; in much the same way as eighteenth-century gallants took coffee, that is, or Victorian wage earners took gin. I don't think this is a distortion of Howard's emphasis; elsewhere she refers to the theatres as 'the new commercial pleasure palaces' (30), a phrase that belittles pleasure by making it a virtual side-effect of commerce and a false aspirant to regal authority. Howard admits that 'Shakespeare openly espoused an aesthetic of pleasure-giving', but having made this admission she hastens to cancel it in her very next sentence: 'This hardly meant, however, that the plays did not perform the work of ideology' (48). When the frivolous aesthetic and the serious work of the theatre are juxtaposed in this way, it's easy to see which of the two really matters to the critic. If pleasure is never a topic of real interest in Howard's critique, sometimes it's a downright nuisance. The female spectator, for instance, might indeed have felt 'the pleasure of aligning with the wit' of Jonson's *Epicoene*, but if she did, 'this is certainly not a "progressive" subject position for women to occupy' (109). I have described Howard's book as admirable, which I believe it to be; and in fact I agree with her about the misogyny of *Epicoene*, as my own discussion of this play in Chapter 3 will confirm. But I am concerned here with the dismissive and unreflective take on the question of pleasure, both in Howard's work and in the critical environment of the last twenty years.

I don't wish to imply either that all new-historicist and feminist critics have been hostile to the idea of pleasure, or that my own practice as a writer and thinker has been immune to the influence of these dominant formations. The first assumption would be simply untrue, the second both untrue and ingenuous. Thomas Cartelli, for example, is a critic who combines a new-historicist commitment to cultural enquiry with a declared interest in the aesthetic gratifications of theatre. 'What we need instead of a critical perspective premised on disapproval and denial', Cartelli writes, 'is a way of understanding why such plays exerted so strong an appeal on their playgoing public.'[25] A comparable position within feminist criticism might with some justice be attributed to Celia R. Daileader, whose clever and at (appropriate) times hilarious interpretations of offstage sex in Renaissance drama are at some level explorations of 'the mystery of female sexual pleasure'.[26] I am happy to join forces with both of these critics, as my subsequent references to their works will show. The critical environment which I have been describing, however, has in general been far less receptive to pleasure and the interpretation of pleasure than these two writers have shown themselves to be.

What then of *The Pleasure of the Text* by Roland Barthes? Here is a book that ought to point the way towards some of the critical explorations that have been declared off-limits by the orthodoxies of the recent past. And indeed it does so, in part by observing exactly the kind of imbalance I have been describing. 'We are always being told about Desire', Barthes writes, 'never about Pleasure; Desire has an epistemic dignity, Pleasure does not. It seems that (our) society refuses (and ends up by ignoring) bliss to such a point that it can produce only epistemologies of the law (and of its contestation), never of its absence, or better still: of its nullity.'[27] Barthes is opening up a space for the discussion of pleasure, and it is clearly an aesthetic space that he wants to liberate. He resists the 'minor mythology' that would identify pleasure as 'a rightist notion' (22), namely, the argument that a critical reading which positions itself as a-political is necessarily serving the interests of the status quo. 'The pleasure of the text does not prefer one ideology to another', he declares; '*However:* this impertinence does not proceed from liberalism but from perversion' (31). This is a cryptic utterance that deserves explanation. The point Barthes is making, I believe, is that aesthetic pleasure precedes and (at least while one is absorbed in reading) disarms the judgements one might otherwise wish to make. And unless this playfulness, this receptive alacrity, is given its opportunity to function, an aesthetic reading will be impossible.

It should be noted that Barthes sees himself defending not only 'pleasure' but also 'bliss', and that the French original of this second key word is once again *jouissance*.[28] It would appear that Barthes is here responding to Lacan, though it is difficult to know exactly how. At times he seems, like Lacan, to be clearly privileging bliss over pleasure, as in this description of two kinds of text:

> Text of pleasure: the text that contents, fills, grants euphoria; the text that comes from culture and does not break with it, is linked to a *comfortable* practice of reading. Text of bliss: the text that imposes a state of loss, the text that discomforts (perhaps to the point of a certain boredom), unsettles the reader's historical, cultural, psychological assumptions, the consistency of his tastes, values, memories, brings to a crisis his relation with language. (14)

Elsewhere he associates pleasure with the experience of feeling at home within a literary tradition, and bliss (by contrast) 'only with the *absolutely new*' (40). Would it be fair to conclude, then, that even for Barthes pleasure is not enough? Perhaps. But I am inclined to the view that there is a slippage of sorts between the two categories: that bliss is indeed a particularly focused and disruptive kind of pleasure, but a pleasure nonetheless.

The Pleasure of the Text has not cast a prominent shadow across the subsequent history of criticism. The reasons for its relative neglect can be suggested by referring to Fredric Jameson's critique in 'Pleasure: a Political Issue'. In rhetorical gestures that reveal his obvious distaste for the object under scrutiny, Jameson calls Barthes' book 'that pamphlet', 'that influential, fragmentary statement'.[29] True, *The Pleasure of the Text* is a playfully arranged series of *aperçus* rather than a fully articulated system, but I think Jameson makes this point with scarcely controlled malice. His view of Barthes is motivated by a need 'to evade the complacencies of hedonism' (2: 74), and for this reason he reinscribes *The Pleasure of the Text* as a 'lesson' which reads as follows: 'the proper political use of pleasure must always be *allegorical* in the sense spelled out above: the thematizing of a particular pleasure as a political issue' (2: 73). This may indeed be Jameson's view, but I doubt that it was ever held by Barthes. In his anxiety to escape hedonism, Jameson has taken refuge in moralism: in exactly the Left puritanism that Barthes is seeking to transcend.

But there are signs of change – signs that pleasure may indeed be re-entering the realm of the permissible in our critical thinking and discourse. Among these is Wendy Steiner's defence of aesthetic pleasure in contemporary art and culture against the various exponents of official or unofficial censorship: 'the experts in the Mapplethorpe trial, the Islamic fundamentalists who could not tolerate Rushdie's wicked fun, the feminists who fear pornography's "rape" and the cinema's fetishism, and the Marxists who denounce beauty as co-optation'.[30] Steiner's defence is made in the name of an aesthetics which finds value in the 'virtuality' of art (a postmodern synonym for mimesis, I suspect) and the pleasure that arises from experiencing it. Another of the signs of change is Stanley Corngold's brief on behalf of 'complex pleasure', a phenomenon he believes to be essential to the experience of literature itself. Such pleasure arises, Corngold argues, from 'a distinctive sort of disclosure'[31] available in literary experience – a disclosure in which our emotional capacities and rational faculties are collaboratively involved. 'One of my concerns', he writes, 'is to reinsert into the forms of literary perception this neglected component – pleasure – in claiming that pleasure is the spur to interpretation' (12). Without the incentive of pleasure, the work of interpretation would in a sense be hollow, and certainly incomplete. There is a comparable concern, though a different set of metaphors, in Roger Kuin's call for 'a relevant relation of pleasure'[32] between ourselves as readers and the early modern texts we are seeking to interpret. For Kuin, criticism is a performance art in which two texts (the one being read and the one doing the reading) are 'accomplished' perhaps not simultaneously but certainly in partnership: 'Criticism is an art of thinking (in counterpoint with) a text. Its first and simplest pleasure, then, is that of participating...in the skill of a good performance and the individuality of the performer. Of feeling the touch, the brush, the breath of the performer's mind in the triple bond between him, the text, and yourself' (22). While the details of my agenda aren't identical with those of any of the three writers just quoted, I certainly do share with all of them a belief that the value of pleasure needs to be recovered; and like them I hope that my own critical performances, in the chapters that follow, will participate in such a recovery. Pleasure may not be *the* good, but it is what we hope to find in the virtuality of art, in the disclosures of literary experience, and in the performance of critical interpretation.

This is not a book about Shakespeare. In a sense this is simply a matter of choice, but there are good reasons for making such a decision. First of all, Shakespeare's unchallenged position as the central figure within Renaissance studies has inevitably marginalized many of the playwrights who, in the sixteenth and seventeenth centuries, were energetic presences in the theatrical culture of London and serious competitors for a share of the spectators' attention. As critics and scholars are observing with increased frequency and (I would hope) anxiety, the nominal commitment to diversity in current critical practice, the legitimate concern for the voices of the 'other' in its many forms, has in fact done nothing to challenge the hegemonic prestige of Shakespeare.[33] The reasons for this anomalous state of affairs are no doubt complicated, and have a great deal to do with institutional pressures and market forces of various kinds. Shakespeare's name is a virtual guarantee that students will enrol in large numbers in courses that bear his imprimatur, that spectators will travel many miles to see productions at one or another of the festivals flying his flag, that scholars will attend conference sessions devoted to interpreting his plays; and the by-product of all this Shakespearean activity, of course, is that academic deans and editors of journals and publishers of scholarly books and, for that matter, taxpaying members of the public are more likely to confer value upon a work that has the name of Shakespeare attached to it. In his review article of books published in the field of Renaissance drama in 1995, James Shapiro takes note of this state of affairs and describes some of its consequences. The concentration of attention on Shakespeare has ensured that 'the canon of plays that we pass on to the next generation is smaller than the one we ourselves inherited', Shapiro claims. 'Scholars looking back at our cultural moment a half-century from now may well regard us as the generation that successfully killed off the study of Shakespeare's fellow dramatists.'[34]

I am not comfortable with this situation; indeed, my book is in one sense a minority report in which I am implicitly arguing that plays by Marston, Webster, Middleton, and Ford deserve the kind of critical attention that is routinely given to Shakespeare. I would like my position here to be understood not as discharging an obligation, but as offering a new and special invitation. What matters about the playwrights I am discussing here is not that we *ought* to study them, but that there are pleasures of many kinds to be discovered in reading them, and that these pleasures are often not the same as those to be found in Shakespeare.

You could argue that I might have included at least a chapter on Shakespeare, perhaps focusing on a few plays that interrogate the experience of pleasure. *Twelfth Night* ('Dost thou think because thou art virtuous there shall be no more cakes and ale?' [2.3.107–8]) and *Anthony and Cleopatra* ('I'th'East my pleasure lies' [2.3.39]) would be pretty obvious candidates for inclusion, and I have no doubt that the results of such an enquiry could be of genuine critical interest. You could argue further that any account of pleasure in Renaissance drama is incomplete without some systematic discussion of Shakespeare. These are legitimate concerns, but I have chosen to exclude Shakespeare nonetheless. Shakespeare's cultural prestige is such that the moment you decide to include him, he has a tendency to take over the agenda. Even a chapter on Shakespeare would quickly and inadvertently become the norm against which the rest of my book would then be read. The attempt to be comprehensive (by including Shakespeare) would in that case backfire: it would probably mean that Marston or Ford would have to be cut to make room for Shakespeare, or at the very least that the less familiar playwrights would come to occupy a diminished place in the shadow of their universally admired competitor. That this is no idle fear can be inferred from the way in which the balance is struck in recent books that lay claim to some of the same territory I am offering to explore.[35] Without Shakespeare I can't claim to have written a comprehensive book, but this has not been my objective in any case. I do claim to have written a diversified and suggestive book, and I believe these goals have been achieved partly because of the decision to write systematically, for once, about playwrights who aren't in the centre of the cultural nomenclature.

None of this should be taken as an expression of aversion to Shakespeare, nor as a denial of my own complicity in the practices of teaching, spectatorship, and scholarship that continue to thrive under his patronage. Nor should it be taken as a self-imposed prohibition; I have already referred to three of Shakespeare's plays, and will continue to make such references in the pages that follow. The one safe assumption to make about readers of this book is that all of them will be familiar with Shakespeare, and for this reason quotations from and references to his plays are often a useful way of suggesting the dimensions of a critical problem. But the usual proportions in the text that follows will be reversed: Shakespeare at the margins, everyone else in the centre. Such an inversion is strategically necessary if I hope to carry out my main purpose, that is, to explore critically the diversity of pleasures in the drama from Marlowe to Ford.

In the critical discussions that follow I try to respect as much as possible and to respond as precisely as I can to a broad range of theatrical texts and to the specific textures of thought and feeling encoded in them. That is the principal reason for dividing my subject (with one exception) into chapters focusing on individual playwrights. What counts as pleasure in Marlowe is radically unlike Jonson's pleasure, or Marston's, and the differences need to be spelled out in detail before meaningful comparisons can be made. Even within the work of a single playwright there can be strategic realignments, fundamental changes, or even contradictions, and part of my critical agenda is to create a map of such fissures and discontinuities. My method for doing so is to select, within the work of each playwright, those texts that explore the question of pleasure in particularly interesting ways, and to comment at some length on these texts. Other works by a particular author (Jonson's poetry and critical writing, for example, or Marston's satires) may be alluded to or even cited if they help to advance a particular argument, but my critical practice as a whole can be described as a phenomenology of pleasure (especially erotic pleasure) in those authors and texts which I've chosen to represent the diversity and special energy of Renaissance drama.

The decision to arrange this book into chapters on individual playwrights should therefore not be misunderstood as taking the road of least resistance. Indeed, it could be more accurately described as itself an act of resistance to a prevailing orthodoxy in which the agency of a particular author is of little or no account within a system of discourse or a cultural history that seems to write and rewrite itself with very little help from personal agents. The mistrust of authors as agents in current critical practice is traceable in part to the influence of Foucault's proposal that the notion of an individual author with personal characteristics and habits of mind be replaced by the 'author function', an entirely impersonal 'mode of existence, circulation, and functioning of certain discourses within a society'.[36] This may have been a good move, and even a necessary one, within the kind of socio/historical critique that preoccupied Foucault. But it is not a step that literary critics should be eager to follow, at least not if the creative energies embodied in a particular text are of any concern to them.

Foucault's position is of course itself a response to a cunning and playful essay by Barthes, 'The Death of the Author'.[37] Barthes is concerned with defining what he calls 'the modern scriptor' (145), a figure who lacks a 'voice' and who produces a text which is not so much a personal statement as a montage, 'a tissue of quotations drawn from innumerable centers of culture' (146). But Barthes makes it clear that this figure is a product of modernist anxiety and aesthetic practice, that indeed the 'scriptor' is the descendant of a far more independent author for whom the prospect of an authentic voice was indeed a desirable goal. Still, the precise differences of emphasis between Barthes and Foucault are not at issue here, so much as the suppression of the author as agent in much subsequent critical writing.

Two examples will suffice. Jeffrey Masten, in *Textual Intercourse: Collaboration, Authorship, and Sexualities in Renaissance Drama*, quotes Foucault on the opening page of Chapter 1 and then cites a great deal of appropriate scholarly evidence to support his claims that collaboration was more frequently practised than single authorship by Renaissance playwrights, that a great many plays were performed without any notice of authorship, that performance by a theatrical company was in itself an act of collaboration, and so on. Such evidence leads to the quick inference that 'collaborative dramatic texts from this period thus strikingly denaturalize the author–text–reader continuum assumed in later methodologies of interpretation'.[38] Thus liberated, Masten is able to write with great sensitivity and wit about some of the plays attributed to Beaumont and Fletcher, and some of the plays (notably *The Two Noble Kinsmen*) in which Shakespeare had a collaborative hand. Masten does acknowledge that printed playscripts bear the marks of individual authorship with increasing frequency in the early decades of the seventeenth century, that Ben Jonson makes a comprehensive claim to single authorship of theatrical texts by publishing his plays as *Workes* (1616), that in short the playwright as author is an emergent category in the period about which he is writing. But he doesn't approve of this development, and therefore resists it with what would seem to be desperate rhetorical strategies: 'it is important not to see the construction of dramatic authorship in the early seventeenth century as anything resembling a *fait accompli*', he writes; 'authorship continued to be negotiated in relation to collaboration' (120–1). When positive evidence is cancelled and reinscribed in this way, it is inevitable that the critic will reach the end of his work with precisely the same idea he had at the outset.

In a book which is itself a work of collaboration, Scott McMillan and Sally-Beth MacLean take as their subject not the works of individual playwrights but the collective work of a single theatrical company, the Queen's Men, over the two decades of its existence (1583–1603). The rationale for doing so is the entirely plausible contention that 'this was an actors' theatre';[39] that is, playscripts were produced in order to promote the quite specific professional and commercial objectives of an entertainment industry in which actors, not script writers, were the dominant figures. This point of departure allows for detailed scholarly enquiry into the composition, touring schedule, and repertoire of a theatrical company that was once the biggest draw in England; it allows for learned commentary on the stylistic preferences of the company, and on the practice of doubling which enabled a company of fourteen actors to produce plays with two or three times as many roles. What it doesn't allow for is the critical interpretation of specific plays. Indeed, the very point at which this prospect suggests itself most forcefully is also the moment when McMillan and MacLean decline the invitation. Having analysed at length the casting requirements and the need for doubling in Peele's *The Old Wives Tale*, they observe that 'the entire play can be read (and produced) as a thematization of this idea [of doubling]'. But instead of offering such a reading, they announce a hasty exit from critical discussion with the gestural observation that 'this is not the place to elaborate on an interpretation' (112). Perhaps not, but only because the terms of their enquiry have been set up in advance to privilege the collective industry of a theatrical company at the expense of whatever achievements an individual playwright might bring into being.

McMillan and MacLean are willing to concede that the Queen's Men were not the wave of the future, that indeed their practices were traditional and conservative, and that they quickly lost their pre-eminence as soon as rival companies could offer plays by such strikingly individual playwrights as Marlowe (in the case of the Lord Admiral's Men) and Shakespeare (in the case of the Lord Chamberlain's). They justify their enquiry by remarking, quite appropriately, that a rich understanding of history includes knowledge not only of the forces and practices that prevailed, but also of those that were superseded. And indeed it is on these terms, as an admirably researched account of a particular moment in English theatrical history, that theirs is an entirely admirable book.

But the inference to be drawn, from the evidence cited by Masten as well as by McMillan and MacLean, and from a great deal of early modern writing for and about the theatre, is that individual playwrights and their distinctive voices did matter a great deal, to the playwrights themselves, to the theatre companies, and to the spectators who paid for admission. When Marlowe burst upon the theatre scene with *Tamburlaine the Great*, Part 1 (*c.*1587), he virtually announced that his art was going to be radically unlike what had gone before: instead of the 'jigging veins of rhyming mother-wits' he offers a hero 'Threat'ning the world with high astounding terms' (Prologue 1, 5). When Jonson suffered the indignity of discovering that an audience didn't like a play of his, he fought back with every rhetorical weapon at his command and asserted the theatrical author's right to educate his audience. When John Webster arranged for the publication of *The Duchess of Malfi* (in 1623), he dedicated this 'work' to a noble patron in words that imply the enduring value of his achievement as a writer: 'for by such *poems* as this, *poets* have kissed the hands of *great princes* and drawn their gentle eyes to look down upon their sheets of paper when the *poets* themselves were bound up in their winding sheets'. When John Ford wrote a brief verse to commend the same play, he titled it 'To the reader of the author, and his *Duchess of Malfi*'.[40] Here Ford is using the term 'author' not in a casual but in an honorific sense, much as he does in the observation that 'it is an easy vanity to bee a conceited Interpreter, but a difficult commendation to bee a serious Author'.[41] The theatrical author was of course not a free-standing individual. He wrote with performance in mind as a first objective, and this meant he was working with (and sometimes against) a great many forces and agencies outside of his immediate control: the actors and management of a particular theatrical company, the structure and resources of a given playhouse, the abilities and wishes (in many instances) of a collaborator, the tastes and attention span of the theatre-going public. Some playwrights appear to have negotiated these constraints and pressures with remarkable alacrity, while others were exasperated or even silenced by them. The experience of being a theatrical author was not identical for every playwright, and for some it was a hazardous enterprise. But the notion that authorship as an institution and as a vocation was unavailable or unimportant to these playwrights is not based on a fair appraisal of the records that survive.

So I have not been reluctant to take the theatrical author as the principle of division in the chapters that follow. To be sure, I have chosen playwrights with unusually distinctive and resonant voices: not everyone is as flamboyant as Marlowe, as belligerent as Jonson, as cunning as Middleton, or as disquieting as Ford. But my selection has been made with a view to representing the quite striking range of theatrical pleasures still available to the reader of Renaissance drama. And it will be justified if the pleasures created by these playwrights are taken as an incentive to share in the pleasure of interpreting the textual performances they have left us.

2
Tobacco and Boys: Christopher Marlowe

I am assuming in what follows that Marlowe was gay. Since this is a judgement about Marlowe's experience (rather than a fact in his biography), it's not the sort of thing you can prove to everybody's satisfaction. Richard Baines, who gave the Privy Council a spectacularly unfavourable appraisal of Marlowe's character, attributes to him the saying 'that all they that love not tobacco & Boyes were fooles'.[1] And Marlowe's written work is often as outrageous, though not as flippant. In *Hero and Leander*, the opening description of the young woman, Hero, is encumbered with frustrating layers of clothing and allegorical decoration; the first view of Leander, the paragon of male beauty, is by contrast a vigorously naked appeal to the senses of sight, and touch, and taste. The most moving love affair in Marlowe is a bond between two men: the king and Gaveston in *Edward II*. These and other instances are something else than proof; but they seem to me persuasive signals of an orientation that today would be called homosexual.[2]

My opening assumption is neither new nor unusual. Havelock Ellis made the first attempt to bring Marlowe the man out of the closet a century ago,[3] and after that readers of the plays and poems have often remarked – sometimes with evasive coyness but also quite openly on occasion – that Marlowe's bias in sexual matters is part of his stance as an artist.[4] This idea, expressed in the language of what used to be called depth psychology, has made its most formal appearance as the subject of a book by Constance Brown Kuriyama.[5] Marlowe's lifelong passion, in Kuriyama's reading, is the quest for a secure masculine identity. Thus, *Tamburlaine* becomes an act of hypermasculine rebellion against real or imaginary father figures; *Dido Queen of Carthage* a defensive retreat from the embrace of an emasculating mother; *Doctor Faustus* an experiment in evading the consequences of being exceptional; *The Jew of Malta* a strategy for justifying the outcast by condemning the orthodox; and *Edward II* a hard-won acceptance of alienation, of otherness, together with a submissive acknowledgement of the need for compassion. The search for a masculine identity is doomed from the outset to failure, but not to futility, since the side-effects of Marlowe's pain endure as works of art.

Kuriyama's Marlowe is not identical with my own: her playwright is both more obsessively neurotic than I would have imagined, and more dismally normal than I could have hoped. His illness has many symptoms in common with the epidemic of Oedipal guilt which took Vienna by storm in the late nineteenth century and swept through the rest of refined society in the twentieth, while the norms he clings to are in large measure those attributed by social scientists to the North American homosexual population of the last generation or two. But even if Kuriyama's Marlowe appears now and then to be oddly dressed in borrowed robes, he is still recognizably the man who wrote the plays. Hers is a book that needed to be written – that cried out to be written. Her final chapter, 'Imagining and Living', is a lucid account of Marlowe's brief and bizarre life written by someone who knows, respects, and understands the documentary evidence, and who isn't afraid of interpreting it.

Still, why bother? Why ransack the records for the skimpiest evidence about Marlowe's private life, when all that can matter today is the works which outlive him? This is a fair question, as indeed the 'so what' question always is. It deserves both a short and a long reply. Briefly, Marlowe's private life was, by his own choosing, anything but private: to judge by the testimony of many contemporary witnesses, what Marlowe felt about the received opinions of Elizabethan society came out in conversation as flagrantly open defiance. A fastidious concern for his privacy is both more than Marlowe deserves and less than he wanted. That is the short reply. The long one is implied in the rest of this chapter, all of which concerns the question of desire. By way of clarification, I might add that for Marlowe the experience of desire is never the same as he presumes it to be for his predominantly 'straight' audience, and by way of provocation that to misinterpret the meaning of desire in Marlowe is to deny access to the complex pleasures that his drama has to offer.

I first read Marlowe's plays when I was the same age as he was when he wrote them (give or take two or three years as appropriate for early and late works). The only critical book I read at the time was Harry Levin's *The Overreacher*, and this now seems to me a lucky if accidental choice. What I found in the book was a coherent presentation of Marlowe's world as a place obsessed by desire: the will to power, the appetite for sensation, the zeal for knowledge. The objects of desire in Marlowe turned out to be the traditional ones: the world, the flesh, and the devil. But the language of desire was something else again: restless, powerful, sensuous, alive with absolute superlatives and blasphemous hyperbole. A great deal of subsequent Marlowe criticism can or should be read as answering or supplementing Levin's persuasively argued position. This is true in a special way of Fred B. Tromly's *Playing with Desire*, a book in which the image of Icarus about to plunge into the sea (which appeared on the title page of *The Overreacher*) is reproduced and answered by an image of Tantalus, immersed in a river from which he is unable to drink, just underneath an apple tree, the fruit of which he is unable to touch or taste.[6]

The quality of desire in Marlowe, the vitality or pressure of the felt experience, strikes me as something that can't be contained either in particular objects or in rhetorical devices. Instead, I believe that the quality of any desire in Marlowe depends on whether or not it counts as an act of defiance. This rule about the inner life, so to speak, is implied in the compulsive rebellion of Marlowe's protagonists, and it is virtually stated as a rule by the Duke of Guise in *The Massacre at Paris*. Having concluded 'That peril is the chiefest way to happiness' (2.35), he's willing to take any risk to get what he wants: 'I'll counterpoise a crown', as he puts it, 'Or with seditions weary all the world' (2.54–5). Even if Marlowe despises the Duke of Guise, I'm certain that he respects this declaration of desire, as he does in all of his overreachers. And what makes the desire of this dirty politician worthy of respect is the stance of defiance to which it commits him.

Elsewhere in Marlowe there are enough cases of ordinary, legitimate desire (dismissed by the Guise as 'common') to set off by contrast the glamour of desire which entails defiance. Often, it is female characters who make the strongest appeal on behalf of ordinary desire: hence, the understandable plea by Zenocrate in *Tamburlaine*, Part 1, that her father be treated with mercy; or Isabel's repeated offer, in *Edward II*, to encircle the truant king with her domestic embrace. Where common desire is neither female nor even sexual, it can take the form of Calyphas' refusal to bear arms, in *Tamburlaine*, Part 2, on the perfectly reasonable grounds that civilized pleasures, like playing cards, are more satisfying to him than a relentless diet of blood, and that in any event, 'my father needs not me' (4.1.15). In describing these ordinary desires I have repeatedly conferred on them the tacit approval of 'understandable', 'reasonable' urges, because that is what they are. But in Marlowe's drama, ordinary desires are either too tame to win the allegiance of men who want the world, or too timid to survive the earthquakes caused by the movers and shakers.

Most of what rings true, emotionally, in a play like *The Jew of Malta* depends on this radical divergence between two levels of desire – the one rebellious, anarchic, egocentric, the other soporific, domestic, self-effacing. Barabas presents himself, in his brilliant opening speech, as the impersonation of a desire that includes but is not confined to the gold in his counting-house. The mere metal is troublesome 'trash' (1.1.7) and the means of getting it 'vulgar trade' (1.1.35), Barabas claims, but the precise reasons why his own desire amounts to anything more than greed remain unclear. He admires the substances of wealth if they are exotic, pure, sensuous, and powerful, but this makes him no more than an aristocrat within the system he claims to despise. In the following scene, when his wealth is confiscated by the authorities of Malta, Barabas shows his true colours for the first time, and he achieves this revelation through an action of defiance. A complacently wealthy Barabas could have surrendered half his estate at once (as indeed his fellow Jews do) in the interests of preserving the remainder. But Barabas identifies himself, by the terms of the Maltese proclamation, as 'he that denies' (1.2.76). And he makes his denial knowingly, openly, courageously. For Barabas, as a Jew and an outsider, the need for wealth has been connected all along with his insistence on living by a code of ethnic defiance in an island of intolerant legalism and conformity. The one desire has been required to guarantee the other. What his act of defiance does for Barabas in theatrical terms is to earn him the respect of the audience. I'm not pre-judging what may happen to the responses of the spectators who stay on Marlowe's roller-coaster to the wild and bitter end. The point here is a simple one: that Barabas earns respect in the early scenes of *The Jew of Malta*, and that he does this through Marlowe's characteristic fusion of defiance and desire.

The typical object of defiance in Marlowe is an emblem of authority: a person, an institution, or a symbol in which authority is vested. In *The Jew of Malta* it is Machevil's responsibility, as the speaker of the Prologue, to ensure that defiance will be directed against such oppressors. Thus the deceptively casual shrug at the authority of the church:

> I count religion but a childish toy,
> And hold there is no sin but ignorance.

(ll. 14–15)

It might be helpful to distinguish between authority (which matters deeply to all of Marlowe's overreachers) and orthodoxy (which doesn't). This should surprise nobody who has read, say, Galileo's letter on his blindness to Diodati of Pisa or Shaw's *Saint Joan* or Umberto Eco's *The Name of the Rose*: orthodoxy is by definition a subject of far greater interest to the inquisitor than the heretic. Marlowe's Machevil counts religion 'a childish toy' not because of any doctrinal questions which need refinement, but because he sees it as a tool in the hands of those who govern society: a notion readily compatible with Marlowe's view as quoted by Richard Baines, to the effect that 'the first beginning of Religioun was only to keep men in awe'.

To rebel intelligently in Marlowe's Malta is to see authority for what it is: self-serving, hypocritical, intolerant, yet fearful of any real challenges. This description applies with almost equal force to the specifically religious authority represented by the abbess and friars, to the political authority exercised by Ferneze and his knights, and to the imperial authority which swaggers into Malta from Turkey (in the form of Selim-Calymath) or from Spain (as Martin del Bosco). Every layer of authority in Malta is utterly conventional, and therefore vulnerable to Barabas' unqualified scorn.[7] Such flawed and commonplace authority appears throughout Marlowe's work – from Mycetes in *Tamburlaine*, Part 1, to the Pope in *Doctor Faustus* – and always with the same emotional result.

But Marlowe isn't simply an *enfant terrible*, and authority needn't be based on convention alone. The authority which commands respect and requires obedience is powerfully felt in Marlowe's imagination, and powerfully invoked by Tamburlaine:

> There is a God full of revenging wrath,
> From whom the thunder and the lightning breaks,
> Whose scourge I am, and him will I obey.
>
> (Part 2, 5.1.182–4)

If Tamburlaine's earthly quest depends on his ability to find opponents qualified to fight him, so his assault on the heavens requires a god who is worthy of Tamburlaine's notice. None of the 'real' deities passes this test: Christ and Mahomet are parochial rivals, and even 'mighty Jove' is merely a 'precedent' whereby Tamburlaine can measure himself (Part 1, 2.7.17). And while the gods, through confusion or mismanagement or lack of interest, are failing to establish their authority, Tamburlaine is magnificently demonstrating his. Small wonder that Theridimas can claim, with no ironic intention, that 'A god is not so glorious as a king' (Part 1, 2.5.57). In *Tamburlaine* real authority is perilously close to tyranny: it requires an invincible army and an unshakable will. It remains impervious to sentiment, it cuts down even reasonable dissent, and it forces declared opponents to submit at length to abject humiliation. There is nothing enlightened about Tamburlaine's despotism, and that is precisely why he is universally feared. By the same token, Tamburlaine can't bother fearing the gods of tradition because they are neither as implacable nor as ruthless as he is. The only authority he can respect is that of the unnamed 'daring god' who at last strikes him down (Part 2, 5.3.42), and this is a god made in Tamburlaine's own image.

Authority. Defiance. Desire. This triad of compulsions is always close to the centre of Marlowe's imagination, even when his mind is reaching to the borders of Tamburlaine's map or charting the course of Barabas' argosies. In the rest of this chapter I hope to explore the dramatic unfolding of this pattern in the two plays by Marlowe which strike me as having lost none of the brightness of their first creation: *Edward II* and *Doctor Faustus*. But first, I want to return to the place where I began: with Marlowe's homosexual bias. In his compendiously researched history of sexual practices in England during the early modern period, Lawrence Stone writes as follows: 'Officially, both Church and state in the sixteenth century regarded male homosexuality as a serious crime: an act of 1533, reissued in 1563, made buggery punishable by death, but there is no evidence of how often, if at all, it was enforced.'[8] I think that a man of Marlowe's idealistic temperament would be quick to recognize in these circumstances a critical divergence of authority: the letter of the law is tyrannical in its intolerance,

but conventional wisdom hedges and allows evasion. And I find it easy
to imagine how a man who was also gay could come to think of himself
as an outlaw, living always in defiance of the sacred and secular code, and
requiring at all times the support of influential protectors against even the
bare possibility of a legal reckoning.[9] Desire, for such a man, would be by
its very nature an act of defiance.

The pleasure of reading or watching Marlowe's plays in performance
is derived in large measure from the pain endured by his protagonists. In
one sense this inverse ratio is among the axioms of tragedy: the reader's or
spectator's aesthetic pleasure is completed by the torment of Oedipus, by
the madness of Hieronimo, by the humiliation of King Lear. But in
Marlowe the protagonist's commitment to a disastrous or unattainable
pursuit is in a special way the condition on which aesthetic pleasure is
built: the protagonist commits himself to a course of action that we as
spectators want to endorse, to objectives that we wish might be achieved,
even if we know them to be unattainable. The failure of the quest in
Marlowe is nonetheless an aesthetic gratification, because (as readers and
spectators) we are carried along by the sheer energy of the overreacher's
desire and thrilled by his defiance of authority. The pleasures Marlowe
offers may leave his audience uncomfortably situated, even today, but
I doubt that such a result would have bothered him. His was an art of
provocation, as he surely knew; and the consequences of provocation, in
life as in art, he submitted to reckless experiment.

Edward II opens with Gaveston, alone on the stage, reading a letter from a
man who has long been his lover and has just become a king. '"My father is
deceased; come, Gaveston, / And share the kingdom with thy dearest friend."'
I don't think anyone, least of all the actor who plays Gaveston, could ask for
more. It's a brilliant way to begin, remarkable even in a writer accustomed to
brilliant beginnings. Look again at what Edward says in his letter, and look at
what he doesn't say. He says, 'My father'. He doesn't say, 'The king, my father'.
And he covers the experience of death – physical, emotional, religious experience – with an evasively euphemistic cerecloth: 'is deceased'. He doesn't
even say, 'The funeral will be held at Westminster Abbey on Monday, beginning at 11 a.m.' There is no hint in Edward's letter of the ritualistic patterns
whereby the dead are honoured and grudgingly returned to ashes or dust.
There is no fear of heaviness as the crown which Longshanks wore passes to
him. There isn't even a trace of mourning. Only relief.

The historical Piers Gaveston grew up at the court of Edward I, in the
company of young Prince Edward, until banished to Gascony by the king.
But even this is more history than you need to know to sense that, for
Edward II, the image of his father is a threatening emblem of authority.
Edward is a decent man who has done what is expected: he is married with
a male heir to his credit, and these are in every sense the right qualifications.

But remove the hand of authority, and Edward knows exactly what it is he wants. 'I'll have my will', he says (1.1.77), in defiance of the barons, the conventions of kingship, the sacrament of marriage, and the wishes of his father.

After the opening words of the play (which are indirectly Edward's), he doesn't mention his father again until he knows that Gaveston is dead. In a world where dynasties are a way of life and fathers are also heads of state, this can't be accidental. The Earl of Kent, Edward's brother, does what he can to keep the memory of their father alive. 'I do remember, in my father's days', he says (1.1.108), believing that such an invocation will be powerful enough to shake the rebellious barons back into their customary places. The habit of acknowledging tradition gives Kent a solidity which his brother lacks, and qualifies him to fill the paternal role which his brother neglects. The young prince, on becoming Edward III at the end of the play, has inherited the kingdom from his father and has learned about authority from his uncle. He speaks with more than a personal voice when he says: 'Go fetch my father's hearse, where it shall lie, / And bring my funeral robes' (5.6.92–3). The new king at the end of the play marking the death of a 'Sweet father' (5.6.98); the new king at the beginning seeking to escape the influence of a hard paternal master: between these boundaries Edward lives, for the present only, unwilling to be bound by the past or the future so long as he can give himself to the bewitching minute of unqualified rapture.

For people accustomed to thinking of sex as an exclusive relationship between a woman and a man, there are two inhibitions that need to be thrown aside before the bond between Edward and Gaveston can be properly appreciated. The first consists of pretending that Edward and Gaveston are just good friends, and that any sexual motivation is incidental. Does anyone make this claim about Othello and Desdemona? About Anthony and Cleopatra? Forget friendship; they are lovers.[10] The second inhibition is more dangerous, because it seems to be based on greater open-mindedness: this is the apparently progressive tendency of seeing homosexuals as a sort of separate class, with qualities of character and habits of thought that appear quite uniform to the naked heterosexual eye. From this point of view, what matters about Edward and Gaveston is that both are, just about equally, queer.

Neither inhibition could survive a good production of *Edward II*. In making this judgement I'm willing to rely on the testimony of Toby Robertson, who directed the Marlowe Society of Cambridge in a production staged at Stratford in 1958, with Derek Jacobi as Edward. In an interview with John Russell Brown, Robertson praises 'the lack of shame about homosexuality in *Edward II*' and points out the unequal balance in the relationship between the lovers: 'one realizes what is particularly horrifying: Edward is totally in love with Gaveston – is dotty about him – but Gaveston is just using Edward'.[11]

Considered apart from his political role, Edward appears to be an ordinary man: well-bred, confident of his good taste, at ease with most people even if they're not his equals, eager to please, anxious to be loved, accustomed to being at the centre of things but not impressed with the importance of it all. Hidden inside this perfectly unobjectionable social self is a need, a hunger, a love for a man quite unlike himself. For Gaveston: showily dressed, ostentatiously vain, flirtatious or bitchy as the mood strikes him, eager to parade his coy submissiveness when the king is at his side, rapaciously greedy for power when he isn't. Gaveston, in short, is a gay stereotype: his attractions and his talents are those which Claude Lemieux would like to claim as his own in Michel Tremblay's *Hosanna*. Change the pronouns and you'll find that Germaine Greer's description of the female stereotype fits him to perfection.[12]

This image of Gaveston, I believe, is required by the nuances of Marlowe's text. It is established in the opening scene where Gaveston, in soliloquy, reveals the quality of his erotic imagination as he anticipates the ways in which Edward will now be entertained: 'I must have wanton poets, pleasant wits, / Musicians that, with touching of a string, / May draw the pliant king which way I please' (1.1.50–2). Aesthetic pleasures will be offered in response to the new king's declared tastes. But the aesthetic will include the sensual, as in the provocative image towards which Gaveston's rhetoric has been teasing us:

> Sometime a lovely boy in Dian's shape,
> With hair that gilds the water as it glides,
> Crownets of pearl about his naked arms,
> And in his sportful hands an olive-tree
> To hide those parts which men delight to see,
> Shall bathe him in a spring....
>
> (1.1.60–5)

This is a kinky passage, and people who pride themselves on ruggedly heterosexual tastes will find it unsettling. Gaveston's idea of a good time is definitely not a wilderness weekend in northern Ontario. Nor, for that matter, is Edward's. Gaveston understands Edward, as Cleopatra understands Anthony, in a genuinely intimate way. He knows how to create a bath of pleasure for his lover, and he relishes the thought of doing it: 'Such things as these best please his majesty' (1.1.70). What saves the passage from pornography is its personal character: Gaveston isn't tarting up his body and inciting his imagination for some unknown stud he hopes to meet at the tavern, but for a man whose desires he knows as well as he knows his own.

Still, even when these allowances have been made for Gaveston, they remain allowances. He's a manipulative lover and an unforgivably selfish man. There's nothing spontaneous in his anticipation of being with Edward again; in fact, the careful premeditation of the scene he imagines has a quality which Marlowe is fond of designating as 'policy'. Gaveston has too much political shrewdness for his own moral good; Edward too little. The distinction is implied whenever the two men speak of their desires. For Edward, love is an unqualified absolute:

> I'll bandy with the barons and the earls,
> And either die or live with Gaveston.
>
> (1.1.136–7)

Gaveston's comparable declaration of love is, rhetorically and morally, composed of flimsier stuff:

> What greater bliss can hap to Gaveston
> Than live and be the favourite of a king?
>
> (1.1.4–5)

This question doesn't require an answer, but a question it remains. And even if you overlook the fact that, in defining the relationship, Gaveston uses his own name and avoids using Edward's, you might still wonder why he wants to be the favourite of *a* king (not *the* king). Will virtually any king do, so long as he's wearing a crown? Perhaps this line of argument is unfair to Gaveston, but it's not irrelevant.

As a political and social being, Gaveston earns his share of hostility. He cherishes the safety of the king's embrace because he thinks it will allow him to thumb his nose at the barons: a tactic he tries with immediate success at the expense of the Bishop of Coventry. 'As for the multitude', they are beneath his notice; he dismisses them with a contemptuous shrug and an Italian farewell: '*Tanti*' (1.1.20–2). Petitioners who bring to Gaveston their poverty or meekness are sent away with scorn: 'These are not men for me' (1.1.49). Once he senses that he has the upper hand, Gaveston is recklessly ungracious. Queen Isabel, whom he has visibly displaced as the ornament around the king's neck, continues to fawn on Edward out of desperation: 'On whom but on my husband should I fawn?' (1.4.146). Gaveston chooses to answer her, in a sniping, insinuating tone of voice that carries more truth in it than anyone could at this point suspect:

> On Mortimer with whom, ungentle queen –
> I say no more; judge you the rest, my lord.
>
> (1.4.147–8)

Gaveston has spent his life as a courtier on the make, and having made it at last to the centre of power, he wants to dish out with imperious disregard the same crap he sucked back in all those years as a sycophant. It's an understandable syndrome, and a tediously common one, but for all that I continue to find it repugnant.

Then why doesn't Edward see through him? Because he loves Gaveston, and love is blind. Because he's not interested in politics, while Gaveston clearly is, so he can't help crediting Gaveston with a degree of political insight that's wildly at variance with reality. Because he can't understand why giving things to a lover should be wrong, especially if the lover wants them, even if the gifts include the office of Lord High Chamberlain and the title Earl of Cornwall. Because he's afraid of Gaveston – desperately afraid of Gaveston's disapproval and shamelessly eager to merit his affection – too fearful to risk the consequences of ruffling his loved one with even the hint of a critical glance. Because he doesn't want to.

Edward's predicament is an understandable one too, but I don't find it repugnant. The extent of his folly is also the depth of his love. The value Edward places on love – to the exclusion of all else if necessary – allows him to score a rhetorical victory over the nobles, who are pressing him to banish Gaveston or else. To the threat of deposition, Edward can reply with a firm sense of what really matters to him:

> Make several kingdoms of this monarchy,
> And share it equally amongst you all,
> So I may have some nook or corner left
> To frolic with my dearest Gaveston.
>
> (1.4.70–3)

Politically, this would be no more than shallow posturing, if it wasn't based on the simple truth: Edward *is* prepared to risk his position for the sake of his lover, and would gladly embrace a private life if escape could be found. The problem is that Gaveston wouldn't. Edward's plan, in the face of open threats from the peers, is to send Gaveston away, to provide him with money, and to see him again as soon as the political heat is off:

> And long thou shalt not stay; or if thou dost,
> I'll come to thee. My love shall ne'er decline.
>
> (1.4.114–15)

To these words of comfort, Gaveston replies: 'Is all my hope turned to this hell of grief?' (1.4.116). To renounce his new power as the king's favourite and his new prestige as Earl of Cornwall before he's had even a decent taste of them: this is Gaveston's hell. And for Edward, the thought of displeasing Gaveston is abhorrent.

This perfectly mismatched set of needs is what holds them together and brings them down. What Gaveston won't give up is the rush of exhibiting himself and flaunting his power; what Edward won't give up is the pleasure of pleasing Gaveston. This is more than the barons can digest. They get rid of Gaveston in what Mortimer would like to be taken as an act of public hygiene, Warwick as a political necessity, Kent as a patriotic duty, but what everyone knows is a lynching.

The heretic is dead. Long live the heresy.

As soon as Gaveston is dead, Marlowe reveals that – for all the flamboyance he has written into the part of the favourite – his real interest has been in Edward's character all along. On hearing the bitter news, Edward is shaken with personal grief (as you'd expect him to be) and with rage: he swears 'By this right hand, and by my father's sword' (3.1.130) to exact the price of bloody revenge on the barons who have thwarted his desire. In one sense this is a new Edward: a man who can accept his father's legacy, a king who cares about the crown, a leader who won't be led. But in another sense he hasn't changed. After kneeling (perhaps) to make his curse of revenge, he rises, turns instinctively to one side, where Gaveston ought to be, and sees the face of young Hugh Spencer:

> Spencer, sweet Spencer, I adopt thee here;
> And merely of our love we do create thee
> Earl of Gloucester and Lord Chamberlain,
> Despite of times, despite of enemies.
>
> (3.1.144–7)

Has Edward learned nothing from his experience? Can't he see that, in repeating his mistake, he's courting deposition? Can't he see that, in adopting Spencer with such alacrity, he's devaluing his love for Gaveston? These are the inevitable questions, both for the barons and for the audience. The barons make up their minds at once; their answer is implied in the swift message they send enjoining the king to get rid of his new minion. But spectators can (and should) proceed with greater care, as the rest of my argument will show. In proposing what I take to be the real answers to my three inevitable questions, I want to invert their order and deal with them one at a time.

To begin with the question of Edward's alarmingly short sexual memory. Why does Marlowe do it? Not, I believe, to discredit the sincerity of Edward's need for Gaveston, but rather to insist that the need will outlive the needed one. You can't turn Edward into a cheerful family man simply by decapitating his lover. With Gaveston forever gone, Edward is going to feel his isolation even more painfully. He's going to miss Gaveston's private love and his public support. He's going to be searching desperately for someone to fill a huge space in his life, and it won't be Isabel he'll fasten on.

The actor who plays Hugh Spencer should be sensitive and skilful enough to take on some of the responsibility for making Edward's choice credible. Marlowe takes the trouble of introducing Spencer – with plenty of fanfare for a minor character – long before he's going to be required by the plot. As a young courtier in search of a new patron, Spencer believes that his best prospect for advancement is to ingratiate himself to Gaveston, 'The liberal Earl of Cornwall' (2.1.10). Until Gaveston's death, Spencer is very much a fringe player, but the kind of player whose every move is calculated to impress: he must be observing Gaveston's tiniest caprice with keen self-interest, and I think he should gradually come to adopt Gaveston's personal style. He might add a flounce to his costume here, the toss of a curl to his manner there, until the resemblance between his patron and himself – which nobody suspected – becomes inescapable. His imitative style should never approach caricature, but should always be the kind of emulation which genuinely flatters.

Edward, knowing that Gaveston is dead, reaches out instinctively and finds – not Gaveston, but someone who reminds him of everything Gaveston meant to him. In his isolation and vulnerability, Edward accepts the replacement at once; it's easy for him to see this choice not as an act of betrayal but as a way of honouring the memory of his dead lover. It's not a wise choice: even after he has defeated the barons in battle, even with Hugh Spencer at his side, Edward continues to remember his 'dearest friend',

> To whom right well you knew our soul was knit,
> Good Pierce of Gaveston, my sweet favourite.
>
> (3.2.42–4)

The image of Gaveston remains with Edward, untouched by the weapons of the barons, undiminished by the comforts of a substitute, untarnished by the long road of humiliation which leads to the dungeon.

The question of Edward's political stance in Act 3 – of his reckless willingness to court deposition by repeating his mistake – is really a small way of introducing the larger question of the relationship between Edward and Mortimer. When it becomes publicly obvious that Edward isn't going to conform, that he'll continue to outface the barons, Mortimer must be the happiest man in the realm. He's built his whole career on the ability to provoke and capitalize on the king's mistakes: now he has Edward caught in what looks like the blunder of his life. Mortimer charges into action, practically singing I-told-you-so to the other nobles: 'Look, Lancaster, / Yonder is Edward among his flatterers' (3.2.11–12).

It has been so from the beginning. In the first confrontation between the king and the barons, when Lancaster and the rest are appealing for the king to sign their ultimatum, to banish Gaveston, to reform his government, Mortimer is looking for provocation: 'Curse him if he refuse, and then may we / Depose him and elect another king' (1.4.54–5). When Edward signs the deed, hoping to send Gaveston to a private retreat in Ireland, Mortimer isn't satisfied: he wants to repeal the act of banishment, murder Gaveston humiliate Edward – he wants to do something, anything it seems, that might lead to the result he longs for: 'Then may we with some colour rise in arms' (1.4.279). Like Edward, Mortimer is driven by a single passion; but his is a political passion, the craving for power which earns him, in Edward's precise description, the title of 'unrelenting Mortimer' (5.1.103).

In a world where politics is everything, Mortimer will always emerge as a leader. Edward's desire – politically dangerous but personally necessary, outrageous but honest – gives to his character a warmth quite outside of Mortimer's range. The contrast between the two men is beautifully condensed into an understated pun on the word which began it all: father. After Edward's military defeat, he seeks refuge with the monks of Neath Abbey, appealing to the Abbot for compassion: 'Good father, on thy lap / Lay I this head, laden with mickle care' (4.7.39–40). Mortimer, on hearing the report of Edward's murder, offers to bury the secret in priestly silence: 'Matrevis, if thou now growest penitent / I'll be thy ghostly father' (5.6.3–4). Edward searches for and thinks he may at last have encountered spiritual authority, while Mortimer offers an ugly threat as a parody of genuine forgiveness.

But how much of this does Edward come to know and understand? To rephrase the last inevitable question, does he learn anything from his experience? There are almost as many ways of answering this question as there would be in the case of *King Lear*. What Edward learns about kingship doesn't amount to much: a generous portion of sentimental nonsense and a bit of popular Machiavellian cynicism, but that's all. A prisoner in Killingworth castle, he resigns the crown at last with a shocking lack of political awareness:

> Commend me to my son, and bid him rule
> Better than I. Yet how have I transgressed
> Unless it be with too much clemency?
>
> (5.1.121–3)

Perhaps he means that he ought to have killed Mortimer while he had the chance, and that if he had he wouldn't be in trouble now. But this is a narrowly technical reading of a much larger claim, namely, that a whole crescendo of political disasters – rebellions, wars and rumours of wars – can be resolved on a single self-serving chord. Too much clemency indeed. Who wouldn't want that as his one significant error? And I think that Edward is playing the same soft music – splendidly, to be sure – in his abdication fantasy:

> But what are kings when regiment is gone
> But perfect shadows in a sunshine day?
>
> (5.1.26–7)

Marlowe is right to withhold the secrets of statecraft from his dejected king. A ruler who provokes crisis upon crisis isn't likely to put it all together just in time for his resignation speech. But I don't want to belittle Edward. Rather, I want to place the emphasis where I think it belongs: not on Edward the king, but on Edward the man.

From Killingwith, Edward is led away and locked in the dungeon of Berkeley castle. He offers no resistance: 'Whither you will; all places are alike, / And every earth is fit for burial' (5.1.145–6). But the dungeon is not like any place he has been before, and his flesh rebels against hunger and thirst, the 'stench' of 'channel water' (5.3.18–27), the sleeplessness inflicted by his jailers. At last comes Lightborn, Marlowe's angel of death. He calls for a featherbed (on which Edward's body will relax involuntarily), a table (with which Gurney and Matrevis hold his body down), and a red-hot spit (which, to paraphrase Holinshed's account, they plunge up Edward's ass). It's a spectacular death by any standards. If the crude and premeditated violence of it seems understated in Marlowe's text, that's because he can and must depend on the actors to make it hurt.[13]

Through all of this, Edward says many of the conventional things: he begs Lightborn to wait until he's properly prepared, he complains of mental and physical lassitude, he admits he's afraid, he commends his soul to God. His last words are, 'Oh spare me! Or dispatch me in a trice!' (5.5.110). Then the terrible screams begin. All of this – however effective as drama – is to be expected from a playwright as gifted as Marlowe. But there's one brilliant moment which stands out. Lightborn, while waiting for the spit to be got ready just offstage, tries to lull Edward into relaxation with reassuring lies. And Edward reaches greedily for hope:

> Forgive my thought for having such a thought.
> One jewel have I left; receive thou this.
>> [*Gives a jewel*]
> Still fear I, and I know not what's the cause,
> But every joint shakes as I give it thee.
> O, if thou harbour'st murder in thy heart,
> Let this gift change thy mind and save thy soul.
>
> (5.5.82–7)

Toby Robertson describes this episode as the last 'love scene' in *Edward II*: 'We played this with Edward almost lying in Lightborn's lap and sort of crooning to him. He's very gently stroking him and it became like a child asking for love, wanting love, affection. And, of course, this is the trouble – this is what Edward needs. You feel it in the beginning of the play.'[14]

Edward learns about the terror of need. In a sense he has known about need – about vulnerability – before: about erotic need when Gaveston is taken from him, restored, and taken away again; about emotional need when Spencer fails to supply the vacancy; about spiritual need when he encounters the gentle father of Neath Abbey; about physical need when he's forced to live in a sewer. And in this last scene he comes to understand pure, unqualified need – the need for life that makes him a supplicant even when he knows what's coming, that speaks in the language of his 'every joint'. This, in a primitive and irreducible form, is the language of desire.

In *Doctor Faustus* the workings of desire are if anything even more devious than in Marlowe's other plays. In a sense this should not be surprising, since here the quest for gratification unfolds under the sign of damnation. The system which Marlowe's protagonist encounters here is by definition one which deprives him of everything even while it promises him he can have anything he wants. Faustus' predicament, while it might appear to arise from the bugbears of medieval tradition, is just as surely the product of a radical deficiency in himself. This inference would be consistent with the interpretation advanced in Edward A. Snow's remarkable essay, 'Marlowe's *Doctor Faustus* and the Ends of Desire'.[15] Snow's Faustus loses respect for the objects of experience as he tries to reduce them to properties or puppets under his control. As soon as external reality is subdued in this way, it becomes unsatisfying: the self remains hollow no matter how fast the appetites try to fill it. Faustus' failure, expressed in phenomenological terms which I think Snow would find acceptable, is his inability to work out a creative engagement between subject and object. More simply, it's a failure of the imagination; the pleasures which Faustus sets out to pursue are never what he really wants, because pleasure itself is for him a solitary and even a solipsistic experience.

Desire is, for Faustus, an uncompromising and ineducable beast that draws down on him 'the heavy wrath of God' (5.2.79)[16] and the implicit smugness of the final Chorus. What makes Marlowe's text outrageous is its insistence on celebrating such a reptile. After setting aside, in his opening soliloquy, the traditional subjects of scholarly enquiry, Faustus turns to magic with rhapsodic anticipation, as if he's just found a new lover:

> These metaphysics of magicians
> And necromantic books are heavenly!
> Lines, circles, seals, letters and characters:
> Ay, these are those that Faustus most desires.
>
> (1.1.50–3)

But it's never quite that simple. He desires magic, of course, but then magic itself is a mode of desire: a way of calling into being whatever you might want later, or as Faustus puts it, of performing 'what desperate enterprise I will' (1.1.82). Desire is a self-begetting experience: having what you think you want puts you in a good position to be wanting something else. I can imagine young John Faustus telling his parents that he's got to leave the provincial backwater of Rhode because what he really wants more than anything else is to study at the University of Wittenberg. God only knows what he says to his teachers as he moves from divinity to law to medicine to philosophy, outstripping both competitors and mentors as he goes. The play tells us what he says to Mephastophilis as soon as the secrets of magic are within his power: surely there's more to it than that, in effect. Faustus can feed the reptile but he can't put it to sleep. That's the sense in which he's right when he tells himself, 'The god thou serv'st is thine own appetite' (2.1.11).

Like Marlowe's other protagonists, Faustus can't make his peace with authority. The Prologue refers to his 'parents base of stock' (l. 11), but from Faustus we learn nothing about them. He mentions them only once, on the verge of damnation, when he knows the clock is about to strike twelve, and he takes this crisis as an occasion to curse them for giving him life. But parental authority is only one – the least prominent one, at that – of his many targets. Having escaped the control of his parents for the freedom of the university, Faustus discovers that the academic establishment is also based on authority – the authority of Aristotle, Galen, Justinian, and St Jerome. Now a splendidly accomplished scholar, he feels both contempt for these authorities and a need for something more. Defiance and desire. Then, on making his first contact with the world of magic, he finds at once that he's dealing with yet another structure of authority. 'I am servant to great Lucifer', Mephastophilis explains; 'No more than he commands must we perform' (1.3.40–2). As if by habit, Faustus begins his relationship with the underworld by trying to subvert it, asserting as a 'principle' that 'There is no chief but only Belzebub' (1.3.56–7). Arrogantly, he claims to know more about the devils than they themselves do, and there should be a little of the just-try-to-tell-me-more-than-I-already-know tone in his next question: 'Tell me, what is that Lucifer thy lord?' (1.3.63). Even among the spirits he so hotly desired moments ago, Faustus will never be a good company man. He's going to persist in asking embarrassing questions, he's going to dictate the terms of his own contract, and he's going to start looking for loopholes from the moment he's signed it. Only naked power – torture and threats of torture – will bring him into line.

A perverse and unmanageable creature, this reptile. Then why, and in what sense, can it be celebrated? Because, in a deep and unavoidable way, it makes us what we are. In the sense that, no matter how skilfully we rationalize, our big choices will be responses – positive or negative, urgent or timid, manifest or latent, but responses nonetheless – to the inarticulate promptings of desire. I'm prepared to argue that Marlowe sees Faustus defining himself in just this way, especially in three scenes: the negotiations between Faustus and Mephastophilis just after the signing of the deed (2.1), Faustus' address to Helen of Troy (5.1), and his damnation speech (5.2).

The hard bargaining between Faustus and Mephastophilis would be worth following from their first encounter, where Faustus has the nerve to begin the relationship with an insult and an order. 'Thou art too ugly to attend on me', he says ingenuously (1.3.24), and sends his devil away to change into an acceptable costume. When Mephastophilis obeys, Faustus congratulates himself on having gained the upper hand – 'How pliant is this Mephastophilis, / Full of obedience and humility' (1.3.29–30) – and he goes on in this mood of belligerent confidence, convinced that he can bully Mephastophilis into accepting a contract which contains all of his own pet clauses. Technically, he is right of course. Mephastophilis receives the scroll without asking for a single change in the language, and it is at this point, in the bargaining that follows ratification, that Faustus reveals all.

Now in a position to ask for anything he wants, Faustus begins, in a deliberate and academic tone of voice, with a metaphysical question:

> First will I question with thee about hell.
> Tell me, where is the place that men call hell?
>
> (2.1.116–17)

From an actor's point of view, this is Marlowe at his most brilliant. Superficially, the question is so perfectly right, so easily compatible with the search for evil knowledge that Faustus began in the opening scene, as to make it seem entirely natural. Why, of course. This is just what somebody who admits he's ravished by magic would say. Inadequately hidden by this cloak of epistemology is naked self-interest. Suppose that it's all real, and that after 24 years of living 'in all voluptuousness' (1.3.92), it's off to hell in a hand-cart; shouldn't you find out as much as you can about your presumed eternal destination? I say presumed, because Faustus never genuinely believes in hell, as his question implies. Not where *is* hell, in fact; but where is the place that men (foolishly, errantly, superstitiously) *call* hell. At a deep level, it's an insincere question, because Faustus thinks he already knows the answer, and the arguments advanced by Mephastophilis don't shake his confidence: 'Come, I think hell's a fable' (2.1.128). It takes some kind of jam to make this announcement to a being whom you've conjured up with magic formulas, whom you've enlisted as your slave, and who in turn claims to be cooperating only out of duty to the prince of hell. It's courage of this kind, both reckless and splendid, that I've been calling defiance.

What Mephastophilis offers in response has its own magnificence. First, an evasive non-answer: hell is, well, 'Under the heavens' (2.1.118). This doesn't satisfy someone as theologically clever as Faustus, and he persists until Mephastophilis delivers his famous definition:

> Hell hath no limits, nor is circumscrib'd
> In one self place, but where we are is hell,
> And where hell is there must we ever be.

> (2.1.122–4)

Beautiful and moving though these lines are, it's easy to see why they don't convince Faustus of the objective reality of the place men call hell; indeed, they can be taken as evidence in support of the view that hell is a fable. And when Faustus draws just this conclusion, Mephastophilis continues answering in riddles: 'Ay, think so still, till experience change thy mind' (2.1.129). At the level of plot, this is a just-wait-and-see response to Faustus the sceptic: once your 24 years are over, hell will be real enough. But I think that both 'fable' and 'experience' are flexible enough to bear more weight than this. Suppose hell *is* a fable; that doesn't make it *merely* a fable. It could – even as a fable, especially as a fable – continue to hold a powerful grip on the imagination. And in this sense, Faustus' experience will be the continuing terror of living with a mighty fable in his heart – a fable which loses none of its potency when assaulted with sceptical jibes and boastful tavern-talk.

In response to the first request he makes, Faustus doesn't get what he bargained for. He asks for information, and the ontological mystification he gets in reply leaves him no wiser than he was before. His second request – for a wife – is flatly denied. 'How, a wife?' says Mephastophilis, 'I prithee Faustus, talk not of a wife!' (2.1.144). The prompt appearance of an ugly demon, dressed as a woman and offering to be a wife, is enough to convince Faustus that, since marriage is a holy sacrament – in the new language, 'a ceremonial toy' (2.1.151) – he shouldn't mess with it. After a token protest, he simply drops his demand. Prudence would insist on the contrary. 'It's no deal', he should now be shouting; 'there's nothing in the contract about wives, and there's plenty to guarantee that I get what I ask for.' But Faustus isn't a prudent man. He's a wanton and lascivious man (by his own admission) for whom an endless string of 'the fairest courtesans' (2.1.153) is a prospect which throws marriage into full eclipse. And he's a reckless man too: having started this game, he wants to continue playing; judging by what he's seen of Mephastophilis so far, he thinks he can win. To expect that Faustus behave prudently at this point is to ask him to violate the self he has chosen to create.

The purest symbol of desire in *Doctor Faustus* is Helen of Troy. Hers is a silent part. This may have been caused accidentally, by Marlowe's unwillingness to trust even a single spoken word to the particular lovely boy actor who would soon be breaking the hardest heterosexual hearts in his Helen of Troy disguise. Even so, there's a wonderful rightness in the decision. Pure desire should be inarticulate. Helen can speak only through the voices of those who admire, those who crave:

> Was this the face that launch'd a thousand ships
> And burnt the topless towers of Illium?
> Sweet Helen, make me immortal with a kiss;
> Her lips suck forth my soul, see where it flies!
> Come Helen, come, give me my soul again;
> Here will I dwell, for heaven be in these lips,
> And all is dross that is not Helena.

> (5.1.91–7)

Desire, taken as a self-begetting experience, as an addiction that requires stronger and stronger dosages, reaches its apex with Helen. She's the perfect fix, the junk that makes the rest of the world look like it's just been snorting cocaine. For the first time, Faustus admits that he feels desire to be destructive – 'her lips suck forth my soul' – but, addict that he's become, he has no will to resist. To get what he wants has always been an easy matter for Faustus. Scholars have sung his praises; women have waited for benediction; devils have danced attendance. The life of desire has come to him naturally. It was easy enough to impress the Duchess of Vanholt by producing a dish of ripe grapes; then why not amuse his old companions with a scholarly glimpse of the image of Helen of Troy? And, once having seen her, why stop there? Why not have her for himself? Because, paragon that she is, Helen is unreal. By a parody of the Platonic ladder, all those years spent living in voluptuousness have led to a craving so strong that it can be satisfied only by an ideal, a form. Call it the great human sickness, or call it the Doctor Faustus syndrome, this habit of desire. Or call it simply wanting most what you know is forever elusive.

In speaking of Faustus as a spiritual junkie, I've been ignoring the question of whether he can or wants to break his habit. From the moment he's initiated by Valdes and Cornelius, Faustus protects himself against repentance (which he thinks of as irresolute softening) with a boyish display of manliness: 'Valdes, as resolute am I in this / As thou to live' (1.1.135–6). When Mephastophilis warns him about the pain of hell, and reminds him that he's renouncing the bliss of heaven, Faustus arrogantly tosses back a piece of advice:

> Learn thou of Faustus manly fortitude
> And scorn those joys thou never shalt possess.

> (1.3.85–6)

This is certainly defiance, and it may be real courage, but it's also a mood. And moods are subject to change. Before he signs the deed, Faustus turns his thoughts longingly to the God he has promised to forget, but manages to silence his inner voice by telling himself that God is now his enemy. After the bargain is a bargain, he's as restless as ever:

> When I behold the heavens then I repent
> And curse thee, wicked Mephastophilis.
>
> (2.3.1–2)

Faustus is chafing under the tyranny of his adopted masters, and would gladly repay them with defiance. But the consequence of such a decision would be to throw himself on the mercy of God the Father, and that would mean submitting to an authority he has taught himself to scorn. Logically, Faustus can repent, in the sense that the possibility exists; theologically he can repent, in the sense that God's mercy is by definition limitless. But he can't repent and continue to be Doctor Faustus; to renounce desire would be to annihilate the person he has become.

Annihilation is what he longs for – as a desperate last resort – at the end of his final speech. Other possibilities, one by one, are vanishing. He begins by demanding a miracle: 'Stand still, you ever-moving spheres of heaven' (5.2.61). Wishful thinking. The period of grace will not be extended, and even the 'one bare hour' (5.2.59) slips away as he speaks. The prospect of repentance shines once more, and brighter now: 'See, see where Christ's blood streams in the firmament' (5.2.71). At this point the desperate cycle begins again. He knows the devils will torment him if he repents. He knows they will torment him if he doesn't. The fable of hell tightens its grip on his mind. And the other fable too: not the infinitely merciful message of Christ's blood, which fades like an oasis in a mirage, but the powerful 'arm' and the 'ireful brows' of a God who knows and punishes (5.2.76–7). Faced with these threatening alternatives, the swagger of manliness and the macho defiance melt away; Faustus becomes a terrified little boy who thinks he can 'hide' from the 'heavy wrath of God' (5.2.79) under a blanket of mountains or hills or earth. The desire to escape, so understandable, so necessary, betrays him into grasping pathetically at the flimsiest straws.

The clock strikes the half hour. He calls on God. He calls on Christ. Not for love and forgiveness and infinite comfort, but for 'some end': 'Impose some end to my incessant pain' (5.2.93). The notion of eternity now threatens him with speculative terror, and he searches for philosophical remedies. Purgatory. Transmigration. Materialism. But these are fables too, and fables that have no power. Anticipating the end of his hour, of his 24 years, of his life on earth, he looks back into the past for beginnings:

> Curst be the parents that engender'd me;
> No Faustus, curse thyself, curse Lucifer
> That hath depriv'd thee of the joys of heaven!
>
> (5.2.105–7)

And the clock strikes twelve.

Only one desire can remain – the desire for absence, for non-being, for cancellation. If the body could be turned to air, and the soul to drops of water, escape might still be possible. Or, if the heretic won't self-destruct, the heresy can be destroyed: 'I'll burn my books.' Repentance, no. But recantation? Will recantation suffice? 'Ah, Mephastophilis!' (5.2.115). These are his last words. Words of terror, of recognition, of celebration. With them, Faustus passes from the world of experience and into the life of fable.

Everything I've said about Marlowe implies that he was a peculiar man: a rebel, an iconoclast, an outsider, a lover and maker of strange fables. Yet, unlike Blake for example, he was also an artist with a popular following. The two parts of *Tamburlaine* could have been called, with very little distortion, *Star Wars* and *The Empire Strikes Back*. There is a paradox here that calls for resolution: how is it that Marlowe can get away with harvesting both the corn and the chaff? I think the answer lies in the unusual nature of the contract between playwright and audience.

Marlowe begins his career as a popular dramatist with a revolution and a seduction. The revolution is a pitiful bit of Persian double-dealing, in which a laughably impotent monarch is replaced by his bombastic brother. But the spectators are unlikely to remember any of this beyond the end of Act 1. What they will remember is the figure of Tamburlaine, soaring above the pettiness of Persia as if he were a god. As for the seduction, it's a further tribute to Tamburlaine's magnificence. Such at least is the testimony of the person who falls victim to his influence. That person is not Zenocrate, but Theridimas. Tamburlaine captures the woman, he seduces the man. And Theridimas gives himself to Tamburlaine in the language of true love: 'Won with thy words and conquered with thy looks, / I yield myself' (Part 1, 1.2.226–7). But for the spectators, who are themselves being swept away by Tamburlaine, the distinction between seduction and capture won't matter greatly. Just how Theridimas yields, or just how Zenocrate resists yielding, is less important than the image of Tamburlaine, who, 'Like his desire, lift upward and divine' (Part 1, 2.1.8), is bound for victory by whatever means. I think the distinction I have drawn is crucial, nonetheless, if what interests you is the bargain which Marlowe strikes with his paying customers. They want their Tamburlaines to be virile, and for most of them, the only acceptable proof of virility will be Zenocrate or someone a lot like her. Very well then, Zenocrate they shall have. But Marlowe needs his own test of Tamburlaine's manliness, and to satisfy himself, he allows Theridimas to be seduced.

In *Edward II* the terms of the bargain are easier to specify, in *Doctor Faustus* more difficult, but the pattern remains consistent. Since Edward and Gaveston are flagrantly out of step with prevailing heterosexual morality, they're going to encounter plenty of hostility. This is what happens in the play, and I have little doubt that it happened in the theatre. Hostility is a powerful instigator. It can release the dragons: social violence, conspiratorial killings, sadism. If you choose to join forces with Mortimer, and Warwick, and Lightborn, Marlowe knows he can't stop you. But I think he's convinced he can jolt you into knowing what you're doing. Don't call it rejuvenating the monarchy, or acting in the public interest, or upholding the tradition of the nuclear family. Take another look at Edward in his dungeon – naked, hungry, bereft of sleep – and if your hostility survives that, call it hatred.

The final Chorus of *Doctor Faustus* is itself a puzzling text. It says both too much and too little: too much to be taken as an oracle, too little to qualify as a sermon. But as a covenant it's just about right, and I think Marlowe is here showing special concern for the delicacy of the agreement which unites him with and divides him from his audience:

> Faustus is gone, regard his hellish fall,
> Whose fiendful fortune may exhort the wise
> Only to wonder at unlawful things,
> Whose deepness doth entice such forward wits
> To practi[s]e more than heavenly power permits.

Like Faustus, Marlowe has to be among the 'forward wits'. That's both his privilege and his curse. But, as a spectator, you might prefer to be among the 'wise'. In that case, you 'may' understand the career of Faustus as an exhortation to prudence, in which case you will only 'wonder', never 'practise'. You may take this conventional path, but you don't have to. The choice is yours. You may, with Faustus, choose to celebrate desire. In this case too, Marlowe wants you to know what you're doing. The old devils have changed their names – to anguish, neurosis, and alienation – but the destination which threatens forward wits, even today, is still the old place that men call hell.

The pleasures of reading and responding to Marlowe's drama are of course not identical with the pleasures represented in the plays themselves. It follows from the readings I have offered here that the recurrent pleasure enacted in the plays is the pleasure of defiance. This principle holds true in various ways throughout Marlowe's career as a playwright; it is resoundingly true of *Edward II* and *Doctor Faustus*, where the claims of the protagonists on our attention rest in large measure on the energy they are prepared to expend in order to defy the conventions of the heterosexual and patriarchal system or the doctrines and assumptions of religious orthodoxy. A terrible price is exacted of the heroes who give themselves to defiance on this scale, but the defiance itself is nonetheless the distinctive pleasure of their lives. It is all the more distinctive for being not entirely chosen: in both Edward's case and Faustus', the world seems to have been arranged in such a way as to ensure that their only real path to pleasure is through defiance. The members of Marlowe's audience would not have been overreachers in the same way that his heroes were. They lived in a culture in which religious beliefs, ethical norms, social hierarchies, and even dress codes set out to regulate all public interaction and a great deal of private behaviour. But they also lived in a culture where the defiance of old limits, in large matters and small, was leading at times to surprising results. They lived in a culture already inflected by the adventurism of Columbus or the daring of Luther and soon to be shaken by the imagination of Galileo. What Marlowe offers his spectators is a complex pleasure which includes both pathos and demystification. Pathos is the aspect of pleasure that links the spectator to the protagonist, that offers us a share in his suffering without obliging us to partake in his defiance. Demystification is the aspect of pleasure that offers to liberate the spectator, not from all the necessary regulations of social life, but at least from the belief that these are immutable and eternal.

3
A Shrew Yet Honest: Ben Jonson

In conversation with Drummond of Hawthornden, Jonson is by turns belligerently scornful, ironically dismissive, intemperately vain, lucidly perceptive, and (on rare and moving occasions) clairvoyantly honest about himself. In one of these moments of deep self-knowledge he reports that, while visiting Sir Robert Cotton's country estate, 'he saw in a vision his eldest sone', who appeared to him with the mark of the cross on his forehead, 'of a Manlie shape', and full-grown, as Jonson believes 'he shall be at the resurrection'.[1] Meanwhile, a letter arrived from Jonson's wife to confirm that the boy had died. The sincerity of this account is beyond question, even without the support of Epigram 45, 'On My First Son'. And it reveals, aside from Jonson's emotional integrity, his belief that the shape of the immortal soul is the perfection of manliness. This idea, though not the striking metaphysical context of the occasion, is always near the centre of Jonson's thinking about life and art. It motivates his choice of a name – Eustace Manly – for the only moral survivor of the social wreckage he dramatizes in *The Devil is an Ass*. It stands behind his public image as the master of a literary circle known as the sons of Ben. It colours his language when, as 'Judge & Professor of *Poesie*', he praises the work of a younger poet 'with some passion' by declaring, '*My Son Cartwright writes all like a Man.*'[2] What Cartwright made of this compliment, or whether he deserved it, are questions that no longer matter. What Jonson meant by it remains a living concern for anyone sufficiently dazzled by *Volpone*, annoyed by *Epicoene*, or bewildered by *Bartholomew Fair* to care about meeting Jonson on his own terms.

To care about meeting Jonson at all, I could have said, because unless you're willing to take him on the terms he prescribes, Jonson will always be somewhere else: not at home, out to lunch, otherwise engaged. So it's best to begin by catching Jonson in his various prescriptive moods: reeling off pronouncements, however spiced with irony or sack, to the recording angel of Hawthornden; jotting down the wit of other men or the products of his own invention, however unsystematically, in a compilation of *Discoveries*; affirming where he stands, however indirectly, in the poems.

'Looke upon an effeminate person', Jonson writes in *Discoveries*; 'his very gate confesseth him. If a man be fiery, his motion is so: if angry, 'tis troubled, and violent. So that wee may conclude: Wheresoever, manners, and fashions are corrupted, Language is. It imitates the publicke riot. The excess of Feasts, and apparell, are the notes of a sick State; and the wantonnesse of language, of a sick mind.'[3] To dismiss the effeminate person with a scornful shrug is authentic Jonson: it's a gesture he animates point-edly at the expense of Inigo Jones, ironically at the expense of Sejanus. But there's more to Jonson's manliness than contempt for men who don't measure up. In the passage just quoted Jonson is attacking three separate kinds of effeminate behaviour as if to define, by opposition, three kinds of manliness. First, the manners and fashions of an effeminate man – and his way of walking – are qualities which belong to his public image. In opposition to the courtly gait of his effete antagonist, Jonson imagines the actions of real men to be fiery, angry, even violent. Secondly, where the health of the state and the individual mind are at stake, manliness is a mark of social and personal sanity. Finally, in relation to language, manliness is a question of style: effeminate language is a form of corruption to be opposed by speaking and writing in the genuine idiom of men. Since each of the territories I've just named – public image, morality, and style – amounts to a Jonsonian obsession, I've chosen them as the basis for the map of Jonson's mental geography which follows.

The public self Jonson created, both for his contemporaries and for pos-terity, is typically engaged in the manly art of competition.[4] In the grandest and pettiest senses of the word, he was a fighter. The motivation for his literary programme – from the *Epigrams* to *The English Grammar* – includes a determination to rival the ancients. In his treatment of John Marston, to take a less elevated example, the same competitive urge expresses itself as a snarl of antagonism. It's a public war of words when Jonson parodies Marston as Hedon (in *Cynthia's Revels*) or as Crispinus (in *Poetaster*), if that indeed is what he's doing. It's still a war of words when he claims that Marston wrote his father-in-law's sermons, and that his father-in-law wrote Marston's plays. This is funny because it's outrageous, and it remains funny even if you realize that Marston deserved better after having dedicated *The Malcontent* to his unappreciative mentor. But competition for Jonson is also a matter of muscular self-assertion. In his late forties he can't resist boasting to Drummond of his 'many quarrells with Marston', in one of which he 'beat him & took his Pistol from him'.[5] Playfulness? Maybe. The same kind of fun he had in the quarrel with his fellow actor, Gabriel Spencer, whom Jonson (by his own account) was able to kill in self-defence despite a hand-icap of ten inches in the length of his weapon.

It's easy to grant the high-mindedness of Jonson's desire to compete with Aristophanes, Horace, Juvenal, and Tacitus. It's easy to understand why a writer born into the same generation as Shakespeare and Donne would wish to disarm comparative judgements, or at least exercise a fair bit of control over them by recording his own evaluations. It's easy to tolerate a satiric writer's need to deface the sacred monuments of the recent past, as in the remark that 'Sidney was no pleasant man in countenance, his face being spoiled with Pimples.'[6] But as you move down the scale, discovering along the way that Jonson's literary enemies included Thomas Middleton, Michael Drayton, Sir John Harington, Edward Sharpham, Abraham Fraunce, Gervase Markham, John Taylor the Water Poet, and somebody called John Owen (epigrammatist), you begin to suspect that forming disinterested judgements isn't the point. Competition seems to have been a compulsive joy for Jonson. He didn't have to look back over his shoulder to see how far he had outstripped the Gervase Markhams of the world, but look back he did.[7]

Jonson's most celebrated quarrel was his protracted assault on Inigo Jones. In this case there were good artistic and ideological reasons for the antagonism; in declaring poetry and picture to be sister arts, 'both...busie about imitation', Jonson appears eager to add the crucial qualification: 'Yet of the two, the Pen is more noble, then the Pencill.'[8] The court masque required intimate collaboration between pen and pencil, and if the pen was convinced of its own superior calling, it's not hard to imagine why the pencil might rebel. But I think Jonson's satiric attacks on Jones are coloured with something darker than artistic rivalry. 'An Expostulation with Inigo Jones' gets most of its energy from Jonson's ability to make an insult stick: 'What makes your wretchedness to bray so loud / In town and court...?' the speaker enquires. Clearly, Jonson hated Jones. He reduces his rival, rhetorically, to a dandified poseur who fails every test of real manhood. Elsewhere, 'Sir Inigo' is caricatured as a butterfly. And if Epigram 115 ('On the Town's Honest Man') is indeed a veiled attack on Jones, then it shows Jonson at his belligerent best: the object of contempt is denied a name, deprived of a sexual identity (by having the neuter pronoun thrust upon 'it'), and stripped of all values, even primary decencies: "Twill see its sister naked, ere a sword.'[9]

The battle with Inigo Jones was part of a larger Jonsonian campaign – the one described by Jonas Barish in 'Jonson and the Loathèd Stage'.[10] Though he spent much of his life writing for the theatre, Jonson was never stage-struck. His repertoire of antitheatrical stances included the willingness to berate his paying customers for their shallowness or to hector them into submission; an active distaste for most of what the London theatres had to offer, especially if the scenic effects were spectacular; a persistent mistrust of shape-shifting in a broad philosophical sense and of the acting profession in particular; and a lifelong suspicion of the seductions of ornament. Not, on balance, the portrait of a natural playwright. To these observations, all of them drawn from Barish's essay, I would add only a speculative question. I wonder how Jonson felt in a world where Celia and Lady Politic Wouldbe and Dol Common and Grace Wellborn weren't 'real' women in any sense of the word, but young men in drag? I think the answer to this question is implied in *Epicoene*, and perhaps that's a sufficient answer in itself. I suspect that Jonson felt far more comfortable when he left the tiring-house at Blackfriars and entered the Apollo Room in the Devil Tavern, where his would be the only show in town, and where men could be trusted to be men.[11]

As soon as you begin thinking about Jonson's cherished moral positions – generosity in friendship, loyalty to king and country, pleasure in moderation, fidelity to truth – you find yourself in the company of someone radically unlike the contentious ruffian who seems to have been asserting himself up to this point. And that's as it should be. Jonson's moral positions were not the casual inferences he drew without effort from a tranquil life; they were, like everything of value in Jonson, won with great labour from the mess of experience.[12] Moderate enjoyment of liquor isn't likely to be a major virtue except for someone who fears the chaos of being endlessly drunk.

It's difficult to catch Jonson the moralist in the act of struggling with experience, because of his habit of stating the truth only after he's sure; but when you do catch him, the results can be rewarding. Epigram 65, 'To My Muse', is the record of one such remarkable moment. It contains the astonishing admission (for Jonson) that he's made a mistake; his muse has 'betrayed' him by prompting him to praise 'a worthless lord', so Jonson repudiates her influence and accepts the consequences:

> With me thou leav'st an happier muse than thee,
> And which thou brought'st me, welcome poverty;
> She shall instruct my after-thoughts to write
> Things manly, and not smelling parasite.[13]

It takes a painful effort for Jonson to admit that he has fallen into the trap of worshipping external greatness; such 'idolatry' as he calls it is false worship (even if only in retrospect). So, although Jonson's error doesn't amount to simple hypocrisy, it still *smells* parasite. And that's enough to taint the experience. The honest way out is to admit the mistake, to renounce the art of the parasite, and to insist that the objects of worship live up to an exacting standard of 'manly' integrity.

The close bond between manliness and virtue in Jonson's thinking might with some justice be taken as a sign of misogyny. This inference would account for an awkward and revealing touch in the portrait of the ideal woman he draws in Epigram 76 ('On Lucy, Countess of Bedford'):

> I meant she should be courteous, facile, sweet,
> Hating that solemn vice of greatness, pride;
> I meant each softest virtue there should meet,
> Fit in that softer bosom to reside.
> Only a learned and a manly soul
> I purposed her....[14]

Jonson's resistance to characterizing the feminine ideal by alluding to beauties of body or face is his way of putting the emphasis where he wants it. There's only one word in the poem (the ubiquitous and uninformative 'fair') which could have the slightest reference to anybody's appearance. Instead, the centre of interest is moral worth in what for Jonson is its female form: the virtues of courtesy and sweetness which become the 'softer bosom' of woman. But, arriving at the soul of his ideal creation, Jonson finds himself in a rhetorical cul de sac. Can he give her a softer soul without endangering his portrait? Not if he wants his ideal to be more durable than the 'easy wax' of antifeminist tradition. So he does the inconsistent thing, and gives her a 'manly' soul instead.

The Jonson who offered this dubious compliment to the Countess of Bedford is the same man who got into trouble with the Countess of Pembroke by backing her husband's dismissive assertion that 'Woemen were mens shadowes'. According to Drummond's account, the Countess gave Jonson 'a pennance to prove it in Verse',[15] and he responded by composing a Song, 'That Woemen Are but Men's Shadowes' (*The Forest* 7). I think Jonson deserves credit for discharging this obligation with more wit than he showed in contracting it. His poem is and is meant to be a trifle, but it still confirms the judgements he offers more soberly elsewhere:

> At morn and even shades are longest;
> At noon they are or short or none:
> So men at weakest, they are strongest,
> But grant us perfect, they're not known.
> Say, are not women truly then
> Styled but the shadows of us men?[16]

Like Milton and many lesser men, Jonson simply can't confer the same moral independence on women as on men. And men become genuinely independent ('perfect') only by escaping the influence of women entirely. Manliness is in part a code of renunciation. Resist flattery. Resist beauty. Resist women. It's worth remembering that two of Jonson's major sexual achievements, as reported to Drummond, were adventures in renunciation. His marriage included a period of '5 yeers' during which he had 'not bedded with' his wife. And among the 'accidents' of his sex life is the account of how he 'lay diverse tymes with a woman, who shew him all that he wished except the last act, which she would never agree unto'.[17] There's nothing preposterous about either of these events, nor anything inherently damaging (either way) to Jonson's sexual reputation. He may have had excellent reasons for deciding to live apart from a woman he described as 'a shrew yet honest'. As for the coy mistress of the anecdote, her thoughts may have ranged anywhere from fear of pregnancy to optimistic support for the view that physical pleasure can be transcended. Still, what remains puzzling is the occasion of Jonson's

recounting these events. Why make these intimate revelations for the benefit of a host as dull as Drummond of Hawthornden? I have no doubt that
drink was a great provoker of eloquence. But I suspect also that Jonson's tone
of voice included a conspiratorial maleness of the kind that expects women
to enter a man's life either as recreation or as trouble.

The moral virtue of manliness, in Jonson, seems to require a defensive
posture in relation to the blandishments of the world and the flesh. To give
in to temptation is to become less than a 'perfect' man. Thomas M. Greene
articulates what I think is the same Jonsonian pattern in 'Ben Jonson and
the Centered Self'.[18] The image of a justly drawn circle with a fixed centre
is, for Jonson, an emblem of positive moral achievement. Centrifugal pressures are by definition threatening to the stability of the centred self; but
these can and should be resisted by exercising the right centripetal forces.
Sufficient moral 'firmness', to adopt the famous language of Donne's
'A Valediction: Forbidding Mourning', will make the human circle 'just'.[19]

To watch Jonson putting manliness to the test of experience, I want to
take a preliminary glance at two of his dramatic works: *Sejanus* (1603) and
the masque entitled *Pleasure Reconciled to Virtue* (1618). In terms of Jonson's
career, these works may be taken as bracketing the period of his greatest creativity: the brief span of years in which he produced *Volpone* (1606), *Epicoene*
(1609), *The Alchemist* (1610), and *Bartholomew Fair* (1614).

In *Sejanus* the paragon of manliness is 'the lofty cedar of the world, /
Germanicus' (5.242–3). He doesn't appear on stage (having been killed
before the action begins), but his influence is never absent. He's the human
standard by which all of the Germanicans judge their own behaviour, and
he seems to have left something of his manly soul to his widow, the 'male-
spirited dame' Agrippina (2.211). At the other end of the scale is Tiberius,
the emperor who seldom appears on stage because he can't be lured away
from the Island of Capri where he lives with his 'stale catamite' (4.404) and
various other groupies of both sexes, acting out 'strange and new commented lusts, / For which wise nature hath not left a name' (4.400–1).

The action forces most of the characters to choose one of the two models:
either the complete manliness of Germanicus, or its degenerate parody,
Tiberius. Rome is thus sharply divided into 'things manly' and those
'smelling parasite'. Sejanus himself, for all his apparent power, fails every
major test of manliness. He began his career as 'the noted pathic of the time'
(1.216); that is, he got his start by selling his ass to the right men.
Subsequently he's been married and divorced. He decides he'll seduce Livia,
not because he finds her attractive – 'Venus hath the smallest share in it', he
coldly admits (1.374) – but because she's a political stepping-stone. When
Drusus openly challenges him with a blow to the face, Sejanus isn't man
enough to strike back. His power is exclusively the kind you borrow from
other powerful people, and his weapons are limited to subterfuge. That's

why, when Tiberius withdraws his support and decides to back Macro, Sejanus crumbles. He's verbally impotent in the final Senate scene, and once offstage he's literally annihilated by the mob. Sejanus has never been a complete man, in the sense that his masquerade of manliness has always relied on second-hand attributes, never on anything integral to himself.[20]

Pleasure Reconciled to Virtue works out a symbolic ritual that reverses the action of *Sejanus*. The Jacobean courtiers who watch or participate in this theatrical event are placed for a moment in the position of Hercules at the crossroads: of choosing, that is 'Twixt Virtue and her noted opposite / Pleasure' (ll. 169–70). But only for a moment because, under the benign influence of King James, these two opposing forces have been 'reconciled' (l. 180). We should not assume that reconciliation brings about a partnership of equals; rather, as Richard S. Peterson has shown, to be 'reconciled' in this context is to yield to a higher authority.[21] In this very act of hierarchical yielding, Pleasure has not been obliterated but has established the credentials which encourage Virtue to trust her. The danger that lovers of pleasure will 'grow soft or wax effeminate' (l. 190), that they'll sink to the level of 'sponges, and not men' (l. 85), has been overcome by giving Virtue the last word: 'in her sight and by her charge all's done, / Pleasure the servant, Virtue looking on' (ll. 191–2). In the Jonsonian system mere self-indulgence threatens to turn men into shadows or sponges; the defence of manliness requires not only allegiance to abstract virtue, but the practical exercise of wit.

To explain what Jonson understood by manliness of style looks like a simple matter. He left plenty of clues in *Discoveries*, like the handy definition: 'Too much pickednesse is not manly'.[22] On 'pickedness' the *Oxford English Dictionary* gives a useful list of synonyms – 'adornment, elegance, trimness, spruceness' – and a string of examples including the sentence from *Discoveries*. If this isn't enough, you can look up the passage in Seneca which Jonson is translating: 'Non est ornamentum virile concinnitas'.[23] So 'pickedness' in style amounts to ornamental elegance. The context for this idea in *Discoveries* isn't explicitly about language at all, but about manners:

> *There* is nothing valiant, or solid to bee hop'd for from such, as are alwayes kemp't, and perfum'd; and every day smell of the Taylor: the exceedingly curious, that are wholly in mending such an imperfection in the face, in taking away the Morphew in the neck; or bleaching their hands at Mid-night, gumming, and bridling their beards; or making the waste small, binding it with hoopes, while the mind runs waste: Too much pickednesse is not manly.

So Jonson himself gives you a rich contextual definition of 'pickedness' and a secure feeling for how much would be too much. And if he's talking about fopperies of character rather than vanities of speech, that shouldn't cancel out the value of the statement. In Jonson, manners and language always go together.

Of course Jonson won't be satisfied with loutishness parading as man-liness. There are some wits, he remarks, 'that in composition are nothing, but what is rough, and broken'. When a sentence threatens to come out smoothly, 'they trouble it of purpose. They would not have it run without rubs, as if that stile were strong and manly, that stroke the eare with a kind of unevennesse.'[24] Like effeminate language, the rough and broken style is an affectation, though at the opposite end of the scale. It's another way of making nature afraid, to borrow a phrase from the Induction to *Bartholomew Fair* (l. 115).

'The true Artificer will not run away from nature, as hee were afraid of her; or depart from life, and the likenesse of Truth.' With these words Jonson begins a passage in *Discoveries* which sounds more like a manifesto than any other. An honest writer must be willing to resist going after flashy effects, Jonson believes, even if this means he'll be called 'barren, dull, leane'. Never mind. Posterity will recognize genuine merit: 'his wisdome, in dividing: his subtilty, in arguing: with what strength hee doth inspire his Readers; with what sweetnesse he strokes them'. The 'sharpenesse' of his satire and the 'urbanity' of his wit will be admired; his ability to 'invade' the minds of his audience will become legendary. As for 'Elocution', he'll be praised for deciding 'what word is proper: which hath ornament: which height: what is beautifully translated: where figures are fit: which gentle, which strong to shew the composition *Manly*. And how he hath avoyded faint, obscure, obscene, sordid, humble, improper, or effeminate *Phrase*.'[25]

There's considerable flexibility in Jonson's programme for the ideal writer. Sweetness and gentleness are not excluded, nor is ornament; used without restraint, these softer qualities could signal an effeminate style, but in themselves they are virtues. The mark of manliness, however, is strength of composition. This I take to be the 'harmonious fitting of parts in a sentence', which can have almost the 'force of knitting, and connexion: As in stones well squar'd, which will rise strong a great way without mortar'.[26] Manly discourse has a strength which comes from the secure integration of well-fitting parts.

The qualities of manly writing as Jonson defines them are consistent with most of his more famous pronouncements about style. When he says that 'the chiefe vertue of a style is perspicuitie',[27] he's defining further the natu-ralness of the manly style, especially in opposition to the vice of obscurity. When he says, 'Pure and neat Language I love, yet plaine and customary',[28] he's working out an agreement between the true artificer and the order of nature. Language won't be plain unless the excrescences of jargon and bombast are chiselled away by art; yet it won't be pure unless the artist is willing to accept what nature supplies. Somewhere near the centre of this paradox stands the manly speaker and writer of the language: as natural as God made him, yet equipped with the tools he needs to make each stone sit square and strong. These are the assumptions that underwrite Jonson's praise of his mentor in the 'Epistle to Master John Selden' (*The Underwood* 14). Selden is singled out for 'the excellent seasoning of your style, / And manly elocution',[29] qualities which tell us at least as much about Jonson as about the person he's commending. The warmest way Jonson can praise a friend is to single out the marks of manliness for which he wants to be admired himself.

For Jonson the poet and Jonson the critic, 'manly elocution' is the model of excellence. For Jonson the playwright, the norm remains the same but the terms of reference alter drastically. The first great pronouncement he makes to his audience at the Globe is to tell them, in the Prologue to *Every Man in his Humour*, that he won't provide romance or spectacle, 'But deeds and language such as men do use' (l. 21). Not the language men *ought* to use, but the language they *do* use. The comic dramatist has a special commitment to the idiom of human folly: that is, to all of the 'faint, obscure, obscene, sordid, humble, improper, or effeminate' registers of speech which the manly stylist makes it his business to condemn and avoid. As a writer of comedy, Jonson repeatedly puts himself into the position of choosing between this commitment to folly and the requirements of his own cherished system of norms. The greatness of his art can be measured by the honesty of the choices he makes.

Even after the sexual revolution, North American society remains prudish as ever on at least one question: affectionate physical contact between hetero-sexual males. Just when you think you can violate this prohibition – with a hand on the shoulder, or something equally innocent – you find yourself shocked into asking the predictable series of questions (Does he think that I think that he thinks...?) and wishing you'd been satisfied with the unambiguous chastity of a handshake. I know of only one circumstance in which the prohibition doesn't apply: the moment after the decisive goal (or home run or touchdown) in team-sport competition. For a few sublime seconds the rules are suspended, and the men who have just become heroes are allowed to embrace like lovers before millions of approving eyes. It's as if Wayne Gretzky and Mark Messier can be permitted to leap into one another's arms after collaborating on the record-setting goal because nobody, not even the most hardened TV cynic, will be able to call them queer. They are exempt from the code – for a moment – by virtue of their status as models of manliness.

This paradigm is a helpful way of getting at one of the special (and otherwise troublesome) qualities in the relationship between Mosca and Volpone. After the duping of the first gull, Voltore, Volpone is wild with excitement: 'Excellent, Mosca!' he says, 'Come hither, let me kiss thee!' (1.3.78–9). He repeats this demonstrative wish after the fleecing of Corbaccio in the following scene; and when they've hoodwinked the entire judicial establishment, Volpone has nothing but praise for his 'Exquisite

Mosca' (5.2.4) who has managed things so deliciously that 'The pleasure of all womankind's not like it' (5.2.11). This looks like an invitation to see the bond between master and parasite in erotic terms,[30] but that's precisely what it is not. The affection and the praise are part of a ritual of high spirits; in each case they follow a major scoring play in the competition between Volpone with his team of dependents and the established order of Venice. Under such conditions, an embrace in which the team captain celebrates his virtuoso performer is a demonstration (not a denial) of manliness.

This is not to say that Volpone is in any sense normal, but only that manliness is a key to the way in which he likes to display himself. True, Jonson qualifies his comic hero's display of self by hedging it about with ironies. But pride cometh before the fall, potency before deflation. The ironies can do their work only to the extent that Volpone wins the right to be their target. This he does by sheer personal magnificence: by being what Jonson calls him in the dramatis personae, 'a Magnifico'. He rises to this potent level (both socially and dramatically) largely because of his urgent and unstoppable desire to compete.

During most of the play, Volpone is the undisputed master, Mosca the endlessly inventive but apparently selfless parasite. They have worked out a relationship based on mutual support (on teamwork, in fact), and they depend on the integrity of this relationship in competing against the sharpers and shysters of Venice. So long as Volpone and Mosca keep in check any suspicion of competition between each other, they remain in control. Working as a team they can predict and capitalize on the competitive urges which divide their antagonists into selfishly isolated competitors. 'But am I sole heir?' asks Voltore, wishing to be reassured that he has outmanoeuvred the other legacy hunters. 'Without a partner, sir', says Mosca; and Voltore's nervous legalism fades behind a smile of complacency: 'Happy, happy me!' (1.3.44–7). When Mosca turns to Corbaccio, he can use the smug departure of the lawyer as a competitive stimulus; only after Corbaccio knows that Voltore has left a handsome bribe does he offer his own bag of chequins which, he believes, 'Will quite weigh down his plate' (1.4.70). As Volpone says, all of the would-be heirs are determined to 'counterwork the one unto the other', to 'contend in gifts, as they would seem in love' (1.1.83–4). The dramatist who designed these opening scenes was on intimate terms with the profit motive (both in himself and in other people). To paraphrase L.C. Knights, Jonson had the clarity of mind to understand the capitalist system even while it was unfolding, and the honesty to admit what competition for gain can do to the human character.[31] For the men in Jonson's Venice, the game of getting and spending is a sophistication of the primitive need to assert manliness as dominance.

In the case of Corvino, competitive zeal expresses itself as violence, misogyny, possessiveness. Jonson allows the ugliness of these distortions to be felt in Corvino's threats to 'chalk a line' beyond which his wife dare not move, or to restrict her motion so that she'll have 'no pleasure...but backwards' (2.5.52–61). Corvino's tactics of surveillance and custody are inherited from a long comic tradition of jealousy and cuckoldry, but the master-stroke is Mosca's (and Jonson's) ability to see the cause underneath the symptoms. When Mosca tells Corvino that Volpone now needs a young woman to coddle him, all he has to do to bring Corvino around is to present the case in competitive terms: 'One o' the doctors offered there his daughter' (2.6.60). Horrified at the thought of being outbid, Corvino indulges in a parody of thinking – 'Wherefore should not I / As well command my blood and my affections / As this dull doctor?' (2.6.70–2) – and reaches the triumphant conclusion that it's all right with him if Mosca uses his wife in the bartering.

Against this background of contemptible elbowing for advantage, both Volpone and Mosca present themselves as competitors on a grand scale. Mosca saves his claim to magnificence for his one soliloquy, where he dismisses the ordinary sycophant, who relies on the 'bare town-art' of flattery, as an opponent unworthy of the true parasite: 'your fine, elegant rascal, that can rise / And stoop, almost together, like an arrow' (3.1.14–24). Even in formulating this hierarchy of parasites and sub-parasites, Mosca is imitating his master's economic snobbery. 'I use no trade, no venture', Volpone says proudly, and he follows this advertisement of his dignity with a derisive list of 'common' strategies for getting rich (1.1.33). In the mountebank scene he's equally anxious to insist that he's not one of the 'rabble of these ground *ciarlitani*' (2.2.48–9) but Scoto of Mantua, knower of 'the rarest secrets' (2.2.159), companion to cardinals, counsellor of princes, the envy of all Italy, the cock of the walk.

Volpone's manliness is a performance based in part on the circulation of rumours about his sex life. He's not married, of course, which is why he has no legitimate heirs. His property includes 'A handsome, pretty, customed bawdy-house' (5.7.12) which he mentions with the kind of affection you'd expect from a pimp who made a big enough killing to retire. Mosca's account of his illegitimate children – 'Some dozen, or more, that he begot on beggars, / Gypsies, and Jews, and black-moors' (1.5.44–5) – may not be the literal truth, but it's part of Volpone's sexual image. According to rumour, the dwarf, eunuch, and hermaphrodite who live with Volpone are his children. 'He's the true father of his family', Mosca says, 'In all save me' (1.5.48–9). It's possible to read this last line as Mosca's claim to be one of Volpone's bastards, though not a 'true' copy of the paternal image. There's no more than a hint to this effect, and that's how it should be; Jonson gives you just the murkiness of possible paternity, much as Beckett does in the pairing of Hamm and Clov in *Endgame*. What the innuendos add up to is a perverse and self-assertive potency for which a phrase like 'dirty old man' is far too mild. Volpone is a man who loves nobody, but can seduce almost anyone and knows that he can.

So all Mosca has to do is mention the fair face and the white skin of Corvino's wife, and Volpone is ready for the old game. It can't be love – or even lust in any immediate sense – because Volpone hasn't so much as laid eyes on her. When Mosca explains that Celia is 'kept as warily as is your gold' (1.5.118), Volpone's eagerness escalates from curiosity ('How might I see her?') to urgency ('I must see her'). Volpone's desire expresses itself as competitive potency: as the need to perform, to dominate, to violate, and (at his time of life) to prove that the old magic still works.

The actors who play Volpone and Celia will need to make assumptions like these to prepare for their first meeting. Volpone swaggers onstage in his showy mountebank disguise, plants himself under Celia's window, and begins a demonstration of circus patter that makes music out of nonsense. Then '*Celia at the window throws down her handkerchief*' (2.2.218.1). The stage direction doesn't say how long Celia has been at her window, or whether Volpone has noticed her presence, or whether she drops her handkerchief naively, deliberately, coquettishly, or accidentally.[32] But the scene brings together a beautiful young woman whose life is a cloistered hell and an experienced magnifico in the full stride of his performance. However intended, the handkerchief is a meaningful sign. Corvino, basing his interpretation on observation instead of fantasy, is for once dead right: 'You were an actor with your handkerchief' (2.5.40).

The next encounter between Celia and Volpone takes place in Volpone's bedroom. Corvino's part in the scene is yet another foolish and artless attempt to control his wife's behaviour, though by now he's pushing and goading her in the direction of Volpone's bed, insisting that a man as old as Volpone can do her no harm. Having destroyed what little credit he may still have enjoyed in his wife's estimation, he allows Mosca to usher him out of the room. Alone with Celia at last, Volpone '*leaps off from the couch*' (3.7.139.1–3) and the seduction begins in earnest. It includes Volpone's praise for the 'miracle' of Celia's beauty which now raises him from his bed (3.7.146), his performance of the song, 'Come, my Celia, let us prove' (3.7.166–83), and his catalogue of anticipated pleasures:

> Thou like Europa now, and I like Jove,
> Then I like Mars, and thou like Erycine;
> So of the rest, till we have quite run through,
> And wearied all the fables of the gods.
> Then will I have thee in more modern forms....
>
> (3.7.222–6)

Celia's part through most of this is infuriatingly passive. What little she does say is designed to keep Volpone at arm's length. I can find in the text no justification for the recurring belief of modern directors that Celia reaches a point of near-seduction.[33] Her one long speech indicates, I think, that

Jonson is far more concerned with Volpone's responses than with hers. She begs to be released, appealing to his pity, and if he has none of that, she says, 'Be bountiful and kill me' (3.7.245). This is little more than an echo of patient Griselda, but what follows hits Volpone with the force of a challenge:

> Yet feed your wrath, sir, rather than your lust,
> It is a vice comes nearer manliness.
>
> (3.7.249–50)

After hearing this provocation, and appreciating the genuine counterforce of her resistance, Volpone calculates his chances, wonders what people will think about him if he fails, and threatens rape. Enter Bonario, with naked weapon drawn, sounding the battle-cry: 'Forbear, foul ravisher! libidinous swine!' (3.7.267).

The ironies are beginning their work, and that is how Jonson has planned it from the start. You can't be a real emblem of manliness if you spend your days lying flat on your back, pretending to be virtually paralysed, and submitting to a heavy treatment of make-up before allowing a visitor to enter. And you're not the Don Juan you thought you were if your carefully orchestrated love scene ends when somebody bigger and younger rushes in just when you're threatening violence. The anticlimax rankles when Volpone next speaks to Mosca, and it continues to hurt. Technically, the old partners make a brilliant recovery in the first courtroom scene by forging and gaining credibility for the big lie: it was all Bonario's fault – he was hoping to kill his father, he'd been openly screwing Celia for months – and in any case Volpone could never have been a real threat. To convince the court, '*Volpone is brought in, as impotent*' (4.6.20.1). Whatever loss of esteem Volpone may feel by publicly declaring impotence he claims to recover when the court accepts and endorses the lie: this is more satisfying, he tells Mosca, 'than if I had enjoyed the wench' (5.2.10). Perhaps. But if that's true, it says more than a man might care to admit about himself.

What brings Volpone down for the last time is the inability to stop competing. Just counting his winnings is no satisfaction; there must be victims for him to spurn, fools for him to scorn. So he invents a tactic to bring back all of the old contestants, because he needs them. He wants the rumour of his death spread through the streets of Venice, because:

> I shall have instantly my vulture, crow,
> Raven, come flying hither on the news
> To peck for carrion.
>
> (5.2.64–6)

So Mosca gets to enter his name in the will, puts on the clarissimo's robe, and makes a point of holding on to the keys. For the first time, Mosca has the competitive edge, and that's enough to shatter the old partnership forever.

In the desperate tension of the final courtroom scenes, Mosca retains his advantage. When he enters, dressed in splendour, declared unbelievably rich, it seems that Volpone's manliness has been conferred on him as well. 'A proper man', muses one of the judges, as he begins to plot the future of his marriageable daughter (5.12.50–1). And in the surreptitious bargaining between Mosca and Volpone (disguised as a courtroom lackey) which occupies real stage centre while the legal guardians of Venice are adjusting to a new set of lies, Mosca proves that he has become Volpone's match. His first offer is an even split: share the money equally, agree to a stand-off. Volpone refuses this with contempt, thinks of the alternatives, and at last agrees. But by this time Mosca has caught the bargaining fever: 'I cannot now / Afford it you so cheap' (5.12.69–70). Between habitual competitors, equality is impossible. Mosca knows now that he's going to be the master in any new alliance. And Volpone, unwilling to see himself in a servile position, throws off his disguise.

Punishment is immediate, severe, and poetic. Mosca is to be whipped and condemned for life to service as a galley slave. Volpone's wealth is confiscated, and he's condemned to prison where he'll be 'cramped with irons' until his body becomes 'sick and lame indeed' (5.12.123–4). Both sentences are external versions of what has already happened in each case to the inner man.

If you live in Volpone's Venice, as everybody does, you can choose not to compete. The price of this choice is to make you either an outsider or an impotent old windbag. Sir Politic Wouldbe (who is both of these) spends his days noting down the occasions when rats get at his spur-leathers or the places where he urinates. And when Peregrine pays a visit to Sir Politic's house, the comings-and-goings prompt him to say, 'I see the family is all female here' (5.4.14).

If you do choose to compete – for as much of the world and the flesh as you can make yours – there's another price to be paid. It is illustrated allegorically in the entertainment put on by the freaks at the outset of the action. The soul of Apollo performs a bewildering series of transmigrations in this interlude, passing indifferently from whores to philosophers, from literal to figurative asses, and coming to rest at last in the body of Androgyno, the hermaphrodite. This is what happens to the human soul if it's allowed to drift, without values, in a world where self-assertion is the only rule. The precise terror of this result can be measured, I think, against the ideal of the 'manly soul' which Jonson saw reflected in the people he loved and admired.

Neither impotence nor androgyny is a tolerable condition for Jonson. Between them stands the good man, Bonario, described sneeringly by Corvino as 'that piece of cedar, / That fine, well-timbered gallant' (4.5.123–4). Here, if anywhere, is a moral point of rest. But Jonson is too much of a competitor himself, too much in love with the game he has created, and too honest an artist to give Bonario more than his nominal assent. So he's artistically stingy with Bonario (giving the poor actor almost nothing more than irate virtue to sustain him) and economically generous (giving him loads of money, as if to say, let's see if that won't corrupt you, too). And he reverses the proportions for Volpone. Economic disaster, imprisonment, immobility. But the artistic approval which lavishes on him the words of a theatrical magnifico, and reserves the last word for him as well. Volpone's final performance is an exercise in the art of competing for applause: 'though the fox be punished by the laws', he comes forward to request that the spectators 'fare jovially, and clap your hands' (5.12.153–7). This ending feels like the work of a man who knows the human cost of competition, but knows as well that he won't and doesn't want to suppress the fighting spirit in himself.

Epicoene is a play of surfaces. Moral questions matter less in this play than they generally do in Jonson, and manners account for more. Given Jonson's view of human character, this is only a change in emphasis – and a pragmatic change at that, since *Epicoene* was first performed by a boys' company, the Children of her Majesty's Revels – but a change it remains nonetheless. Distortions of character in *Epicoene* have less to do with inner compulsions than with outward affectations. Morose himself, determined as he is to find a wife who will speak seldom, softly, and only when spoken to, is ingenuously open in declaring exactly what it is he wants. The play as a whole makes sense only if you recognize that caricature can become art in the hands of a great satiric writer.

So it's artistically right that manliness comes closer to the surface in this play than in any other of the comedies. In the final scene, Morose the bridegroom confronts his wife and the party of wedding celebrants with a shocking announcement: 'I am no man, ladies' (5.4.40). For Morose, this is the emotional climax of a wedding day on which everything has gone wrong, and I think it should be played as a moment of great (comic) solemnity. The declaration isn't literally true, of course; Morose wants out of this marriage in the worst way, and he's now willing to take Truewit's advice to 'confess yourself but a man unable, and she will sue to be divorced first' (5.3.159–60). But there's a real sense in which Morose has spent the whole day revealing his impotence. He can't prevent Truewit from entering his house armed with a post-horn and a sermon of such length and cynicism as to blight anyone's honeymoon for weeks. He can't stop the parade of wits, braveries, fops, and musicians which parodies the spirit of the marriage festival. He can't escape from the noise even by retreating to his acoustically insulated attic and sitting on the rafters, next to his 'treble ceilings' (1.1.167). He can't prevent the silent woman, whom he has found only after a troublesome and expensive search, from turning into a talkative shrew as soon as she's married him. When Morose takes centre stage at the end of all this to affirm his impotence, he's virtually acting out the scenario that his nephew, Dauphine, has flippantly predicted: 'Marry, God forbid, sir, that you should geld yourself to anger your wife' (4.4.9–10). The next step in Morose's degradation is his acceptance of cuckoldry; be brays with approval when Daw and La Foole both pretend they've been getting it on with his new wife. And if this isn't enough, Jonson hides the final unmanning in the plot. When all else fails, when even the claims of absolute impotence and manifest cuckoldry don't secure the desired divorce, Dauphine pulls off Epicoene's peruke and says with a flourish: 'Here is your release, sir; you have married a boy' (5.4.181–2). The tacit annulment which accompanies this gesture is enough to reclaim the solitude which Morose thought he had lost, but not to restore the manliness he's publicly given away.

If *Epicoene* is a play about manners, it follows (for Jonson) that it's also a play about language.[34] This connection is implicit throughout Jonson's critical programme. '*Language* most shewes a man', he writes in *Discoveries*: 'speake that I may see thee. It springs out of the most retired, and inmost parts of us, and is the Image of the Parent of it, the mind. No glasse renders a mans forme, or likenesse, so true as his speech.'[35] Just as manners are the art of man as a social being, so language is the intellectual art. The connection is given the status and weight of a principle in the Jonsonian judgement on the 'effeminate person' which I've already discussed: 'Wheresoever, manners, and fashions are corrupted, Language is.'

The most flagrant offender against the linguistic ideal of manliness is Sir Amorous La Foole. Listen to him talk for five minutes and you'll find yourself thinking about Osric. He can't say good morning without putting on airs. There's a breathy quality in his every phrase, which he supposes will mark him as interested in other people, but which anyone who's not tone deaf can identify as the puff of self-importance. 'Good faith', he says as he enters Clerimont's house, 'it is a fine lodging, almost as delicate a lodging as mine' (1.4.4–5). Conversation is a difficult art for Sir Amorous, though he thinks it's easy, largely because he makes no effort to listen to what anyone else is saying while he composes himself for the next instalment of his serial recitation. When Clerimont tells him that he's likely to be beaten up for the 'doubtfulness o' your phrase' (1.4.14), Sir Amorous continues gushing just as if the insult had missed him completely: 'It should be extremely against my will, sir, if I contested with any man' (1.4.17). Mention any of his relatives to Sir Amorous, and you've got to prepare yourself for the aria which begins, 'They all come out of our house, the La Fooles o' the north, the La Fooles of the west, the La Fooles of the east and south' (1.4.34–6), and which won't end until you've heard more than you can stand about heraldry, dining on pheasant, getting knighted in Ireland, or what to wear if you're travelling to Cadiz. When Sir Amorous bustles offstage – at last – Clerimont turns to Dauphine and says: 'Did you ever hear such a wind-fucker as this?' (1.4.69). I suppose it's a sense of decorum that prompts editors to gloss this by pointing out that the windhover used to be known by a racier name. For me, 'wind-fucker' is perfect as it stands; there could be no better image for the frenetic, self-absorbed and yet aimless verbal pumping which La Foole tries to pass off as real speech.

Sir Amorous, a brilliant demonstration of the principle that too much pickedness isn't manly, is only one voice in a crowd of linguistic offenders. John Daw's masquerade as the man of letters lurches into bathos whenever he reads his own poetry or talks about the books he obviously hasn't read. Captain Otter's invective at his wife's expense melts into servile apology the moment he's confronted with his princess. The Collegiate ladies, artlessly exercising their wits 'with most masculine or rather hermaphroditical authority' (1.1.72–3), are imperfect usurpers of manliness. Jonson is observing and recreating in the society of the play a state of affairs he found threatening: namely, a world where epicene manners are dominant, where distinctions between male and female have been subverted, where the voice of manliness (when it tries to speak) is likely to sound the false notes of foppery, stridency, or androgyny.[36]

So the only real competitors are Truewit (seconded by Clerimont, supported by Dauphine) and Morose. The first meeting between them is a verbal joust where nothing is at stake except manliness. Pretending to be the bearer of news from court, Truewit elbows his way into Morose's house and begins to talk, and talk, and talk. He's chosen the perfect strategy for evading Morose's angry interruptions: 'Alas, sir, I am but a messenger', he can say with a shrug; 'I but tell you what you must hear' (2.2.46–7). Before this confrontation occurs, the spectators have been told that the one thing Morose can't abide is noise, and they've seen for themselves the imperious conversational tyranny whereby Morose dictates expansively to a servant who must answer him only in rigidly prescribed gestures. Truewit gains the dramatic, moral, and verbal initiative simply by ignoring all the silly rules by means of which Morose manages to intimidate everyone else. He enters as if on a delightful social mission, pretends that his antagonist's rage is good-natured badinage, and invents new reasons for talking each time he's challenged.

If language best shows a man, what it reveals about Morose is that here is a person unfit for human companionship. Having cut himself off from the outside world, Morose has only one standard of measurement left: himself. When he inspects the putative woman he's intending to marry, Morose approves of her attractive appearance only in the sense that she's 'well fitted' to 'me' (2.5.18). Speaking as a bridegroom having a first look at his prospective wife, what strikes Morose as worth talking about is himself – dissected into psychological attributes, personal idiosyncrasies, parts of the body. When he mentions her, it's in general terms: she's fine 'without', so let's 'try her within' (2.5.18). To give the woman a body and a soul would at least salvage her dignity, but for Morose an outside and an inside will do. There's an emotional coarseness in this procedure – a coarseness made harsher by the sexual insensitivity which allows Morose to speak of inspecting his bride 'within' while apparently missing the gynaecological flavour of the remark. Here is a rhetoric founded on sensationally poor judgement; the speaker is a bull who makes a complete inspection of his 'heifer' (2.5.60) without being able to distinguish between female and male.

The Truewit style, by contrast, is based on the speaker's ability to control the medium of language in order to draw subtle distinctions, suggest comparative judgements, and engage in the pleasure of social interaction. If Sir Amorous hopes to get by with nothing but manners to recommend him, and Morose tries to construct a life in which manners will be irrelevant, Truewit understands the shallowness of the one position, the indecency of the other. As a social being, Truewit occupies an acceptably human position between the butterfly and the bull; as a speaker of the language, he avoids both fluttering and bellowing. When Dauphine expresses admiration for Truewit's knowledge of women, and an eagerness to learn from the master, Truewit replies that meeting women is a social art that has to be conducted in public assemblies – in playhouses and churches, for example – not in the privacy of seclusion: 'A wench to please a man comes not down dropping from the ceiling, as he lies on his back droning a tobacco pipe. He must go where she is' (4.1.57–9). Despite the care with which he constructs his sentences, there's an easy naturalness in Truewit's speech. He achieves this conversational tone partly through sheer dexterity; when you're as skilful a speaker as Truewit is, you can hide art with art. But there's an additional dramatic quality that contributes to the tone. Truewit isn't so much making a speech as talking to someone whose literary tastes and cultural preferences he knows well enough to make them part of the conversation.

Unlike Morose, Truewit is a man of superior judgement. He's the sharpest and most discerning judge of character in Jonson's London. While John Daw is collecting a reputation as a poet and a scholar, Truewit trusts his experience and his independence of mind to tell him that the man is a fool. As the trickster of the comedy, Truewit relies on a practised eye for seeing in advance how the fools and gulls are going to behave. And his language is alive with the kind of intelligence that isn't afraid of making decisions. The man who has plenty of experience with women, Truewit says, will know 'whom to love, whom to play with, whom to touch once, whom to hold ever' (4.1.55–6).

But there's one sense in which Truewit is no more intelligent than Morose: he's no better than Morose (or anyone else) at guessing the secret of Epicoene's gender. Both Truewit and Morose are engaged, frequently and perhaps obsessively, in evaluating the deportment of women. And the social world of the play gives them plenty of opportunities to judge and find wanting. The Collegiate ladies (Madam Haughty, Madam Centaure, and Mrs Mavis) are clever enough, but vain and pretentious; their lives are vapidly devoted to the arts of conspicuous consumption. Mrs Otter is an energetic virago who extracts unquestioned servitude from her husband in exchange for a beer allowance. Epicoene, by contrast, is the perfect woman: receptive, beautiful, and silent. As Karen Newman has persuasively shown, the play as a whole is filled with anxiety about disruptive female behaviour in general, and disruptive female speech in particular.[37] As proponents of manliness, both Truewit and Morose are in a sense protecting themselves against the threat of female initiative. Morose's need for such protection is so comprehensive as to ensure that the perfect woman, by his own definition, won't be a woman at all.

Both Truewit's position in the play and his style are in one sense privileges conferred on him by Jonson; he's a discerning observer and speaker because Jonson wants him to be. Since *Epicoene* is a play of surfaces, privileges of this kind are permitted to characters who happen to be born with the right names. In the dedicatory letter which offers *Epicoene* to the attention of Sir Francis Stuart, Jonson describes the ability to exercise wise and impartial judgement as 'that noblest and manliest virtue' (ll. 7–8). There's no good reason to blame Jonson for coveting this virtue himself, or for allowing Truewit to express it in manliness of speech. And if, in his attitude towards women especially, Truewit fails to rise above his environment, the same can be said of his creator.

In *The Alchemist* and *Bartholomew Fair* Jonson revisits some of the pleasures and anxieties of his previous comedies, but with greater generosity of spirit. The chicanery by which the world is run in *Volpone* and *Epicoene* goes through a further stage of refinement and emerges in *The Alchemist* as absurdity. What happens to manliness in a world made over by alchemical fantasy is suggested, with emblematic authority, by Lovewit's allusion to 'The boy of six year old, with the great thing' (5.1.24). This mental icon appears in Lovewit's list of the items that might well attract curious crowds to his otherwise vacant house. And it's the perfect image of what the men of the play look like when sexually aroused.

Sir Epicure Mammon's dream is an absurdly literal fantasy of how it would feel to be the complete man. The great thing for Mammon is to be endowed with limitless potency:

> For I do mean
> To have a list of wives and concubines
> Equal with Solomon, who had the stone
> Alike with me; and I will make me a back
> With the elixir, that shall be as tough
> As Hercules', to encounter fifty a night.
>
> (2.2.34–9)

Here the dream of potency discredits itself through rhetorical overkill particularly when Mammon adds to it special safeguards (such as gelding Face and all of the gallants who might be sexual competitors), self-conscious voyeurism (in wishing to see multiple mirror-images of himself, walking 'Naked between my succubae'), and the sadistic pleasure of humiliating those who serve him (as in his refusal to accept anyone but 'fathers and mothers' to do his pimping and procuring). What Mammon wants to project as manliness is in fact childishness: the sort of potency appropriate to a six-year-old imagination. In describing the restorative properties of the elixir, Mammon gives himself away by claiming that 'In eight-and-twenty days / I'll make an old man of fourscore a child' (2.1.52–3). That's as good a description as any of what Mammon has been able to do to himself. He puffs out his pretentious lust to Dol Common, supposing her to be the sister of some great lord, by announcing that she's made him 'the happiest man in Europe' (4.1.112). Minutes later he cowers in a corner, desperately afraid of losing his hope, appealing for Subtle's forgiveness on the grounds that he didn't mean to do it: 'Nay, good, dear father, / There was no' unchaste purpose' (4.5.44–5). The boy of six years old has been caught red-handed with the great thing.

Sir Epicure's fraudulent manliness is an extreme case, but not so different in kind from what happens to the lesser fools in *The Alchemist* or to the pleasure seekers of *Bartholomew Fair*. Dapper thinks he can prove himself a man by mounting the Faery Queen, but all he earns is a symbolic unmanning: he's dressed in Fortune's petticoat and thrown into her 'privy lodgings' (3.5.79) where he remains (utterly forgotten) until Subtle rescues him by accident at the end of the play. In *Bartholomew Fair* the manliness of Littlewit is fraudulent on two counts: neither his cloying uxoriousness nor his ludicrous pride in authorship can be justified by what we are able to learn about his wife and his puppet play. Both strands of paternalism are nicely undercut when Littlewit arrives at the premiere of his puppet play, is asked for the price of admission by the doorkeeper, and then can't locate his wife in the audience because she's masked and accompanied by a pimp.

The concluding action in each of Jonson's major comedies is provoked by a symbol of impotence. In *Volpone*, the magnifico is carried into the courtroom '*as impotent*'; in *Epicoene* Morose declares that he's not a man only to find that his wife isn't a woman; in *The Alchemist* a great offstage explosion destroys the alchemical laboratory and deflates the psychological priapism of Sir Epicure and his fellow dreamers. The radical paradigm of this pattern occurs in the puppet play at the end of *Bartholomew Fair*. Zeal-of-the-land Busy brings the puppet play to a halt with the last of his thundering denunciations: 'Down with Dagon, down with Dagon!' (5.5.1). In the disputation which follows, the puritan's 'main argument' against the miniature players 'is that you are an abomination; for the male among you putteth on the apparel of the female, and the female of the male' (5.5.86–8). The perversity of the players is threatening to Busy's patriarchal notion of exact sexual walking. But the Puppet Dionysius has a ready answer: 'It is your old stale argument against the players, but it will not hold against the puppets; for we have neither male nor female amongst us' (5.5.91–3). And with that, '*The puppet takes up his garment*' (5.5.94.1) to reveal the absence of the great thing.[38] Confronted by sexlessness, Busy knows that he must resign: 'I am confuted; the cause hath failed me', he admits. As for the puppet play, 'Let it go on' (5.5.101–4).

I think the puppet's derisive gesture is an accurate measurement of the relationship between *Bartholomew Fair* and the comedies which precede it. On the one hand, *Bartholomew Fair* expands and enriches what has gone before: the world of the fair is itself a hotbed of desire in which the competing interests and jargons of the vendors and seekers of pleasure are absurdly orchestrated. But *Bartholomew Fair* is also an outrageously comprehensive act of self-parody.[39] The Induction is a piece of writing which only someone with a whimsical awareness of his reputation for self-assertion could have produced. 'These master-poets, they will ha' their own absurd courses', says the Stage-keeper by way of apology for an author who has 'kicked me three or four times about the tiring-house, I thank him, for but offering to put in, with my experience' (ll. 23–6). The elaborately technical contract between playwright and audience which follows, solemnly read out by the Scrivener, is the closest thing in Jonson to a genuinely collective agreement. Like all such agreements, it follows a tacit admission that authoritative paternalism hasn't been an entirely blessed arrangement.

I'm not proposing that *Bartholomew Fair* be read as a Jonsonian recantation; the master-poet of the Induction, however he may have changed, 'prays you to believe his ware is still the same' (l. 143). But there is in this play an uncharacteristic letting-go, a feeling for the world as a circus of appetites which won't be controlled by calling on principle. Zeal-of-the-land Busy typifies the new Jonsonian mood which is willing to say, 'Let it go on.'

The new mood is what allows Jonson to tolerate, forgive, and enjoy the two great spirits of the fair – Ursula the pig-woman and Bartholomew Cokes – both of whom transcend the distinction between male and female as surely as the puppets do. Ursula is technically female, and most of the references to her nourishing capacities make her explicitly maternal. To Overdo she's 'the very womb and bed of enormity' (2.2.101), to Knockem 'she's mother o' the pigs' (2.5.70). But her femaleness defies heterosexual conventions; as Quarlous observes, to embrace her would be 'like falling into a whole shire of butter' (2.5.90). And when Ursula talks or drinks (as she does incessantly), her style is a parody of manliness: 'two stone o' suet a day is my proportion. I can but hold life and soul together with this (here's to you, Nightingale) and a whiff of tobacco, at most. Where's my pipe now?' (2.2.77–80). Dripping with sweat and fat, presiding greedily over her passionately roasting pigs, Ursula stands for appetite at a level more primitive than sexual desire. She is the sexless goddess whose nature it is to offer the promise of limitless indulgence.

The ideal consumer in the fair world is Cokes, for whom every desire is a whim of the moment: each new hobbyhorse or ballad or gingerbread-man eclipses whatever it was he bought last, so he buys them all. Though he's nineteen years old and comically tall, Cokes can't be trusted to visit the fair except in the company of his 'dry nurse', Humphrey Wasp (1.5.45). Even so, his childishness makes him the easiest mark for every purveyor and snapper-up of trifles. The litany of items he loses includes his money, his cloak, his hat, his sword, his sister, his fiancée, but above all 'my bargain o' hobby-horses and gingerbread, which grieves me worst of all' (4.2.78–9). For an experienced cutpurse like Edgworth, Cokes represents asexual desire: in his case, the caprices which lead him from one trinket to the next keep him blissfully unaware of adult responsibilities. He's hopeless at defending either himself or his engagement to Grace Wellborn, but in his view of things, these are not matters worth caring about.

Despite the greasy sensuality of the one and the vacuous simplicity of the other, Ursula and Cokes are the spirits whom Jonson is indulgently cele-brating in *Bartholomew Fair*. I'd be less confident about making this claim if it weren't for Michael Bogdanov's energetic and thoughtful production at the Young Vic in 1978.[40] The authority given to Ursula in this modern-dress interpretation was earned in part by the acting of Laura Cox. But it was supported by the mannishness of her costume, the dominant placing of her booth at the centre of the set, and even by the icon which decorated the programme – '*the pig's head with a large writing under it*' (3.2.53–5) – appro-priately modelled on Jonson's stage direction. Cokes, as played by Phillip Bowen, was a faultless fool. Ostentatiously overdressed for a circus, indelibly upper-class in language and manners, he danced through his disastrous day at the fair without for a moment losing his conviction that nothing could go wrong. In the puppet play at the close, Cokes's insipid commentary was greeted with laughter and applause of the kind you reserve for the artless comic who makes the best jokes when he doesn't understand them himself.

The representatives of manliness who encounter the pleasures of the fair get harsher treatment from Jonson than either his amorphously female provider or his promiscuously childish consumer. In various ways, Adam Overdo, Zeal-of-the-land Busy, Quarlous, Edgworth, and a handful of lesser competitors adopt the stances and the styles of manliness either to defend themselves against the perils of pleasure or to exploit the fair to their own advantage. Overdo, the justice who hopes to smell out enormities by visit-ing the fair in disguise, could have emerged for a younger Jonson as a voice of sanity, comparable to Lovewit or Truewit. But in *Bartholomew Fair* the 'manliest virtue' of justice is helpless; the only person who places absolute trust in the warrant of Justice Overdo is a certifiable madman, Trouble-all.

Jonson the man may have felt that in *Bartholomew Fair* he had gone too far in allowing pleasure to dissolve the potency of the manly soul. If this is the case, then it appears he tried to set matters right by including the virtu-ous but clumsy character, Manly, in his next comedy, *The Devil is an Ass*.[41] But whatever his private thoughts, Jonson the comic artist was aware of the limits of manliness. In *Bartholomew Fair*, more completely than anywhere

else, he understood that manliness, in its confrontation with the entice-
ments of pleasure, can be self-defeating, fraudulent, ridiculous. That wasn't
Jonson's only or final view of the matter, but it was the deepest and most
frightening admission he would make.

The pleasures which Jonson dramatizes in his comedies are multifarious
and multivalent: the succulence of roast pork, the stimulus of bottle-ale,
the seductions of erotic fantasy, the gratifications of wealth, the delights
of jargon, the blandishments of theatrical mimesis. But there's a sense in
which all of these are included in the single pleasure of competition. The
birds of prey in *Volpone*, the gallants in *Epicoene*, the customers in
The Alchemist, and the circus barkers in *Bartholomew Fair* are competing
shamelessly for every small verbal advantage, sexual acknowledgement, or
economic reward. The magnificoes of Jonson's comedy appear to renounce
these lesser lures to compete in the comprehensive game of manliness, in
which the particular object of pleasure is less valuable than the thrill of
winning. That's why Volpone is happier to have won the game of discred-
iting Bonario and Celia 'than if I had enjoyed the wench' (5.2.10). That's
why Truewit, the champion of the language games in *Epicoene*, is given
greater authority than Dauphine, the recipient of the contested inheritance. In *Bartholomew Fair* it is no longer possible for manliness to assert
itself, even temporarily, above the hubbub of carnival voices. When it tries
to do so, in the denunciations of Zeal-of-the-land Busy, it is confuted by the
derisive gestures of the puppet play.

The spectators of Jonsonian comedy are also engaged in a game, as the
contractual Induction to *Bartholomew Fair* implies. As always, Jonson puts
himself into an adversarial relationship with the spectators, but he is now
surprisingly generous in the role he offers them. Each spectator has the right
to judge what he sees and hears, 'provided always his place get not above his
wit' (ll. 80–1) and that 'every man here exercise his own judgment, and not
censure by contagion' (ll. 87–8). Even the 'grounded judgments here', that
is, the groundlings, are given their place as the author's 'play-fellows in wit'
(ll. 50–1). This is a facetious rather than a real contract, of course, but even
in its mockery it clears a space in which the spectators can participate.
Jonsonian comedy is a game of wit, and the pleasure of spectatorship is
contained in the simple (and highly demanding) act of playing. And since
this is an adversarial sport, playing implies resistance. The spectator who
trusts his own judgement will not simply fall in line with all of Jonson's
opinions nor share all of his presuppositions. There were times in his career
when such resistance would have infuriated Jonson. But here, for once, he
acknowledges that aesthetic pleasure arises not from winning but from the
activity of playfulness itself. Let it go on.

4
The Adverse Body: John Marston

My favourite line in Marston is from *The Dutch Courtesan*: 'Every man's turd smells well in's own nose' (3.3.45). Marston didn't invent this image; he found it in Florio's translation of Montaigne, a book he read with keen interest soon after its publication in 1603, where it appears as a bathetically unheroic couplet: 'Ev'ry mans ordure well, To his owne sense doth smell'.[1] Florio of course found it in the text he was translating, not in Montaigne's racy French, but in a Latin epigram, 'Stercus cuisque suum bene olet',[2] which Montaigne was quoting inaccurately by memory from the *Adages* of Erasmus.[3] Marston's most striking images will often turn out to have intertextual pedigrees that say more for his bookishness than his originality. But in this instance as elsewhere, if he didn't invent something new, he certainly gave it an idiomatic English crudeness that nobody else did. Vulgarity, in fact, was the gift for which he became notorious and for which he was lampooned by the students of St John's College, Cambridge, in *The Return from Parnassus*, Part 2: 'What, *Monsier Kinsayder*, lifting up your legge and pissing against the world? Put up man, put up for shame' (1.2.267–8). I wish I could claim that Marston's vulgarity was a sign of uninhibited personal warmth or communal glee, but no such happy interpretation could survive much absorption in his writing.[4] The pleasure of smelling one's own turd is a fairly specialized form of narcissism, just as the gesture of pissing against the world is a pretty calculated form of exhibitionism. Marston's vulgarity was not a celebration of but a revulsion against the body.

He targets the female body in particular because of its subversive power over man's will. Marston's short career as a writer began with one erotic fantasy, *The Metamorphosis of Pigmalion's Image* (1598), and ended with another, *The Insatiate Countess* (c.1608). In the first case the woman's body is the contrivance of male 'workmanship' and 'Art'.[5] Pigmalion constructs his ideal mate precisely because he's not prepared to engage in the 'servile' acts of courtship that real women would require. And once he's made her, she's entirely under his control: he gazes at her 'parts of secrecie', he kisses her lips, he fondles her breasts, he takes her into his bed, and in all of these rituals

'She with her silence, seemes to graunt his sute.' Only after he's got exactly the female body he wants does Pigmalion begin to wish for its animation, and even then he desires that his own soul be divided in two, one half for his own body, one for the ivory maiden. When the transformation to flesh occurs it's clearly not the creation of an independent person but the completion of a wet dream; 'And now, oh now, he finds how he is graced / By his owne worke.'[6] *The Insatiate Countess* is the obverse of this same fantasy; here the woman – Isabella, Countess of Swevia – makes her own erotic choices in exactly the way that the title implies. Having recently been left a widow, she's free to denounce her late husband's jealousy while she courts his successor. But during the festivities which celebrate her hasty second marriage, she falls in love with the bridegroom's best friend. She approaches her wedding night with reluctance and ingenuity: 'when my loathed mate / Shall struggle in due pleasure for his right', she says, 'I'll think't my love, and die in that delight' (2.1.256–8). Before long she has begun an affair with her desired lover so spectacular that the new husband goes into retirement as a hermit. She now takes a second lover, whom she fails to incite to the point that he'll kill the first. So she finds a Spanish colonel who's more compliant, and so it goes, roughly in this vein, until she dies on the scaffold surrounded by admiring and forgiving men. Controlling the actions of the female body is a decisive item of the male agenda in Marston's writing. Complete control yields absolute bliss; the absence of control invites painful humiliation.

Both of these texts, to be sure, are problematic or marginal members of the Marston canon: *Pigmalion's Image* he disowned almost as soon as he had written it, and *The Insatiate Countess* he abandoned long before it was finished. *Pigmalion's Image* was published together with *Certaine Satyres* in a single octavo volume (1598). Between the two Marston puts an apology of sorts, 'The Author in Praise of his Precedent Poem'. The tone is defensive; Marston argues that the readers who ridiculed *Pigmalion's Image* have missed the point – the irony – of his 'dissembling shifts'. The problem has arisen because his intentions have been misrepresented: 'as if I had deni'd / Or thought my Poem good, when that I see / My lines are froth, my stanzaes saplesse be.'[7] But you don't understand, it's *supposed* to be funny. This might look like a good defence until you ask: then why wasn't it?[8] Marston was a young man of twenty-one when he got into this cul de sac: not yet enough of an artist to anticipate the problem, and too much of an intellectual to let it go. A decade later, while working on *The Insatiate Countess*, he must have reached a point of saturation he regarded as final. By this time his efforts as a writer had earned him the insult of having his books banned and burned; the humiliation of being publicly scorned by his literary idol, Ben Jonson; and the inconvenience of being put in prison for allegedly offensive passages in his plays. He left his last play unfinished (later Lewis Machin and William Barksted would work it up into a performable script)[9] and sold his shares in the Blackfriars theatre company, the Children of the Queen's Revels. During the next 26 years of his life (1608–34) Marston wrote nothing. He was ordained deacon (1608) and priest (1609) in the Church of England, and held the living of Christchurch, Hampshire, for fifteen years (1616–31). He married a clergyman's daughter, Mary Wilkes; their only child, a son, died in infancy. When a collection of his plays reached print in 1633, Marston must have intervened in some way to get the book reissued in the same year by the same publisher but without his name on the title page. What looks like a comprehensive renunciation of his past extends to his burial, in 1634, under a tombstone marked only with the words, 'Oblivioni Sacrum'.[10]

These acts of disavowal, both early and late, are of interest today only because they bracket a body of work which Marston needed to disown. Among the distinctive marks of this work is a recurring image which could stand for everything I've said so far – the image of vomiting. W. Kinsayder, the satiric persona Marston invented for the purpose of lancing the ills and corruptions of society, is on the whole an angry and combative presence who snarls at vice. But he has his sensitive moods too, as in this passage from *The Scourge of Villainie*:

> From a sickly bed,
> And from a moodie mind distempered,
> I vomit foorth my love, now turn'd to hate,
> Scorning the honour of a Poets state.[11]

The satires as a rule ask us to presume the sickness of a parade of lechers, hypocrites, and poetasters who stand for society, and the health or sanity of Kinsayder, the privileged observer. But Kinsayder isn't immune to the general infection; something he ingests turns love to hate, and he reacts with visceral revulsion which cleanses him and prepares him for the next encounter with vice. In *Antonio and Mellida* (c.1599) the satiric voice has become a dramatic character, Feliche, who makes much the same point in reverse:

> O that the stomach of this queasy age
> Digests or brooks such raw unseasoned gobs
> And vomits not them forth.

> (2.1.87–9)

In *Antonio's Revenge* (c.1600) the crimes of Piero Sforza, Duke of Venice, are poisoning the body politic; the results, explains one of the revengers, will amount to a collective upheaval by means of which the citizens will 'cast / And vomit him from off their government' (5.2.34–5). Among Piero's crimes is the slander of his own daughter, Mellida, which Antonio redresses with countervailing rhetoric: 'Dog, I will make thee eat thy vomit up, / Which thou hast belk't 'gainst taintless Mellida' (1.2.204–5). This example goes a step beyond the others on the grossness scale for two reasons: vomiting here is a premeditated act of hypocrisy instead of a natural reflex, and it's also reversible if Antonio gets his way and forces Piero to lick up his own slime.

Vomiting is a specialized instance of a more general tendency in Marston. It is sometimes accompanied by spitting, for example, or by its opposite, sucking. Noses, aside from smelling turds and other bodily stench, can exude blood and drivel: 'madam', says the fool Balurdo in *Antonio's Revenge*, 'I have taken a murr, which makes my nose run most pathetically and unvulgarly' (3.2.40–1). The anus, as a less respectable bodily orifice, has to appear under various metonymic disguises; we know it's there because of the turds and farts it produces, and because it offers a special temptation 'To snort in source of Sodom vilainie'.[12] The genital organs too are alluded to with some coyness, often by one of their many nicknames. The penis is simply Priapus in the satiric poems;[13] more imaginatively, as in *The Fawn* (*c*.1605), it can become the 'unsanctified member' of mock-puritan rhetoric (2.1.326). In *Antonio and Mellida* Marston supplies the two comic leads with a pageboy each, calling them Catzo and Dildo. For a young man setting out as a playwright, this is one way of acknowledging his multicultural background; perhaps he imagined his Italian-born mother, Marie Fuarsi, explaining 'Catzo' to his proper English father, and the other way round for 'Dildo'. In any case, these are in their way appropriate personifications of a ubiquitous energy in Marston's drama.

The female sexual organs are often conflated with the womb (in the case of mature women) or identified with the maidenhead (in the case of virgins), but the many oblique references are more interesting, as in the case of the lady's 'tender breech' which only her farthingale is lucky enough to touch.[14] The metaphors which encode female desire are often so fanciful as to make you wonder if the body is present in them at all, except when they're spoken by Isabella, the insatiate countess herself; after alienating her third lover (by insisting that he kill the second) she longs to have him 'once more here, / Within this prison, made of flesh and bone' (4.2.131–2). The figure of the body as prison is conventional, but since the object to be contained is the lover (not the soul, for example), the site of imprisonment becomes gender-specific in a way that corresponds to male fears and fantasies. A similar release of male horror is at work in *Antonio's Revenge* in the words Piero uses, albeit hypocritically, to accuse his daughter of sexual impurity: 'The flux of sin / Flows from thy tainted body' (4.1.127–8). A more sensitive father might have worried, I think, about the implicit equation here between menstrual blood and sexual guilt. But the precise physiology of the vulva is less important in Marston than its presumed attributes of looseness, openness, flexibility, and eternal readiness.

What all of this adds up to is an unusual interest in the threshold areas of the body – in the bodily orifices, the fluids the body might expel, the matter it might ingest. These thresholds are what make the body vulnerable to invasion by disease or vice, because they are open to the world at large.

Readers of Bakhtin will recognize in this description a version of the grotesque body: 'All these convexities and orifices have a common characteristic; it is within them that the confines between bodies and between the body and the world are overcome', Bakhtin writes; and the escape from confinement is a version of carnival, embodied in such activities as 'eating, drinking, defecation and other elimination (sweating, blowing of the nose, sneezing), as well as copulation, pregnancy, dismemberment, swallowing up by another body'.[15] Marston of course finds the grotesque body threatening rather than exhilarating; he wants reason, the moral faculty of the soul, to be in control of the body's activities. But how good are the odds of maintaining such control in a world where the slime of corruption is forever threatening to seep in through one aperture or another, and over a body, moreover, that insists on vomiting or flaming into lust regardless of what reason is telling it to do? The anxiety I've just described is never very far below the surface in Marston's writing. It's outlined explicitly in Satire 8 ('Inamorato Curio') of *The Scourge of Villainie*. The speaker laments the decline in brightness (and hence power) of the soul, and proposes an explanation for the present state of affairs:

> Our adverse body, being earthly, cold,
> Heavie, dull, mortal, would not long infold
> A stranger inmate, that was backward still
> To all his dungie, brutish, sensuall will:
> Now here-upon our Intellectual,
> Compact of fire and all celestiall,
> Invisible, immortall, and divine,
> Grewe straight to scorne his Land-lordes muddy slime.
> And therefore now is closely slunk away....

Abandoned by its rightful governor, the body now is ruled by 'sencelesse will'. The satire concludes with a plea for the immortal soul to return, to 'Inspire our trunks', and to raise humanity out of the corruption into which it has sunk.[16] The part played by the body in Marston's ontology is adversarial: because it is open to new experience, it threatens the wholeness of the person; because it is mired in filth, it resists the governance of reason; and because it has expelled the soul, it can only engender alienation and guilt. This is a line of argument which Marston might have used without much editing in his second career as a priest. But the argument itself is less interesting than the obsessions on which it is based, and these are what matter in the greatest achievements of his first career: *The Malcontent* (*c*.1603) and *The Dutch Courtesan* (*c*.1604).

The Malcontent, like so much of what Marston wrote, gets its strongest energies from the comprehensive feeling of revulsion it creates. Here the feeling is mediated most powerfully by the satiric spokesman, Malevole, whose nickname gives the play its title. Malevole's contempt for the world and its inhabitants has its nominal origin in recent political events; he is really Altofronto, the rightful Duke of Genoa, and his stance of malcontentedness, like his *nom de guerre*, is a technique he's using to recover the position from which he has recently been deposed. But there's something in his language which goes far beyond these immediate circumstances. Though he's adopting a pose and self-consciously creating a malcontent language to go with it, there's a quality in his speeches that's close to absolute conviction:

> Think this – this earth is the only grave and Golgotha wherein all things that live must rot; 'tis but the draught wherein the heavenly bodies discharge their corruption; the very muck-hill on which the sublunary orbs cast their excrements. Man is the slime of this dung-pit, and princes are the governors of these men; for, for our souls, they are as free as emperors', all of one piece; there goes but a pair of shears betwixt an emperor and the son of a bagpiper; only the dyeing, dressing, pressing, glossing, makes the difference. (4.5.110–19)

The rhetorical kick in this speech depends largely on exaggeration: the earth isn't just a cesspool, human life isn't merely animated slime, and the differences between people aren't exclusively sartorial. But the exaggerations are clearly based on something that is true, and it's tempting to accept them as the nearest approximation to truth, especially when they're introduced by the gloomy but incontrovertible statement that all things that live must rot. And there's a further dramatic reason which confers authenticity (if not literal truth) on this diatribe. Everything that Malevole has been able to observe about life in Genoa, and everything we've been observing over his shoulder, would support a distressingly low evaluation of what goes on in the human zoo.

After the Induction, written by Webster to help transfer the play to the Globe, the opening scene begins with '*The vilest out-of-tune music*' (1.1.0.1) emanating from Malevole's chamber. Two court hangers-on try to shout the music down with rhetorical questions like, 'You think you are in a brothel-house, do you not?' (1.1.6). Duke Pietro (the usurper) then enters with some of his courtiers, notably Ferrado, who calls out Malevole's name. Finally, silence. But not for long, because Malevole's vocal music begins at this point. He speaks '*Out of his chamber*' (1.2.5.1), which must mean either from the upper level of the stage or from an offstage location. He keeps his distance, even when he does answer: 'Yaugh, god-a'-man, what dost thou there? Duke's Ganymede, Juno's jealous of thy long stockings! shadow of a woman, what wouldst, weasel? thou lamb a' court, what dost thou bleat for? ah, you smooth-chinned catamite!' (1.2.5–9). Ferrado says nothing to refute these accusations, and Pietro surprisingly invites Malevole to join his circle of courtiers, where he may 'bespurtle' whomever he wants to (1.2.12). Before long Malevole is attacking Ferrado again, calling him a 'lecherous animal' and a 'little ferret' who 'goes sucking up and down the palace into every hen's nest, like a weasel' (1.3.22–4), and asking him how he's spending his time aside from practising the usual arts of the sexual sycophant. To this Ferrado replies, 'I study languages' (1.3.28). There's an infuriating smugness about this response, and about much of the behaviour of the court party. The play doesn't reveal anything about the presumed intimacy between Pietro and his *'minion'*, as Ferrado is designated in the dramatis personae, but the initial impression of a court run by unflinching favouritism and unhesitating flattery is going to last.[17]

The Duchess Aurelia will do her part to ensure that it does. She has no sexual interest in her husband, nor much respect for him as a man, so she depends on the expert assistance of the court bawd, Maquerelle, to keep her sex life interesting. As the play opens the current stud is Mendoza, a notorious social climber who's determined to use every ounce of leverage he gets from screwing the duchess for his political advantage. But by the time we see Aurelia she's already convinced that Mendoza has been slighting her, and Maquerelle is leading her, step by careful step, to the conclusion that she ought to sleep with Ferneze instead. 'I will love thee, be it but in despite / Of that Mendoza', she says to the new aspirant: 'Ferneze, thou art the Duchess' favourite' (1.6.46–7). This resolution, expressed in the language of tactical diplomacy, is a bland illustration of a key principle of Marston's Genoa: sex is political, politics are sexual. And it gives impetus to a complicated intrigue which ends when Pietro, goaded on by Mendoza and Malevole, frightens Ferneze out of Aurelia's bedroom in the dead of night. 'I am sorry for our shame', says Pietro to his wife with surprising dignity. 'Go to your bed: / Weep not too much, but leave some tears to shed / When I am dead' (2.5.16–18). She, thinking Ferneze has been killed, finds this a risible request: 'What, weep for thee?' (2.5.18). There's a sense in which this reaction is the right one. Why should she weep for a man whom she probably didn't choose, who prefers the company of his hunting dogs and his catamite to hers, and for whom she's shown no visible sign of feeling so far?

The tactician who makes Aurelia's conduct possible, and the theoretician who makes it plausible, is Maquerelle. She treats women's bodies as if they were a valuable and only partly renewable resource. She shares a restorative 'posset' with two ladies-in-waiting, Emilia and Bianca, and describes its beneficial effects: 'it purifieth the blood, smootheth the skin, enliveneth the eye, strengtheneth the veins, mundifieth the teeth, comforteth the stomach, fortifieth the back, and quickeneth the wit; that's all' (2.4.19–22). The recipe for making this wonderful concoction she divulges in full; it includes 'the juice of cock-sparrow bones' and 'lamb-stones of Muscovia' among its exotic ingredients (2.4.10, 15). And she recommends to her protégées the further attentions of Doctor Plaster-face, whose prescriptions will do their work if a lady spends two hours every morning 'pruning, pinching, and painting' (2.4.52) so as to offset the effects of ageing. Nobody lavishes all this care on a resource without expecting a profit. When Bianca's old husband leaves court on a diplomatic mission, Maquerelle quips that Bianca should be able to earn the money for a new gown before his return. And in choosing a lover, Maquerelle advises, the first thing to look for is the ability to pay: 'he loves ye, pish! he is witty, bubble! fair-proportioned, mew! nobly born, wind! Let this be still your fixed position: esteem me every man according to his good gifts' (4.1.28–31). Laughable and grotesque she may be, but Maquerelle is also a person of considerable authority at the court of Genoa, and she uses her unofficial power to create a climate in which prostitution is both glamorous and normal. When Malevole claims that he'd 'sooner leave my lady singled in a bordello than in the Genoa palace' (3.2.28–9), he has a point. The network of sexual conventions, of which Maquerelle is both product and exponent, has a way of subverting the desire to live in any other way. Once you've internalized it by learning to live with 'impudent custom' (3.2.43), as Malevole puts it, there's no real chance of escape.

The most powerful catalyst of Malevole's outrage is the self-made politician, Mendoza. The nominal ally of Pietro, Mendoza has played his role so cleverly that Pietro, being childless, designates Mendoza his successor. On learning that he's being cuckolded, Pietro finds that grief 'sucks the veins dry, / Rivels the skin', and prompts a general deterioration of the body (2.3.66–7). Mendoza by contrast bristles with the physical energy of a true sexual predator. While he's cuckolding the duke, he's enraptured with himself and exuberant in his praise of women:

> O, how full of ravishing attraction is your pretty, petulant, languishing, lasciviously-composed countenance!...in body how delicate, in soul how witty, in discourse how pregnant, in life how wary, in favours how judicious, in day how sociable, and in night how – O pleasure unutterable! (1.5.41–8)

When Aurelia ditches him for Ferneze he changes his tune but suffers no loss of energy; women are now 'monsters in nature, models of hell' as he suspected all along, 'their looks counterfeit, their hair false, their given hopes deceitful, their very breath artificial' (1.6.85–94). Sex being a political strategy for him in any case, and a wonderfully enjoyable strategy at that, the loss of one woman is just a temporary setback. Soon he's busy making mental plans to marry Maria, the wife of the former Duke Altofronto, not because he loves her in particular, 'but as wise men do love great women, to ennoble their blood and augment their revenue' (3.3.102–3). Mendoza has the unprincipled vitality of the Machiavel, and as in the case of Richard III or Tamburlaine, body language is a crucial weapon in his quest for dominance. It is also central to his inflated self-image, which gains its grandness from the subservience of others, as captured in Mendoza's fantasy of 'petitionary vassals licking the pavement with their slavish knees' (1.5.28–9). Arrogance of this order can go a long way even without other talents, and Mendoza has enough cunning to make himself both likeable and dangerous.

For Malevole, disgusted as he is with what he sees, the typical courtly activities amount to vomiting and sucking. As he explains to his companion Celso (the one uncorrupted straight-man in Genoa), court behaviour is not only immoral but stupidly self-destructive:

> What profit, nay, what nature would keep down,
> Are heaved to them are minions to a crown.
> Envious ambition never sates his thirst,
> Till sucking all, he swells and swells, and bursts.
>
> (1.4.77–80)

Servile courtiers heave up their substance to domineering masters as if by reflex, no matter what self-interest (profit) or sanity (nature) would suggest they ought to do. And the appetite of the great, equally irrational, continues to suck in the substance so offered to the point of explosion. By the social equivalents of indigestion and dropsy the submissive and dominant orders reinforce one another to their mutual detriment. Malevole stands apart from this whole repugnant system:

> In night all creatures sleep;
> Only the malcontent, that 'gainst his fate
> Repines and quarrels – alas, he's goodman tell-clock!
>
> (3.2.10–12)

Less poetically but more characteristically he takes his distance by saying, 'I had rather follow a drunkard, and live by licking up his vomit, than by servile flattery' (4.5.66–8). When the world is as bad as this, to stand apart from it is the only guarantee of personal integrity.

Or is it? This question arises most urgently because of Malevole's double-ness.[18] The malcontent has all along been a pose adopted by Duke Altofronto in order to protect himself while bringing about many desirable goals: the abdication of Pietro, the exposure of Mendoza, the repentance of Aurelia, the vindication of Maria, but most of all the restoration of Duke Altofronto. When all of these goals have been reached the requirements of the plot have been satisfied, but the status of Malevole/Altofronto has been dangerously undercut by ambiguity. If the disguise of Malevole has been merely a cover for Altofronto's manipulations, then isn't he guilty of exactly the same hypocrisy that he finds so loathsome in everyone else? If the disguise is necessary, even as a tactic, then doesn't its deployment show that the way to preserve integrity in a degraded world is to invent some strategy to engage in its machinations? And if the social world is as foul as Malevole all along has made it out to be, then why does Altofronto want to regain his leadership of it to begin with?

I don't think Marston solves these problems except through a strategy – a dramatic strategy – of his own. *The Malcontent* is unlike most Jacobean plays insofar as a single person's viewpoint colours the whole and alternative voices, however loudly they may be heard, are never allowed to seriously challenge it. The doubleness of this single person ensures that his viewpoint will be genuinely more comprehensive than anyone else's. He is both the deposed idealist and the embittered cynic; both the rightful ruler and the underdog; both the last hope for Genoa and the snarling observer of its corruption; both the one just man and the cleverest manipulator. The only comparable instance of such forceful dramatic authority given to a single character is *Hamlet*, a text which has left a deep and recent imprint on the mind which conceived *The Malcontent*. This isn't so much a matter of direct borrowing as of genuine creative influence, as if Marston were writing not with a book open before him but with a deeply felt experience in his memory. To Hamlet's question, 'yet, to me, what is this quintessence of dust?' (2.2.305–6), Malevole has an answer: 'Man is the slime of this dung-pit.' Or try this one: 'Dost thou think Alexander looked o' this fashion i'th' earth?' (5.1.191–2). Malevole again: 'Think this – this earth is the only grave and Golgotha wherein all things that live must rot.' The *'out-of-tune music'* with which the play began is the voice of Hamlet, the voice of the malcontent, and the voice of the adverse body.

And then Marston read Montaigne and wrote *The Dutch Courtesan*. It wasn't quite that simple, but it was one of those rare decisive moments in a writer's career. Imagine Marston as a young man in his late twenties, already well known as the author of *The Malcontent* and much else besides, a leading member of the circle of writers and intellectuals who lived at the Inns of Court, a professed admirer of Ben Jonson and a virulent antagonist of what he saw as the moral indolence of his day – imagine such a person encountering Montaigne's book. He must have felt at once that he was in the presence of someone totally unlike himself, someone old enough to be his father who remembered what it was like to be young, someone who didn't much care about picking a defensible position and surrounding it with impregnable arguments, but who preferred trying on a whole series of apparently unrelated arguments, for the nonce, to see where they might lead.

'What's so terrible about prostitution?' Montaigne asks in effect in the essay which preoccupied Marston most intensely while he was working on *The Dutch Courtesan*, 'Upon Some Verses of Virgil'; or, to quote the words that Marston read, 'Are there not women daily seen amongst us, who for the only profit of their husbands, and by their express order and brokage make sale of their honesty?'[19] And what's at the root of all the irrational fuss about cuckoldry? 'I know a hundred Cockolds, which are so, honestly and little undecently.'[20] To expect absolute chastity from women is 'ridiculous', especially when men place no such demands on themselves. The double standard is only reinforced by the social education of women: 'Even from their infancy wee frame them to the sports of love: their instruction, behaviour, attire, grace, learning and all their words aimeth onely at love, respects onely affection. Their nurces and their keepers imprint no other thing in them.'[21] But when some woman takes the initiative and puts these talents to use, men are the first to complain. And although Montaigne spends much of this essay differentiating between the behaviour of men (us) and women (them), he's aware that what he's describing is a socially constructed reality: '*I say, that both male and female, are cast in one same moulde; instruction and custome excepted, there is not great difference between them.*'[22]

Montaigne's attitude towards the body is not adversarial, at least not in Marston's way. If it were, I don't think he would be able to write digressively and casually, as he does, about his sexual experiences, his dining habits and tastes, his illnesses, his propensity for sneezing, his preference for 'a commodious *Ajax* or easie close-stool' which can at times become 'troublesome with long sitting and nice observation'.[23] When Montaigne remembers the sexual misadventures of his youth, he does so with pleasurable bemusement. He claims that at his age the body no longer delivers pleasure in the same spontaneous way, so he compensates by remembering the enjoyments of the past. What he's looking for is a happy collaboration between body and mind, in which the mind helps to regulate the body's excessive energies (especially in youth), and the body helps to enliven the mind's sombre moods (in advanced age). 'Were my body directly by me, as is my minde', he writes, 'we should march a little more at our ease.'[24] This last image, though it places some distance between mind and body, certainly implies their companionship. Montaigne can believe in a healthful dialectic between the mental and the physical because he doubts their absolute separation to begin with: 'May we not say, that there is nothing in us, during this earthly prison, simply corporall, or purely spirituall?'[25] It's typical of Montaigne that this thought should appear as a question, not a precept, and it need hardly be added that in his case we're never dealing with fixed positions but with a mind (and a life) in movement.[26]

In the use he makes of Montaigne in *The Dutch Courtesan*, Marston shows both the resilience of someone who values novelty and the stubbornness of someone who wants to hold his own ground. He allows Montaigne to define the 'argument' of his comedy, to influence his interpretation of character, and to contribute (at length, and verbatim) to the dialogue. What Marston refuses to grant to his new mentor is the authority to deliver him from loathing.

The printed text of *The Dutch Courtesan* includes, just after the Prologue, a declaration of its argument: '*The difference betwixt the love of a courtesan and a wife is the full scope of the play.*' This idea, however frequently it may have been discussed in the social set to which Marston belonged, owes its prominence in Marston's agenda to the essay by Montaigne from which I've been liberally quoting. The love of a courtesan is motivated by a precise appetite, Montaigne observes: 'Voluptuousness is a quality little ambitious; it holds it selfe rich enough of it selfe without any accesse of reputation; and is best affected where it is most obscured.'[27] Marriage is by contrast a public institution with wide-ranging consequences. 'A man doth not marry for himselfe, whatsoever he aleageth; but as much or more for his posteritie and familie.' So the physical love between husband and wife ought to be sober and discreet; pleasure called into being by 'tickling too lasciviously' would, within marriage, amount to 'a kind of incest'.[28] Montaigne pictures himself as a man who takes marriage seriously, who values the intense erotic experience of his past, but who doesn't expect his wife to recreate it for him. He points out that marriages based on physical attraction often turn out badly, and says he prefers the system whereby marital alliances are negotiated by a third party.

Marston's protagonist in *The Dutch Courtesan*, Freevill, is in the process of living through the kind of change that Montaigne attributes to himself. By all accounts his relationship with Franceschina, the courtesan of the play's title, has been wonderfully voluptuous. And though he's now prepared to marry the virtuous Beatrice, he pays Franceschina that one last visit as if to console himself for what he's losing. Even worse, he takes with him his friend Malheureux – a frosty young ascetic with no sexual experience – because he wants Malheureux to grow up and acknowledge the pleasures of the body. When Franceschina enters, Freevill nudges his companion and says: 'See, sir, this is she' (1.2.74). It's clear from the awkwardness of Malheureux, from his monosyllabic shyness, and from his asides, that he's monstrously stricken with Franceschina at once. And while the woman goes out to fetch her lute, Freevill explains his position with unctuous confidence: 'I loved her with my heart until my soul showed me the imperfection of my body, and placed my affection on a lawful love, my modest Beatrice, which if this short-heels knew, there were no being for me with eyes before her face' (1.2.89–93). Freevill's sharp division of experience into past and future, body and soul, is among his least endearing qualities. The following day, when he finds out that Malheureux has nothing but sex on his mind, Freevill teases him without mercy: 'She's an arrant strumpet', he says of Franceschina; 'as good make use of a statue, a body without a soul, a carcass three months dead' (2.1.130–4). When the prostitute is objectified in this way, there's nothing wrong with her trade; whorehouses are 'Most necessary buildings', Freevill explains; they guarantee the stability of the family by taking lust out of the home: 'I would have married men love the stews as Englishmen lov'd the Low Countries: wish war should be maintain'd there lest it should come home to their own doors' (1.1.59–65).

Next to this callous and self-satisfied permissiveness, the anxieties of Malheureux attract more respect than they might on merit alone. From the outset he believes that lust is both sinful and destructive of nobler pursuits; when he agrees to accompany Freevil to the brothel he believes (naively) that the sight of a whore will augment his loathing of sin. But of course temptation has the opposite effect; suddenly the whole structure of human morality and inhibition seems like the useless baggage of 'custom', and sex is no longer a 'sin' but 'Nature's highest virtue' (2.1.67–78). He returns to Franceschina, propositions her in the most oafish deadpan way, and gets her provisional consent: all he has to do is kill Freevill. Left to himself, Malheureux debates the question: 'To kill my friend! Oh, 'tis to kill myself! / Yet man's but man's excrement, man breeding man / As he does worms, or this' (2.2.198–200). Then, to demonstrate what 'this' means, '*He spits*'. The vision of harmless natural fornication is turning to loathing in earnest, but without reducing his lust. He tells Freevill what has happened, and they agree to arrange a plot whereby Malheureux will get what he wants. By now Malheureux is understandably confused about himself: 'yet I must use her', he says with something approaching self-hatred; 'That I, a man of sense, should conceive endless pleasure in a body whose soul I know to be so hideously black!' (3.1.234–6). You feel almost sorry for Malheureux at the end of the play when you realize he still hasn't made it with Franceschina (or with anyone else), and the kind of advice he's been getting from his best friend has only reinforced his loathing of sex. Almost sorry, but not quite, because Malheureux insists on moralizing his experience in such a way as to pretend that he's been the luckiest of men to evade contact with the sinful flesh of a whore.

The weaknesses of this play – of which there are many – are due in part to Marston's portrait of Franceschina. Why, you might ask, a *Dutch* courtesan? There seems to be no real answer to this question, unless it's Marston's desire to keep her as inarticulate as possible.[29] She speaks a mixture of bad English and nonsense which might pass for a Dutch accent in some quarters, but probably not on Goldsmith's Row, a street which all of the characters would think of as belonging to their neighbourhood. She does have a certain animal vitality, as when, having learned of Freevill's betrothal to Beatrice, she rounds on him with a curse and an empty threat: 'God's sacrament, ick could scratch out her eyes and suck the holes!' (2.2.81–2). She can be witty, as she is in sending Freevill back to Beatrice, his 'unprov'd sluttery' (2.2.91). But the problem with this is that it corresponds too closely to the men's fantasies about the moral nature of the whore. If any doubts remain, these are put to rest when, having set in motion the plot to murder Freevill, she turns into a creature of utter hatred and malice. There's not a hint of an attempt to understand her situation, either in social or any other terms.

Freevill's permissive attitude towards prostitution is far more generous to the buyers than to the sellers. True, he asks Malheureux to imagine this scenario: 'A poor, decayed mechanical man's wife, her husband is laid up; may not she lawfully be laid down when her husband's only rising is by his wife's falling?' (1.1.95–8). But this is an elaboration of Montaigne's tolerance, and has nothing to do with Franceschina. She is, when the men of the play have finished their commerce with her, just a 'comely damnation', a 'woman merely made of blood' (5.3.48, 50). The last glimpse we get of her is when she's led away to prison at the command of Freevill's father.

The play rises above the level of smugness I've been describing, partly because of two special inventions of Marston's. The first is the character of Crispenella, the articulate sister he provides for the blandly conventional Beatrice. When Beatrice makes one of her many appeals to modesty as the quintessential female virtue, Crispenella has a quick reply: 'this froward, ignorant coyness, sour, austere, lumpish, uncivil privateness, that promises nothing but rough skins and hard stools – ha! fie on't!' (3.1.49–52). Like Montaigne she thinks it's ridiculous to idealize chastity, and again like him she's annoyed by the custom of routine kissing as a mode of greeting: 'Marry, if a nobleman or a knight with one lock visit us, though his unclean goose-turd-green teeth ha' the palsy, his nostrils smell worse than a putrefied maribone, and his loose beard drops into our bosom, yet we must kiss him with a cursy' (3.1.18–22). She makes some of her cleverest speeches on the subject of marriage, being careful to reassure Beatrice that *her* marriage will be an exception. She's not nearly as cautious with Tysefew, the gallant whom she does agree to marry at the end, and whom, by the way, she is quite happy to greet with a kiss. But before she promises to marry she gives her suitor a clear idea of what not to expect: 'To hear this word *must!*' she says; 'If our husbands be proud, we must bear his contempt; if noisome, we must bear with the goat under his armholes; if a fool, we must bear his babble; and, which is worse, if a loose liver, we must live upon unwholesome reversions. Where, on the contrary side, our husbands – because they may, and we must – care not for us' (4.1.31–6). Crispenella is by far the most independent-minded, and the wittiest female character anywhere in Marston. That he needed Montaigne's help to create her does not diminish her stature, or lessen her impact on the play. She's so clearly a third alternative to both the voracious vixen and the modest ideal that Freevill's father, a widower, proposes to her within minutes of meeting her. She rejects him of course, and in the process gives a string of witty reasons for doing so. Whether Marston planned it or not, this event adds weight to the growing conviction that Freevill has shown the same bad judgement in choosing both his wife and his courtesan.

Even more important than Crispenella, at least structurally, is the presence of Cocledemoy. He's the instigator and clown in a subplot that jostles subversively against the pieties and certainties that the main plot seeks to endorse. After fleecing the vintner Mulligrub of his favourite goblet, Cocledemoy returns to his victim disguised as a barber's apprentice, alias Andrew Shark, and performs the ceremony of shaving with a vengeance. While Mulligrub closes his eyes to avoid being stung by the soap, Cocledemoy puts a coxcomb on Mulligrub's head, picks up a bag containing £15 which the vintner has ready to deposit, and sneaks out. Mulligrub meanwhile is busily gossiping about, among other things, his loss of the goblet to one Cocledemoy. Suspecting that something has gone wrong, Mulligrub stops himself with: 'Andrew – why Andrew, Andrew, dost leave me in the suds?' (2.3.78–9). When he next appears, dressed as a French pedlar, Cocledemoy is enjoying his conquest and planning more: 'I'll shave ye smoother yet! Turd on a tile-stone! my lips have a kind of rheum at this bowl – I'll hav't! I'll gargalize my throat with this vintner; and when I have done with him, spit him out' (3.2.29–33). Mulligrub is a more suitable prey than even a parson who has 'but one good stool in a fortnight' (3.2.36). So the game continues, with Mulligrub never getting any wiser, but certainly more and more frustrated. Hearing Cocledemoy's voice offstage, Mulligrub impotently threatens to kill him, adding: 'and when he is dead, I'll piss on his grave' (4.5.13–14). Cocledemoy can give as well as he gets, usually better: 'I'll make him fart crackers before I ha' done with him' (4.5.122–3).

I'm not going to follow this subplot any further, partly because it's not nearly as funny in the retelling as in the reading, which in turn isn't as funny as it could be in performance. But there's a true carnival spirit in the language of Cocledemoy's role in particular that deserves special comment. The body is liberally represented in Cocledemoy's idiom, orifices and all, but for once the vulgarity isn't threatening. His remarks about women too, though gross and sensual, are (I think) appreciative rather than exploitative. To him Franceschina is 'a plump-rump'd wench, with a breast softer than a courtier's tongue' (4.3.2–3), 'a clean instep, sound leg, smooth thigh, and the nimble devil in her buttock' (2.1.151–2). These descriptions may not be precisely what every woman would want said of her, but they're closer to the truth and more generous in their way than anything other men say about Franceschina. As Freevill and Malheureux enter the brothel, Cocledemoy greets them with knowing sexual banter that leaves both of them far behind, and he sends Freevill off to his assignation with the cheerful invocation: 'grace and mercy keep your syringe straight and your lotium unspilt!' (1.2.72–3). For once in Marston, vulgarity is just plain fun. And since it's fun at the expense of the straight characters, some of the time, you wonder what Marston was up to. I think he had come to realize, after reading Montaigne, that a more forgiving attitude towards the body could have its advantages, but I don't think he had counted on what such relaxation might imply about his view of sexual experience as a whole.

It would be fair to say in general that the ground Marston didn't yield to Montaigne was the ideology of the adverse body.[30] This would seem to be the case in his subsequent writing where lust is again a ravenous killer of human integrity, and where virtue consists of renouncing the body entirely. I'm thinking not only of *The Insatiate Countess* but of *Sophonisba* (1606) – the most chilling representation of principled victory over the body that Marston created. But I want to stop complaining about Marston's failures; they were many, and they should be obvious by now. Marston's unhappy place in the canon of Renaissance drama is rather like the role he gave to Malheureux in *The Dutch Courtesan*. His work shows a temperamental reluctance to be open to the experience of otherness, and a need to guard the portals of the body as if they were the sacred guarantors of personal identity. As the artist of revulsion, he was able to make his strongest statement in *The Malcontent*. There are signs in *The Dutch Courtesan* that he might have gone beyond this, but he chose instead a path of retreat which quickly led to the final renunciation of silence.

In what sense can revulsion qualify as the characteristic pleasure offered by a playwright to his spectators and readers? This is a question that ought to be addressed in two stages: one which refers in large measure to the intellectual and theatrical culture in which Marston worked; one which refers to the critical environment of our own time.

Unlike Shakespeare, and unlike Marlowe or Jonson in most of their work, Marston didn't write for the celebrated popular theatre companies with their large outdoor playhouses, but for a theatrical system in which adolescent boys (notably the Children at Blackfriars, in Marston's case) played all of the parts in indoor theatres that catered to an intellectually sophisticated audience. The young men who lived at the Inns of Court, of whom Marston was one during his entire career as a playwright, are known to have been a conspicuous fraction of the audience in the boys' theatres, and their tastes seem to have encouraged the production of satirically inflected scripts. If satire always walks a tightrope between denunciation of and fascination with the vices it exposes, in Marston this ambivalent posture was especially awkward and entirely characteristic. The revulsion he provokes in his all-too-knowing spectator is always imbricated in the pleasure of turning away in disgust.

The very ambivalence I have been describing has led Lynda E. Boose, on the basis of her study of Marston's verse satires, to credit him with inventing the distinctive voice of English pornography: 'a language not of lascivious delight but of sexual scatology', a language in which the 'obscene' can emerge in a text 'that purports to be an outraged attack on sexual writing spoken in the voice of the offended moralist'.[31] This is perhaps too strict a paradigm for what happens in Marston's drama, but it is highly suggestive nonetheless. As critical readers have been pointing out for several decades, Marston the playwright is unusually driven to calling attention to the theatrical artifice that we as spectators are observing.[32] Yet these metatheatrical interventions, in Marston, do not have the effect of prescribing or even situating our aesthetic responses with any precision. Instead, they open up the already troublesome divergence between revulsion and fascination: revulsion provoked by the material represented, and fascination with the mode of representation. Marston simply conflated these divergent energies without resolving the ways in which they might (or ought to be) mutually exclusive or complementary. In aesthetic terms, this is the pleasure of having it both ways.

5
One Wench between Them: Thomas Heywood, Francis Beaumont and John Fletcher

The crudest and most repugnant way of showing allegiance to the double standard of sexual morality is to assume that women – and women only – deserve to die for sexual offences. This principle is never stated quite so nakedly, even in Jacobean drama where, in general, crude and repugnant positions are likely to have their adherents. But the assumption is a pervasive one nonetheless. Think of Othello, who repents of his violence to Desdemona only because he discovers that she was, after all, a faithful wife. Or think of Heywood's great summation of the double standard in all its tearful agony: *A Woman Killed with Kindness* (1603). The guilty wife is banished from her husband's bed and board, denied any further contact with her children, and exiled to a country house where she has the sense to do the only decent thing: starve herself to death. The guilty lover is exiled too – but to Europe, where he intends to study the languages with a view to rehabilitating himself someday as a courtier. The message is inescapable: for the man, adultery is a fault that can be mended; for the woman the damage is permanent, the loss beyond repair.

A Woman Killed with Kindness is not a perplexing or a complicated play. The assumptions it endorses are never questioned; the conflicts it raises are capable of being settled with fairly simple changes in behaviour. But I do want to begin with two problems that arise not so much from the text itself as from its interpretations, theatrical and literary. After describing these problems I'll be suggesting ways in which they are related to each other and to the concerns of the play as a whole. But first each problem will have to stand on its own.

Some thirty years ago at the Old Vic I saw a wonderful production of *A Woman Killed with Kindness*. Anthony Hopkins played Master Frankford with a gentle authority that made the very idea of crossing his will seem like sacrilege. Joan Plowright, as Anne Frankford, was a woman capable of exuding happiness and inspiring tenderness in everyone around her. The wedding celebration which opens the play was unambiguously joyful: this *is* the perfect couple, the wedding guests were saying in many different ways. The servants were saying it too, more boisterously, when they danced their percussive clog-dance in the next scene. The actors were not condescending to the text, but conferring upon it the integrity of a performance true to its own assumptions. The rural and provincial environment was created with techniques that stamped themselves at once as natural: all characters spoke in Yorkshire accents, for example, regardless of class; and at the beginning of the hawking scene, two falconers entered with glittering live hawks perched on their hands. The understated brilliance of the production should be attributed in large measure to the cunning and creativity of its director, John Dexter, who knew from the start that this is a text of genuine theatrical power if taken on its own terms.

But the moment I remember most vividly was a disruptive one. During the scene in which Frankford confronts Anne with the enormity of her offence, while she laments the loss of all things dear to her and prepares to receive her punishment, there is a pause in the action while Frankford retires to his study to decide the sentence. Alone on stage, Anne turns to the audience and says:

> O women, women, you that have yet kept
> Your holy matrimonial vow unstain'd,
> Make me your instance: when you tread awry,
> Your sins like mine will on your conscience lie.
>
> (13.141–4)

The cultured and well-behaved people at the Old Vic on the evening I was there greeted this speech with a chorus of hissing protestation. And that brings me to my first problem of interpretation, which is really a problem of audience response.

Why? Why such a hostile reaction to this moment in the performance? You can invent a variety of provisional answers, many of them doubtless true. The people I saw eating their Italian ice-cream during the intermission in the summer of 1971 were probably the same people who eagerly read the first paperback edition of *The Female Eunuch* during their coffee breaks. The hostile reaction clearly had something to do with the emerging rhetoric of feminism. Still, why did it happen in this play, during this production, and at this precise moment? Why didn't it happen, for example, when Othello was strangling Desdemona at the Royal Shakespeare Company? And if feminist antagonism to Heywood was so strong, why wasn't there a picket outside the Old Vic with placards reading 'Liberate Anne Frankford' or 'Who Needs Kindness'?

To move just one step beyond the provisional – the fanciful, if you like – I want to quote from an unattributed article on this production which appeared in *Plays and Players* magazine.

A Woman Killed with Kindness...is, to almost anyone who has read and studied it with care and devotion, a most uninteresting work. The plots of it seem contrived but purposeless, as do the characters....To one who has observed the play in rehearsal by the National Theatre company, however, the characters seem to live even from the first scene, as does, curiously enough, the play itself.[1]

I'm convinced that the excellence of the production, the integrity and vitality of the theatrical experience itself, was required to provoke the hostile response. People were drawn into the story of adultery by its authenticity, its remoteness, its sadness. What appeared to be the perfect marriage is being ruined by a sexually exhilarating but ultimately disappointing affair between a conventionally attractive bachelor (Master Wendoll, played by Frank Barrie) and an inexperienced young wife. It's a familiar story – so familiar, in fact, from the fiction we all read, that it doesn't have to be told in detail so long as it's played with unimpeachably honest emotion. If it is, then Wendoll's attraction to Anne, like her receptivity towards him, will be not quite excusable but understandable; to err is human, to forgive the divine prerogative of every well-prepared spectator.

And at the moment of maximum empathy for Anne, when she's aroused the desire to understand and the need to forgive in every sympathetic observer, what does she do? She turns to the audience directly and says: don't forgive me, and whatever you do, don't follow in my footsteps. In a sense it's a moment of betrayal, at least for spectators who have been inclined (for reasons of gender, perhaps) to take her part. And it was doubly unnerving to the twentieth-century spectator who had been taught that morality is complicated and that drama doesn't moralize. Here the morality is as simple as you like (keep those marriage vows, before all else) and the rhyming couplet ('tread awry...on your conscience lie') calls attention to itself as a formula which governs proper domestic behaviour.

The disruptive moment I've been describing is an example, I believe, of a divergence between the dramatic energy and the cultural meaning of the play. The staff writer for *Plays and Players* was in a sense calling attention to this divergence by expressing indifference to the meaning of the text and at the same time admiring its energy in performance. More about this later, after an account of a second problem of interpretation. This one too arises from responses to the play, more particularly from the responses of literary critics.

Master Frankford does decide on a sentence, which he deliberately announces to his wife:

> I'll not martyr thee
> Nor mark thee for a strumpet, but with usage

> Of more humility torment thy soul
> And kill thee even with kindness.

(13.153–6)

Just what this means in practical terms he spells out at some length: she is
to remove from their home every sign of her residence there; she is to move
to a house seven miles away where she can live, at Frankford's expense, and
be waited on by household servants of her choice; she must not seek to
re-establish contact in any way either with Frankford, or with their two
young children, whose moral natures might be contaminated by further
contact with their mother.

Everyone agrees that Frankford is behaving in a wonderfully generous
way. Anne herself calls it 'A mild sentence' (13.171), though these words are
spoken before she learns that she must give up the children forever. And
when Anne dies, fairly soon after her banishment we must assume, since
she resolves at once to starve herself and sticks to her plan, Frankford's
treatment of her is again singled out as exemplary. Anne's brother,
Sir Francis Acton, thinks that Frankford has shown unusual restraint: 'I am
so far from blaming his revenge / That I commend it' (17.19–20). A tearful,
enervated, guilt-ridden shadow of her former self, Anne Frankford begs
her husband's forgiveness as she lies on her death-bed. He grants it, conde-
scends to kiss her one last time, and she dies with humble gratitude for
these final gestures of acknowledgement. Sir Francis Acton again praises
Frankford's conduct:

> Brother, had you with threats and usage bad
> Punish'd her sin, the grief of her offence
> Had not with such true sorrow touch'd her heart.

(17.133–5)

It turns out that Frankford's policy has been not only generous but damned
effective; instead of inflicting pain with violence, he has encouraged the set
of attitudes and pattern of behaviour by which she inflicts torment on herself. So Frankford can only agree with his brother-in-law's assessment of the
matter, promising to memorialize it with this inscription on her tomb: 'Here
lies she whom her husband's kindness kill'd' (17.140). Except for the
Epilogue, these are the final words of the play.

I don't find it surprising that Frankford's view of his own behaviour and of
his wife's death is the one authorized by the play. But I do find it surprising
that critics are eager to accept Frankford's evaluation of his own conduct
and of Anne's sad end. The case made on Frankford's behalf, both by
characters within the play and by critical readers, is that at least he doesn't
kill her outright. The assumption made, by critic after critic, is that he had
a perfect right to do so:

The 'unwritten law' justifies a husband in taking immediate revenge on an erring wife and her lover; it has even, in drama, justified prolonged and ingenious revenge. Mistress Frankford has betrayed her honor as a wife; Wendoll has betrayed his as a friend; we may expect Master Frankford to uphold his honor as a husband.[2]

Short shrift was given the unfaithful woman, whose husband had the right to kill her.[3]

For centuries the unwritten law had allowed a husband the right of private vengeance on his faithless wife.[4]

Even if he were to demand Anne's life, he would be acting within his rights as a representative of God in his home by judging her sin and exacting penance.[5]

Frankford *is* 'kind', demanding no public degradation. Nor does anyone else in the scene voice disapproval of his sentence, including Anne. Indeed, his refusal to kill Anne immediately and hence send her to damnation is later praised by Acton as exceptionally kind and patient.[6]

There was an established belief that a husband might lawfully kill an adulterous wife, or her lover, caught *in flagrante delicto*.[7]

I have my doubts about this unwritten law, this putative right, this established belief. For one thing, its existence is alluded to again and again without the documentary evidence you'd expect if you wanted to support it. Where, after all, are you going to find documentary evidence for an unwritten law? Occasionally claims of this kind are supported by appealing to earlier critics, or to an authority such as Chilton Latham Powell's *English Domestic Relations, 1487–1653*. But if you follow this trail of citations, the strongest claim you can find (in Powell) is that 'the fallen woman...as a rule got but scant sympathy in either the drama or the life of the time';[8] and Powell's documentary evidence for this claim is...*A Woman Killed with Kindness*. The most recent of the critics quoted above (Atkinson) supports his assertion by appealing to the work of a social historian, Keith Thomas, who speaks of 'a well-established tradition that a husband could lawfully kill an adulterous wife caught *in flagrante delicto*'.[9] But the tradition alluded to here is a very old one indeed. The legal authority cited by Thomas is Pollock and Maitland's *History of the English Law before the Time of Edward I*: 'There are signs that the outraged husband who found his wife in the act of adultery might no longer slay the guilty pair or either of them, but might emasculate the adulterer.'[10] What we have here is a tradition that seems to have been dying out in the thirteenth century, but that somehow prevails in the seventeenth nonetheless. I find it remarkable that the scholars who maintain this position don't cite a single instance of a man who actually killed his unfaithful wife and who was legally exonerated. They do cite the case of a man from Essex who caught his wife in the act, stabbed her in the heart, and was hanged in 1602.[11]

Let me state my position. I believe that *A Woman Killed with Kindness* depends upon, and evokes in its readers, not a legal practice or a code of social behaviour, but a fantasy – a fantasy of male omnipotence. My wife belongs to me and to me alone. If she doesn't live up to this expectation, I will not only renounce her; I will annihilate her. To do so, under those circumstances, would at least restore my legitimate power, my absolute control over her sexual being. The play itself invents this fantasy, out of a vast array of cultural material, to be sure; but it isn't just reproducing social practice. It is creating ideology: the ideology of absolute patriarchy for the ordinary seventeenth-century man.

This ideological position is a specific articulation of a pattern designated as the 'sex/gender system' by Gayle Rubin. Basing her argument in part on the studies of kinship structures by Claude Lévi-Strauss, Rubin observes that the oppression of women follows necessarily from the practice of treating marriage as 'a form of gift exchange in which it is women who are the most precious gifts'.[12] Such an arrangement precludes meaningful agency on the part of women: 'If it is women who are being transacted, then it is the men who give and take them who are linked, the woman being a conduit of a relationship rather than a partner to it' (174). The system sketched in outline by Rubin has been elaborated as a critical paradigm under the rubric of the 'homosocial' by Eve Kosofsky Sedgwick. 'To cuckold', Sedgwick argues, 'is by definition a sexual act, performed on a man, by another man. Its central position means that the play emphasizes heterosexual love chiefly as a strategy of homosocial desire.'[13] These words were written explicitly about Wycherley's *The Country Wife*, but they might without much revision be applied to *A Woman Killed with Kindness*. Indeed, two recent critics have done exactly that, by arguing in effect that the bonds which really matter to Frankford are those between him and the other male characters, and that Anne is no more than the conduit of these relationships.[14] It is certainly true, as so often in stories of adultery, that the husband (Frankford) welcomes into his home the man who will cuckold him (Wendoll) and confers upon him the special marks of friendship. After offering Wendoll access to his entire household, he asks for his wife's collaboration: 'Prithee, Nan, / Use him with all the loving'st courtesy' (4.79–80). In a sense it is true (and of course more true than Frankford knows) that he is treating Anne as a gift to be given at his behest, not as a partner or as an independent agent. But the ideological fantasy which troubles me does not stop with the circulation of women, either within marriage or outside it. The fantasy of male omnipotence requires that a woman who has not met the expectations of her husband be done away with.

So the play creates the illusion that one of Frankford's real alternatives would be to execute his wife, no questions asked. It does this by using a variety of dramatic techniques, some of which I've already alluded to. Sir Francis Acton's pronouncements carry considerable weight because he, as Anne's brother, might be expected to take a lenient position. But no:

> had it been my case
> Their souls at once had from their breasts been freed;
> Death to such deeds of shame is the due meed.
>
> (17.20–2)

More subtly, the desire to lash out with physical violence is presented as Frankford's instinctive response to the sight of his wife and lover asleep in the master bedroom. After taking in this shattering sight, Frankford moans with the understandable pain of hurt, anger, loss. And he explains at once why he did not kill them:

> But that I would not damn two precious souls
> Bought with my Saviour's blood and send them laden
> With all their scarlet sins upon their backs
> Unto a fearful Judgement, their two lives
> Had met upon my rapier.
>
> (13.44–8)

He returns to his bedroom to wake the culprits. The next image we see of him is a violent one: he runs after Wendoll *'with his sword drawn'*, but *'the Maid in her smock stays his hand and clasps hold on him. He pauses awhile'* (13.67.2–3). This moment of suspension is a wonderful dramatic touch; it allows Frankford to think.[15] And as soon as he does so, violence recedes to the realm of the psychological; to kill is what he might but will not do.

The dramatic energies of the play are organized to suggest that violence would be an appropriate response, and that to resist it requires great powers of restraint. While violence is in this way kept alive as an alternative, other ways of coping with such a crisis – even socially sanctioned ways – are excluded. In Heywood's day, adultery was not a crime but an offence under canon law. The church courts tended to subject offenders to a variety of shame punishments, such as those listed in William Harrison's *Description of England*: 'carting, ducking, and doing of open penance in sheets, in churches and marketsteads'.[16] Notice that as soon as he's spelled out what is common practice, Harrison indulges a wish (a fantasy) far less lenient: 'I would wish adultery and fornication to have some sharper law. For what great smart is it to be turned out of an hot sheet into a cold...?' But shame punishments were the norm, and there's plenty of evidence, including some richly documented narratives, to confirm that women taken in adultery were required by the courts to exhibit themselves, wrapped in sheets, to the gaze of their communities.[17] What strikes me as odd about this important strand in the social context is that the play never so much as alludes to it. For some reason Frankford obviously does not want the case against his wife to proceed, in what would have been recognized as the normal way, to an archdeacon's court. Nor does anyone suggest that he take this course of action. Perhaps he is too acutely aware that public shame directed at his wife would be an indirect humiliation for him too. Or perhaps he is unwilling to countenance a way of proceeding that would place his wife outside his absolute control.

A further alternative for Frankford, an acceptable one even by seventeenth-century standards, would be the far more radical step of simply forgiving Anne and taking her back into his home and his heart's embrace. William Perkins counsels this course of action, with great gravity and circumspection, in *Of Christian Oeconomie*:

> If the innocent partie be willing to receive the adulterer againe, in regard of his repentance; lest he should seeme to favour and maintaine sin, and to be himselfe a practiser of uncleannesse, he is to repaire to the Congregation, and declare the whole matter to the Minister, that he may understand the parties repentance, and desire of forgivenesse.[18]

The same goes for the 'adultresse' who is truly repentant; 'adulterie is such a sin, as doth quite break off not only the use, but the bond and covenant of marriage....And yet the same bond may be continued, and grow up againe by the good will of the partie innocent, and consequently they may be reconciled, and dwell together still' (14).

In a sense the whole play is about Frankford's inability to forgive, 'to follow his heart far enough, or daringly enough'.[19] But I should add that forgiveness is an alternative that the play *excludes*. Anne mentions it, but without any real hope or expectation of seeing it practised:

> He cannot be so base as to forgive me,
> Nor I so shameless to accept his pardon.
>
> (13.139–40)

In what sense base? In what sense shameless? For Frankford, to forgive would be to accept something less than absolute perfection in a wife, and hence to lower his expectations, his standards. These have been clear from the scene of their marriage in which Anne is described as 'beauty and perfection's eldest daughter' by an onlooker, as 'A perfect wife already, meek and patient' by her brother (1.23, 37). To accept flawed moral behaviour in a woman is to give up the fantasy of absolute male control. This fantasy has been seriously challenged by Anne's action, and it now needs to be reconstituted as Frankford's unqualified and uncontested right to be her judge. Forgiveness would be shameless for Anne because she believes she deserves punishment, pain, humiliation. She describes the expected punishments with breathless urgency on the night of her exposure: 'When do you spurn me like a dog? When tread me / Under your feet? When drag me by the hair?' (13.92–3). By Anne's own reckoning, these acts of chastisement would be less than she deserves. The best she can hope for is to die without disfigurement: 'mark not my face / Nor hack me with your sword', she begs, 'but let me go / Perfect and undeformed to my tomb' (13.97–100). To escape with none of these punishments, with none of these marks of shame, would be unthinkably cheapening for a woman who has always believed that her chastity is everything.

In short, Anne has completely internalized the ideology of absolute male control. She believes that her life is now worth nothing, and that Frankford has the moral right to end it. When he doesn't, she determines to do it herself, in perfect consistency with the principle that women – and women only – deserve to die for sexual offences. And this brings me back to the disruptive moment in the Old Vic production, when spectators heckled Anne for reading them a moral lesson on matrimonial fidelity. What rankles, I think, is the degree to which this woman's culture – through her husband, her brother, and her church – has taught her to love and value her own subservience. It would be one thing to hear Frankford making such a speech; the smugness might be expected from a small-time patriarch who would be, after all, just aping his betters by reading out the clichés which endorse his own position of dominance. But to hear Anne ventriloquize the sermon that ought to be Frankford's: this is asking too much.

A postscript about the subplot, which I've mentioned only in passing so far. Anne's brother, Sir Francis Acton, quarrels with Sir Charles Mountford over the results of the hawking competition they enter on the morning after the Frankford wedding. The quarrel turns ugly, and Mountford kills two of Acton's servants. He is arrested for manslaughter, imprisoned, and eventually pardoned. But the legal costs have been enormous; all Mountford has left is one small house and its grounds, and even this property he now stands to lose to an unscrupulous creditor, Shafton.

Acton gloats over the misfortunes of his enemy, until he encounters his sister, Susan Mountford. Awestruck by Susan's beauty, by her 'divine and chaste perfections' no less (9.61), Acton wants to court her but can't, because of the hostility between households. So he adopts the pose of the not-so-anonymous donor: he discharges Mountford's remaining debts, thus rescuing both Mountford and Susan from certain ruin. Mountford is mortified at the thought of owing his liberty to a sworn rival, so he proposes to settle the account by offering the only disposable property he now controls: his sister. 'What do you think', he asks her, 'Would Acton give might he enjoy your bed?' (14.41–2). She, having noticed the fervour of Acton's attentions, estimates her own sexual value at £1000. Since this is double the amount of Acton's charitable bequest, the problem is virtually solved. There's only one hitch: Susan is prepared to go along with the proposal as far as she can, but when the moment of truth comes she'll kill herself rather than lose her maidenhead: 'But here's a knife, / To save mine honour, shall slice out my life' (14.84–5). Undeterred by this resolution, indeed positively delighted with the moral character it shows, Mountford proceeds to make his offer nonetheless. Acton, doubly impressed now with the chivalric generosity of his opponent and the acquiescence of the sister he desires, proposes marriage instead of a merely carnal exchange. None of the parties has any reservations about this magical solution to a tangled mess that threatened, moments ago, to end in some combination of poverty, unrequited love, rape, and suicide.

This subplot has attracted more than its share of critical attention, most of it showing, predictably if ingeniously, that it is indeed a significant variation on Heywood's theme, whatever that is taken to be.[20] For my purposes, it's enough to point out that in both plots a woman is prepared to kill herself. And for what cause? For sexual reasons, of course. Anne kills herself because, 'spotted strumpet' that she now takes herself to be (17.78), her death is required to rehabilitate Frankford's honour. Susan offers to kill herself to restore her brother's place in what he calls 'the bead-roll of gentility' (7.37). The ideology of the play has moved beyond overt male violence – beyond the need for bloodshed to endorse the power and maintain the dignity of a husband and a gentleman. Why fight for your honour when there's a woman who will eagerly die for it? The dramatic energies of this text place women at the centre of a system of cultural meanings which they sustain at the cost of their own lives.

Like *A Woman Killed with Kindness*, *The Maid's Tragedy* (c.1610) begins with a marriage, though here it is an opulent and courtly masque that ends the festivities rather than a rustic dance. After siblings and friends have given their last round of good wishes, and the servants have been dismissed, the bride (Evadne) and groom (Amintor) are alone in private for the first time. We all know what's going to happen next. He's a bit nervous, of course, as he makes the first suggestion that they might go to bed now. She's decidedly reticent: she's not feeling well, she's not sleepy, in fact she's taken an oath which prevents her compliance. He's quick to interpret all of these signals as feminine bashfulness; when she frowns he tells her that all of her expressions, including this one, just make her more attractive. And he's careful to respect her mood; he will be patient, he assures her, if she's made a commitment to preserve her maidenhead for another night. She looks at him directly now and says: 'A maidenhead, Amintor, / At my years?' (2.1.194–5).

This is my favourite moment in *The Maid's Tragedy*, for reasons that I want to explain at some length. For one thing, it's vintage Beaumont and Fletcher: it's a theatrically stunning moment of exactly the kind that gave these playwrights their inflated reputation in the seventeenth century. Even today I would guess that Evadne's line is capable of making an actor's eyes light up at the prospect of playing her part. And it's not just the lure of a cheap thrill that makes this a mouth-watering line. It's the feeling that with one bold stroke of honesty Evadne has set in motion a process which is going to roll on towards devastating consequences: the utter demoralization of her new husband, the exposure of a social network built on corruption and hypocrisy, the demystification of patriarchal notions about female chastity, the unravelling of the assumptions and norms of a whole culture. These are very high hopes to pin on a small, intimate scene in a text that most readers would place somewhere between the marginal and the trivial. I should admit at once that Evadne isn't a revolutionary; the larger goals are in no real sense her achievement, or even her intention. But the process that begins with her moment of cruel frankness doesn't stop with her, as the rest of my argument will show. For the present it's enough to observe that in this scene the woman for once has the sexual initiative and knows that she has it. Behaviour like this would be inconceivable in *A Woman Killed with Kindness*; no female character in Marlowe or Jonson or Marston (or in Shakespeare for that matter) can speak of her own sexuality with such confidence in the power it confers upon her.

The consequences of Evadne's revelation are easiest to trace in the lineaments of her pitiable bridegroom, Amintor. He enters the scene with all of his beliefs intact, including the youthful arrogance which assumes that any woman would be lucky to have him for a husband. Recent events have caused him some restless misgivings, but they haven't shaken his faith either in the great chain of being or in his own enviable position within the grand design. True, he had been intending to marry his old sweetheart Aspatia until it became obvious that the King wanted him to marry Evadne. Aspatia's mournful presence at the wedding prompts him to admit that he treated her badly, but he's quick to rationalize (it was the King's will, after all) and eager to forget (he now finds Evadne much more to his taste anyway).

In this mood of expectation and youthful self-assurance he encounters his bride: 'O, my Evadne, spare / That tender body; let it not take cold!' (2.1.140–1). It seems perfectly natural for him to be using the possessive *my*, because women do indeed belong to men. And the concern about her 'tender body' has just the right chivalric touch because women, as the weaker, softer sex, need the guidance of a firm, decisive hand. But Evadne's first word in the scene is 'No' (144). Only gradually does Amintor learn that she means what she says. When she tells him she's not a virgin, he refuses to believe her. When she tells him she'll never sleep with him – ever – he begins to realize that he's in trouble. He prays, he pleads, he tells her that her oath is invalid and that he intends to cancel it by force: 'I'll drag thee to my bed, and make thy tongue / Undo this wicked oath' (277–8). But she's not intimidated by any of this because, as she now explains, she has a lover who can protect her, namely, the King. Once again he can't believe his ears, until she helps him: 'What did he make this match for, dull Amintor?' (306). For the first time Amintor can see the trap into which he has fallen, and he knows he can do nothing about it: 'in that sacred name / "The King" there lies a terror' (308–9). To raise his hand against the King would violate the very structure that Amintor believes in with such innocence; all he can do now is endure his misery.

But even his plan to endure is a remarkably shabby one. That's why he 'seems to shrivel visibly', as John F. Danby observes in a perfectly articulated judgement.[21] 'What a strange thing am I!' Amintor says (319) as he measures the distance between the full expectations with which he entered the scene and the bitter accommodations he must make now. But he knows how to rationalize, as he proves once again: 'Methinks I am not wronged / Nor is it aught, if from the censuring world / I can but hide it' (332–4). Given the circumstances, it's difficult to blame Amintor: he hasn't chosen his disgrace, he's being manipulated by powers he never susupected of existing (Evadne's) and by powers he's been taught all his life to obey without question (the King's). But it is possible to recognize the position he now occupies as completely degraded. By the end of the scene he has only 'one desire' (346): the desire to hide his shame. He'll sleep on the floor, he tells Evadne, and in the morning he wants her to pretend that their wedding-night was everything it should be. This is all he has left to ask for, and, for the first time in the history of their conjugal relationship, she gives her consent: 'Fear not, I will do this' (356). So he suggests that they 'practise' (357) at being man and wife. They link arms and leave the stage, she having gained the knowledge that her spaniel will never again seriously challenge her will, he having settled for a charade in which his only role is to impersonate the man he once believed himself to be.

When you look at this couple in isolation, Evadne has all the power. She has a confidence which comes from knowledge of her own sexuality – a sexuality she radiates even in the act of rejecting Amintor:

> I sooner will find out the beds of snakes,
> And with my youthful blood warm their cold flesh,
> Letting them curl themselves about my limbs,
> Than sleep one night with thee.
>
> (2.1.209–12)

She's not for a moment vulnerable to Amintor, even when he threatens her with violence. As she watches him wilt before her eyes, all she can feel for him is pity. But as soon as you think of this empty marriage as one link in a chain, as one strategic move in a pattern of social relationships, it's obvious that Evadne has no independent power whatsoever. She, like everyone else on the island of Rhodes, is acting out the will of the King. What looks like female power turns out to be just male power in drag.[22]

Because this King is a virtual personification of male ego, he doesn't need to be given an individual character or even a proper name. The rules of the game as he plays it are openly declared when he meets the officially married couple on the morning after their miserable wedding night. His treatment of both Amintor and Evadne is an exercise in naked self-assertion and appalling bad taste. His every word is designed to pose a single (ironic) question: Well, did you have a nice time? And of course he's scrutinizing them with a sexual connoisseur's eye for the slightest hint of behaviour that might indicate they did.

First he makes a point of kissing the new bride in front of her husband. Nobody could object to this, even if he wasn't the King, because to do so would be to imply that the marriage isn't secure. But the kiss is a gesture which claims her, in public, as is his next remark: 'How liked you your night's rest?' (3.1.121). Whether or not this line of enquiry makes Evadne uncomfortable, or even furious, doesn't seem to matter to him. He turns his attention to Amintor now: 'Tell me, then, / How shows the sport unto thee?' (126–7). As the scene unfolds the King's tactless interrogation turns into blatant phallic display. He sends the courtiers offstage and, just to eliminate the possibility that he's being double-crossed, he speaks to Evadne and Amintor directly. It would be worthwhile to follow him through each step of this menacing interview, but it's more important to recognize the object of the game: the complete humiliation of Amintor. The King holds his ground while Amintor squirms with frustration, and having accomplished his ugly task he leaves abruptly: 'Well, I am resolute you lay not with her, / And so I leave you' (276–7).

It's easy enough to see what the King is up to, even though he makes no attempt to explain why he sets up this repulsive little game in the first place. But then he doesn't have to say why because he's a king, and he couldn't say why because he's undifferentiated male ego. He's a radical form of the desiring self described by René Girard in *Deceit, Desire, and the Novel*. Indeed, the situation at the centre of *The Maid's Tragedy* is a nearly perfect paradigm of Girard's 'triangular desire': the pattern whereby the value of the object of desire is established and maintained not by qualities intrinsic to the object but by the competing desire of a rival (the mediator) for the same thing. In some versions of this pattern, Girard writes, the hero 'pushes the loved woman into the mediator's arms in order to arouse his desire and then triumph over the rival desire. He does not desire *in* his mediator but rather *against* him. The hero only desires the object which will frustrate his mediator. Ultimately all that interests him is a decisive victory over his insolent mediator.'[23] What sets this King apart from the heroes of middle-class fiction is his access to an ideological apparatus (divine right monarchy) which gives his desires the force of law. Instead of just participating in a charade, he can manufacture it at will; instead of negotiating the differences between the lives of other people and the scenarios of his fantasy life, he can simply dictate a script that conforms to his will alone.

The women's roles in *The Maid's Tragedy* make sense only when measured against this icon of phallic authority called the King. The text represents two female positions: passive self-pity and collaboration. The second alternative is Evadne's, and I want to return to her dilemma in a moment. But first there are three things that need to be said about Aspatia, the forsaken woman of the play.

The first is that she takes on the role of a spokesperson for womankind. Jilted by Amintor for no reason comprehensible to her, she comes to the understandable conclusion that men are just like that:

> There is a vile dishonest trick in man,
> More than in women. All the men I meet
> Appear thus to me, are harsh and rude,
> And have a subtlety in everything,
> Which love could never know.
>
> (5.3.22–6)

By contrast, 'we fond women' are morally quite different, Aspatia asserts; women's minds are filled with 'the easiest and the smoothest thoughts' (26–7), and this feminine serenity is exactly what makes women into victims when they encounter devious men. I find it remarkable that this position gets a hearing *at all* in a Jacobean play, where casual misogyny is far more likely than tributes to the moral superiority of women. But even for spectators who resist Aspatia's starting assumption, there should be room enough to respect her conclusion: 'It is unjust / That men and women should be matched together' (28–9).

The second thing to notice about Aspatia is her masochism. You'd expect her to attend the wedding of her old lover and Evadne, perhaps, if only as a way of reasserting her dignity. But she doesn't stop there; she insinuates her grief-stricken presence into the ritual of undressing the bride. And of course she has only one thought in her mind: 'This should have been / My night' (2.1.44–5). When Amintor enters, it's Aspatia (not the bride) who greets him with a kiss. These are the gestures of a woman in love with sorrow, and her language is a virtual song of self-pity, 'an artificial way to grieve' (2.1.95), as she herself puts it. Everything she does says, in effect: Look at me, my suffering is beautiful; listen to me, my sorrow is exquisite. Such self-absorption is preferable, she believes, to the compromises of ordinary living, as she explains to Amintor:

> Thus I wind myself
> Into this willow garland, and am prouder
> That I was once your love, though now refused,
> Than to have had another true to me.
>
> (2.1.119–22)

Aspatia is writing a martyrdom script for herself from the outset, and it's no great surprise when she chooses the final ecstasy of death.

The way in which she brings about her suicide, however, is a surprise. She disguises herself as a young man, pretends to be her brother, and in this borrowed shape she challenges Amintor to a duel. Paralysed by guilt, Amintor refuses to fight. But Aspatia persists; she strikes Amintor, then kicks him, and at last gets what she wants. The fight is brief because Aspatia opens her arms to receive Amintor's sword. Hers is indeed an artificial way to die: 'I have got enough, / And my desire', she says. 'There is no place so fit / For me to die as here' (5.3.103–5). Suicide is her one real action in the entire play, and in order to bring it off she has to disguise herself as a man. Her belief in the polarities of gender is absolute: man is active, aggressive, devious, dangerous; woman is passive, receptive, innocent, vulnerable. The pretence of manliness provokes a moment of self-directed violence which vindicates her female nature. And so she dies, proud of her suffering to the end.

Evadne's share in the violence which ends *The Maid's Tragedy* is nominally quite unlike Aspatia's. What she does is this. She enters the King's bedroom while he's asleep. She '*Ties his arms to the bed*' (5.1.35.1) and awakens him. He thinks she's developing an interest in bondage games: 'What pretty new device is this, Evadne?' (47). But while he's getting carried away with erotic anticipation, she pulls a knife on him. 'I am a tiger', she announces; 'I am any thing / That knows not pity' (67–8). Now she unloads on him the full cargo of her revulsion:

> Thou art a shameless villain,
> A thing out of the overcharge of nature,
> Sent like a thick cloud to disperse a plague
> Upon weak catching women; such a tyrant
> That for his lust would sell away his subjects,
> Ay, all his heaven hereafter.
>
> (91–6)

And she stabs him, repeatedly, until he dies, claiming the final stroke as vengeance for herself, 'the most wronged of women' (112).

Aspatia couldn't have done any of this; for that matter, she couldn't have called herself a tiger without sounding ridiculous. But she certainly could have called herself 'the most wronged of women'. The point of contact between the two is their perception of themselves as victims in a male-governed sexual game. That Aspatia has the right to see herself this way is glaringly obvious. Evadne's claim to status as a victim is an unexpected turn, but I think it's basically sound.

Everything in Evadne's experience has taught her that her role is to gratify a superior (male) power. You can quibble about the way she does this, but you can't really deny that that's what she's up to. There's a confrontation between her and the King on the morning after her marriage to Amintor that reveals just how this syndrome works. Suspecting her fidelity, the King reminds her of her oath to love nobody but him. She corrects him at once:

> I swore indeed that I would never love
> A man of lower place, but if your fortune
> Should throw you from this height, I bade you trust
> I would forsake you and would bend to him
> That won your throne. I love with my ambition,
> Not with my eyes.
>
> (3.1.170–5)

I can't help feeling outrage at this clear-headed statement of a repugnant morality. But outrage is pointless. The King reacts to this not by lecturing Evadne, a strategy he knows would fail, but by threatening her: 'Why, thou dissemblest, and it is in me / To punish thee' (179–80). It doesn't seem to bother him at all that what she loves most is naked power. In fact, her worship of power is his best guarantee of her fidelity. All he needs to do is demonstrate Amintor's impotence, which he does at length in the rest of the scene, and he can rest assured that Evadne will never waste a sexual thought on him. Indeed, she soon plays her role in the arrangement with sadistic brio; she begs the King to watch while she shows him just how eagerly she can make Amintor crawl. Power is what both the King and Evadne understand to perfection: he how to use it on her, she how to use it on his behalf.

The destabilizing force in this otherwise perfectly articulated structure is a character I haven't mentioned so far, Evadne's brother Melantius. A military hero whose good fortunes abroad are sustaining the prosperity of Rhodes, Melantius returns home to help celebrate the wedding of his best friend, Amintor. There's a fair bit of throat-clearing as the courtiers explain to him that the bride is not Aspatia, as he had expected, but his own sister. It takes Melantius some time to get a forthright explanation for this revision of events. But as soon as he knows the truth, he has a double reason for directing his hatred against the King and exacting revenge. Both as Amintor's friend and as Evadne's brother he feels that his honour has been implicated, and no ideological magic (such as divine right) is going to prevent him from acting: 'from his iron den I'll waken Death /And hurl him on this King' (3.2.189–90). It's not quite so easy, however, because Amintor's shame as the designated cuckold would remain unrequited if Melantius were to act on his own. So Melantius determines to act by indirections, that is, through the agency of his sister Evadne.

The scene in which Melantius convinces Evadne to carry out his mission is a difficult and disturbing one. However high-minded Melantius' objectives may be, his tactics are as vicious and more crude than what he might be expected to use to break down an enemy spy. First he isolates her, by having her dismiss her maids; then he locks the door. He threatens her, insults her, and draws his sword. Now he's on a roll:

> Speak, you whore, speak truth,
> Or, by the dear soul of thy sleeping father,
> This sword shall be thy lover; tell, or I'll kill thee.
>
> (4.1.95–7)

Having killed her, he says, he'll leave her naked body behind to publicize her shame. She tells him the truth, which of course he already knows. But in making her admission she has yielded to yet another icon of masculine power: the patriarchal order as represented by her brother and the memory of their dead father which he invokes. There is no independent position for Evadne, and there hasn't been since the moment she became the King's mistress. The competition for control of her sexuality has escalated into a virtual civil war. She can decide to switch sides, which of course she does, but she can't declare neutrality. One way or another, she has to enter the service of a dominant male champion.

I'm not claiming that her repentance is insincere, only that it makes her into an 'instrument' of Melantius' power. This is exactly the word used to describe her role by Strato, the shrewdest of the courtiers, the moment the murder of the King is discovered (5.1.139). And Evadne herself would agree with this description. Having submitted to the influence of Melantius, she knows that any positive act she performs will be merely an imitation of what he would do. She takes the decision to act nonetheless, on precisely these terms:

> I will,
> Since I can do no good because a woman,
> Reach constantly at something that is near it.
>
> (4.1.254–6)

Two anonymous gentlemen discover the King's lacerated body moments after Evadne leaves the bedchamber. 'This will be laid on us', says one of them; 'who can believe / A woman could do this?' (5.1.128–9). In the end nobody does believe in female power. The tiger Evadne turns out to be like the lost Aspatia in this respect: both of them can perform heroic actions only when they masquerade as men.

Aubrey describes the collaboration between Beaumont and Fletcher as follows: 'They lived together on the Banke side, not far from the Play-house, both batchelors; lay together; had one Wench in the house between them which they did so admire; the same cloathes and cloake, &c. betweene them. I value this portrait not for its historical accuracy, which is unverifiable, but for its semiological generosity. Aubrey has them sharing material possessions

including the one available 'Wench', as if to imply a happy nonchalance about
vulgar competitive and acquisitive urges. But it's a marriage of true minds as
well: 'There was a wonderfull consimility of phansey between [Beaumont] and
Mr John Fletcher, which caused that dearenesse of friendship between them.'[24]
This notion of friendship, still broad enough in the seventeenth century to
include most of what used to be called male bonding and some of what's now
known as homosocial desire,[25] is the one distinctive landmark in the sexual
topography of *The Maid's Tragedy* that requires further comment.

The bond of friendship between Melantius and Amintor is by a long
stretch the deepest mutual commitment in the play. When Melantius,
having been abroad in military service for months on end, sees Amintor for
the first time, there's a powerful embracing of bodies and words: 'I might
run fiercely, not more hastily / Upon my foe', says Melantius; and he gets
this in return: 'Thou art Melantius: / All love is spoke in that' (1.1.112–18).
Such open declarations of reciprocal feeling simply don't happen between
men and women in this play. When Melantius discovers that his sister has
married Amintor, he warmly approves her choice in words that replace her
attachment to Amintor with his own: 'You looked with my eyes when you
took that man; / Be happy in him' (1.2.114–15). When Melantius feels that
some secret grief is troubling Amintor, he can't have a tranquil thought until
he knows the reason. When he's forced to choose between loyalty to Evadne
and love for Amintor, the grounds for his decision are given the weight of
absolute conviction: 'The name of friend is more than family / Or all the
world besides' (3.2.167–8).

No woman can hope to compete with the undisputed star of the script
Melantius is writing. He does take an unnamed 'Lady' to the wedding
masque, but this feels like pure bravado. The moment he's found her a
place to sit, which he does with more of a flourish than strictly required,
he excuses himself in order to meet someone who does matter – the King.
The metaphors which animate his script assign value to only one sex.
When he's annoyed with someone's behaviour, he's likely to describe it as
'unmanly' or 'womanish' (1.2.63, 70). Genuine value for Melantius is
what he can find, partly inflected by nostalgia, in his relationship to
Amintor:

> When he was a boy,
> As oft as I returned (as, without boast,
> I brought home conquest) he would gaze upon me
> And view me round, to find in what one limb
> The virtue lay to do those things he heard;
> Then would he wish to see my sword, and feel
> The quickness of the edge, and in his hand
> Weigh it; he oft would make me smile at this.
>
> (1.1.49–56)

I resist analysis here; it would be too easy. And in any case my argument doesn't require homosexuality, either blatant or latent. The principle I want to establish is that men in this text are busily excluding women from the centre of their emotional lives.

With this thought in mind I return to the ending of the play. Aspatia has just received her eagerly awaited mortal wound at Amintor's hand. Who should enter now but Evadne, *'her hands bloody, with a knife'* (5.3.105.1). As always, Evadne is completely dependent on how men see her. She turns to Amintor for confirmation, for approval, for recognition of the value of the great sacrifice she has made: 'Am I not fair? / Looks not Evadne beauteous with these rites now?' (116–17). This great gift is not what Amintor needs. Nor is the gift of her body, which she now offers lavishly: 'Forgive me, then, / And take me to thy bed' (150–1). As the truth dawns on Amintor's astonished mind, he registers it not from Evadne's point of view at all, but from the King's:

> Those have most power to hurt us that we love;
> We lay our sleeping lives within their arms.
>
> (127–8)

These are lines of incredible beauty, but they do nothing for Evadne. To her double request Amintor has a single answer: no. In a final bid for his approval, she does the one thing left to her: she kills herself.

Amintor's suicide is next, motivated by his discovery that the youth he's just killed in a duel is really Aspatia. And while Amintor is dying, it's Melantius' turn to arrive. He has no trouble finding what he wants among all the bleeding corpses. 'This is Amintor!' he cries, as he gathers up the remnants of his friend in a final embrace. Don't bother to point out to him that his sister is also dead: 'Why, Diphilus, it is / A thing to laugh at in respect of this: / Here was my sister, father, brother, son, / All that I had' (263–6). Evadne's short life, the site of such competitive anxiety about honour, chastity, revenge, and power, turns out to have been just an interruption of the homosocial bond between two men. Her position at the end is with Aspatia, on the margin.

So what, in the last analysis, are Beaumont and Fletcher up to in *The Maid's Tragedy*? Are they taking a position on the use of women as instruments in the games of violence that men believe themselves destined to play? I don't think there's an answer to this question, except by way of evasion. What were Beaumont and Fletcher up to when they chose to represent a King destroyed by members of his own court in recompense for his deeds of gross corruption and exploitation? Were they speaking through Amintor, when he attributes to the King a sacred influence which charms him into obedience against every moral principle? Or were they endorsing Melantius when he argues that obedience has its limits and tyrants must be held to account? Was Beaumont on the side of Melantius, perhaps, Fletcher on the side of Amintor?[26]

Taking a position is exactly what Beaumont and Fletcher are most skilful at avoiding. If this were not the case, they couldn't have written a play about regicide with any hope of having it performed. Their achievement is to enter a debate, without taking a stand, at precisely the moment when consensus is no longer possible. When a monarch feels called upon to assert his own divine right, as King James repeatedly did, it's a sign that not all of his subjects are taking this doctrine for granted. When a playwright endorses the absolute patriarchal authority of husbands over wives, as I think Heywood was doing, that's a warning signal too.

The sexual politics of *The Maid's Tragedy* add up to a demystification of the patriarchal consensus. The violence women suffer has become a feature of their social entanglements, a function of being the one wench in a house occupied by two men. In *A Woman Killed with Kindness*, it's the sexually transgressing woman who dies, while chastity pays the big dividend for the woman who knows how to invest it. In *The Maid's Tragedy* it no longer matters whether you're a virgin or a vixen. You end up as a corpse not because you were a good girl or a bad, but because you were expendable from the beginning. Hardly a reassuring thought, for a woman, but at least it's a recognition that the system isn't working as it stands.

Exactly where to locate Beaumont and Fletcher's position is in one sense not the point. In this chapter my concern has not been with individual authors and their distinctive strategies or voices, but with a cultural pattern as inflected by two particularly revealing theatrical texts. The authorial stance in both of these cases is of less interest than the positioning of these plays within a cultural semiology. Heywood's claim on our attention (and that of his contemporaries) is largely as a theatrical craftsman; by his own count he wrote or had '*at the least a maine finger*' in some 220 plays.[27] He was clearly the kind of playwright who allowed his culture to speak through him, as I think it did with especial clarity in *A Woman Killed with Kindness*. The Beaumont and Fletcher collaboration, as Jeffrey Masten has shown, implies a set of assumptions about artistic practice quite alien to the single author paradigm that Ben Jonson, for example, made a point of endorsing.[28]

So the overall question in this instance is not about the distinctive pleasures that authors might be advertising, but about the kinds of pleasure that a theatrical culture is offering for inspection. Here it is obvious that both texts are representing, in divergent ways, the pleasures of sexual power. This power is disguised as ideology in *A Woman Killed with Kindness*, but it is power nonetheless: absolute power in the sense that it kills; sexual power in the sense that it singles out the object of erotic attachment for its victim; and power inflected as pleasure in the sense that it achieves its goal with a special satisfaction coded as kindness. The new element in *The Maid's Tragedy*, as its title would imply, is the shift of emphasis whereby woman becomes the subject, not just the object, of tragic action. Here male sexual aggression is answered by suicidal masochism in the case of Aspatia, and by arrogant complicity in the case of Evadne. The pleasure of this text derives in large measure from the thrill of resistance, however incomplete or temporary, to a sexual power that believes itself to be unquestioned and unquestionable.

The aesthetic pleasure arising from these theatrical representations is far more difficult to describe, and indeed it may have been quite different for seventeenth-century spectators or readers than for their counterparts today. In its own day *A Woman Killed with Kindness* had a reputation as a tear-jerker, an effect that can still be recognized in its dramatic structure but probably no longer experienced. The effect that remains is a version of the pleasure of discovery: the dubious but considerable enjoyment of watching a seventeenth-century marriage created and destroyed in exact accordance with the governing assumptions of gender ideology. *The Maid's Tragedy* brings into focus the difficult and disturbing problem of the aesthetic appeal of sexual violence. Granted that the manipulations of the King and the savagery of Evadne in *The Maid's Tragedy* are shown to be shallow and self-defeating, why do they nonetheless provoke pleasure in the spectator? In a sense this question is unanswerable: it simply locates aesthetic pleasure (correctly) outside the domain of the explicitly rational and ethical. In another sense it suggests that what is at work here is the pleasure of recognition: however painful or shocking the sexual violence of these scripts may be, they speak to us of a danger we can recognize within ourselves.

6
Impossible Desire: John Webster

'Sooner murder an infant in its cradle', said Blake, 'than nurse unacted desires.'[1] Webster would have agreed. More important, he would have understood. In *The Devil's Law-Case* – an uninspired play by Webster's standards or anyone else's – the darker purposes of art repeatedly spill out as discursive thought. On one such occasion Leonora, having been told that the man she craves is dead, breaks into an oddly philosophical moan: 'There is no plague i'th' world can be compared / To impossible desire' (3.3.236–7). Here Webster is no match for Blake: instead of the choice between hateful contraries, the one shockingly concrete and the other evasively abstract, he is content to announce his character's feelings as if they were a generally binding principle. At his best – which is where he is in *The Duchess of Malfi* – Webster can be spectacularly better than this: 'Cover her face: mine eyes dazzle: she died young' (4.2.264). Spoken by Ferdinand as he looks down at his sister's corpse, this line is fat with whatever it is that he's been nursing inside himself. Impossible desire is still a principle, but not a slogan; you have to infer it from the guilt in Ferdinand's eyes.

Most of what matters in Webster can be found in *The Duchess of Malfi*: it's the one play of his that can still move and enrapture students and spectators. But Webster was a laborious writer who grew up to be a master playwright with great effort. People made fun of him for being a slow worker; Henry Fitzjeffrey called him 'Crabbed (*Websterio*)' and scoffed at his creative heaviness by asking, 'Was ever man so mangl'd with a *Poem*?'[2] To judge by the frequent allusions, quotations, and thefts in his verse, Webster must have been addicted to the commonplace-book habit; he stored what he could find of value in Plutarch, Erasmus, Montaigne, Camden, Sidney, Jonson, Donne, and Marston; he spent his hoard as an artist should – at will.[3] After learning the craft of making plays in the Henslowe studio, Webster set out on his own in his early thirties and produced what every dramatist fears: a near miss. *The White Devil* was acted at the Red Bull where, Webster complains in his address 'To the Reader' of the published play, it didn't stand a chance. You don't get 'a full and understanding auditory' when your play premieres 'in so dull a time of winter' and 'in so open and black a theatre'. Webster needed excuses, because he wasn't about to give up. *The White Devil* was a great step forward – but an intermediate step – on the way to creating a masterpiece.

Reading Webster is hard work; reading *The White Devil* is exhausting. What makes this play so demanding isn't really its length (*Othello* is longer) nor its relative unfamiliarity (it doesn't get much easier the seventh time round). It's Webster's technique that causes the difficulty; because of his habit of constructing a theatrical scene out of prevarications, self-deceptions, interruptions, and misinterpretations, it's almost impossible to know whom to trust. Dena Goldberg is making a similar point when she claims that, in *The White Devil*, Webster offers us a universe largely created by rumours, insinuations, and gossip; as spectators, we find ourselves in the position of the voyeur, 'in the sense that, like everyone on stage, we eavesdrop, we spy, and we are confused by conflicting rumors, opinions, and even visual and verbal evidence'.[4] Nobody in *The White Devil* makes a full disclosure of his or her motives, partly because there is virtually no privacy for any of the principal characters. These glamorous courtly people are always playing to an audience, to the point where they themselves are unsure of the difference between an authentic response and a fabricated stance. 'Not the least pitiable aspect of their lives', Goldberg argues, 'is the submergence – or even loss – of the private self in the public role' (83). The spectator's confusion or disorientation is therefore just partly the result of a particular dramatic technique; it is also the result of a hermeneutical dilemma shared by spectators and characters alike. Both inhabit a world in which dialogue is untrustworthy; what appears to be casual or unremarkable at first glance may be full of significant weight; and in this world, where almost everything happens by indirections, the gap left over for ulterior motives is as large as it is in life.

   The White Devil is based on a great love story – a crime of passion story, to be legally precise – and in such cases it's especially important to know exactly what it is that brings and binds the lovers together. Does Vittoria love Bracciano? From the outset, it's impossible to be sure. Her first moment onstage is a public one: she's playing the part of the great lady while she extends to Bracciano 'The best of welcome' (1.2.2) as if there were nothing warmer than civility between them. But before half an hour has passed, she has given Bracciano her sexual consent. She accomplishes this under circumstances that are still public: her maid (Zanche), her mother (Cornelia), and her brother (Flamineo) are present while she entertains Bracciano's proposal. Her husband Camillo has been hustled offstage moments before, with tasteless expedition, and at Vittoria's prompting to Flamineo: 'How shall's rid him hence?' (1.2.161). While Bracciano makes his appeal, Vittoria responds with calculated ambiguities. When he claims he'll be lost forever without her, she says: 'Sir in the way of pity / I wish you heart-whole (1.2.208–9). Is this the Chaucerian 'pitee' that 'renneth soone in genti herte' and opens the way for love?[5] Or is it a modern survivor: the word that specifies feelings precisely other than and inferior to love? Nothing Vittoria says in this scene tips the balance; her ability to evade emotional commitment is astonishing. What she does offer can be inferred, not from anything she says, but from the comments of observers. 'See now they close', says Zanche with a schoolgirlish feeling for the narrative ('And then she..., and then he...'). Flamineo, speaking ironically as always, declares it a 'Most happy union'. And Cornelia makes the first of her many complaining predictions of 'ruin' (1.2.215–20). There's not a pinprick of evidence about how Vittoria feels, but it's clear that sexual communication has begun.

And this is going to be the rule from now on. The same pattern is at work in Vittoria's account of her dream, a narrative she offers Bracciano 'To pass away the time' (1.2.229). At midnight, while Vittoria (in her dream) 'sat sadly leaning on a grave' under 'a goodly yew-tree', who should accost her but 'Your duchess and my husband' armed with a 'pick-axe' and a 'rusty spade'. They accuse her of wanting to uproot the tree; they threaten to 'bury' her 'alive' (1.2.233–44). Terrified, unable to pray, Vittoria dreams on:

> When to my rescue there arose methought
> A whirlwind, which let fall a massy arm
> From that strong plant,
> And both were struck dead by that sacred yew
> In that base shallow grave that was their due.
>
> (1.2.251–5)

The dream could be either a fabrication from beginning to end, or a clearly remembered nocturnal event, but either way, it's an expression of Vittoria's wish. And her wish isn't murder, of course, or anything with so ugly a name; it's just a desire to remove unpleasant obstacles. To counsel murder with conscious intent would make Vittoria responsible; to admit her hatred would make her vulnerable. But she knows how to take evasive steps in advance. That's why the dream is introduced with such studied casualness; 'A foolish idle dream' she calls it parenthetically (1.2.231), as if its consequences or its meaning were nowhere to be found. The tree becomes 'This harmless yew' (1.2.240) on the same grounds; why it's impossible I could have shabby motives, they'd never occur to me, and the people who see them everywhere are disgusting. The only emotions she assigns to herself are the ones that display her to best advantage: pensiveness and fear. In her own words, she 'walk'd' into the graveyard and 'sat sadly leaning on a grave'. Pensiveness. The duchess and husband, by contrast, 'came stealing in' (1.2.232–6) with no perceptible motive but to threaten her to within an inch of her life. 'Lord how methought / I trembled' (1.2.247–8). Fear, expressed viscerally and evocatively, but without any hideous outburst or want of composure. In her own eyes, Vittoria always looks her best.

Taking responsibility is one of the things men are allowed to do for Vittoria. Flamineo understands: 'She hath taught him in a dream / To make away his duchess and her husband' (1.2.257–8). Bracciano understands:

> Sweetly shall I interpret this your dream, –
> You are lodged within his arms who shall protect you,
> From all the fevers of a jealous husband,
> From the poor envy of our phlegmatic duchess, –
> I'll seat you above law and above scandal.
>
> (1.2.259–63)

Flamineo's euphemism is perfect: 'To make away' the intruders is exactly what she wants. And Bracciano by now knows her well enough to interpret 'Sweetly', so the people who shouldn't have come to the party are assigned their diseases and deformities, while the star gets legal, physical, and moral protection. And what does Vittoria say while such sweetness is being offered? Nothing. She doesn't have to risk saying a thing. Just a simple smile of gratitude is all she needs to throw Bracciano's way to reassure him that his kind of chivalry is the right kind. To judge by this first scene of Vittoria Corombona's, she'll take whatever she's offered before she gives anything away. It's not that she enters the game in bad faith, but (more sadly) that she plays without any faith at all.

Does Bracciano love Vittoria? This time there's too much verbal evidence rather than too little; Bracciano has a habit of letting people know exactly how he feels, or at least how he thinks they think he ought to feel. In Vittoria's presence, he's enraptured; without her, he's impatient, unsure of himself. 'Quite lost Flamineo', he says as he watches her move away from him on Camillo's arm (1.2.3). Flamineo's whispered promise that she'll return brings a wave of pleasure – 'Are we so happy?' (1.2.10) – and a twinge of insecurity: 'O should she fail to come' (1.2.38). There's a heavy sexual tension in all of his behaviour as he moves in for the kill. Does he love her? Impossible to say. Does he want to get laid in the style he thinks he deserves? No question about that.

So the moment of opportunity arises, made all the more pleasant by the '*carpet*' and the '*two fair cushions*' which Zanche arranges to ritualize the occasion (1.2.204.1–2). Bracciano knows he's got to move quickly now, but without seeming too eager. 'Let me into your bosom happy lady, / Pour out instead of eloquence my vows', he begs; 'for if you forego me / I am lost eternally' (1.2.205–8). I'm here as a petitioner, as a gentle and vulnerable person. 'Let me'. All I need is your permission, and then I'll be able to survive. And while the form of the request is ever so civil, the language is loaded with voluptuous feeling. Let me go where? Into your bosom lady. To do what? To pour out. Desire is a tactile experience for him whether he's talking to her, kissing her, or decorating her with his jewel. 'Nay let me see you wear it', he says as she accepts the jewel (1.2.226). Again the perfectly pitched 'let me'. But in asking and gaining permission, Bracciano is claiming her and taking over what he assumes is his right: the right to control and command. 'Here sir', she says as she displays the ornament. Now the verbs change their moods to show exactly how sexual pressure works. 'Nay lower, you shall wear my jewel lower', he says. And Flamineo does the rest: 'That's better – she must wear his jewel lower' (1.2.226–8). Let me see you wear it. You shall wear it. She must wear it. The descent from princess to puppet happens with only a few rhetorical dance-steps.

Bracciano's moods run up and down the scale I've suggested so often that you wonder if he sees himself as a prince or a puppeteer. While he's anticipating her submission, he offers her the world: 'you shall to me at once / Be dukedom, health, wife, children, friends and all' (1.2.267–8). But when bliss doesn't simply unfold as he expects – because of Cornelia's interference – he throws a tantrum, and storms out of the room protesting that whatever happens now it won't be his fault. When Vittoria is taken from him by legal force and sentenced to the house of convertites, Bracciano follows her, true to his word. But the moment he finds there's a letter addressed to her from the Duke of Florence, he's enraged. He rips open the letter, jumps to his own hasty conclusions, calls her 'A stately and advanced whore' (4.2.76), and wonders why he ever found it necessary to do away with his long-suffering wife. Vittoria protests, tells him the truth, accuses him of talking big but providing little, and breaks down. Having endured the long innuendo of her so-called trial, she's in no condition to put up with more of the same from the man who said, in effect: trust me; I'm going to protect you; I'm sincere. So '*She throws herself upon a bed*' (4.2.128.1–2). As soon as she's down, submissive, helpless, at his mercy, Bracciano's feeling for her revives. 'Is not this lip mine?' he croons (4.2.134). But she's in no frame of mind to relent. 'Am I not low enough?' she asks (4.2.185). Haven't you seen me suffer enough humiliation? Must you add to your malice the further insult of your no-longer-welcome desire? And by the way, 'What have I gain'd by thee but infamy?' (4.2.107). Obviously, Bracciano has got to reach into his bag of promises and come up with something good. While he's coddling and cajoling and kissing her, she resists him with bitter accusations of betrayal. Then comes the last promise: 'for you Vittoria, / Think of a duchess' title' (4.2.220–1). She remains silent after hearing this proposal. Once again she avoids revealing how she feels. But the next time she appears she will be – officially, incontrovertibly – his.

What Bracciano needs from Vittoria is for her to be seen wearing his jewel in the movie that he's directing. What Vittoria needs is to be the unrivalled star of the show. Up to a point, these are compatible fantasies – up to the point, that is, where one partner's ego makes gains at the expense of the other partner's self-esteem. That's when they become competing fantasies, as they do in the trial scene. Bracciano chooses to attend, as Vittoria's protector. To draw attention to his special role, he refuses the offer of a chair and '*Lays a rich gown under him*' instead (3.2.3.1). It's clear that he wants to prove he can make his rattling stand up as something more than rhetoric: 'were she a whore of mine', he had said in reply to Francisco's insinuations, 'All thy loud cannons, and thy borrowed Switzers, / Thy galleys, nor thy sworn confederates, / Durst not supplant her' (2.1.60–3). The phrasing of this challenge is telling: in conversation with another dominant male Bracciano declares that he will defend what he considers 'mine'; the question of whether or not a woman is a 'whore' doesn't seem to matter when placed next to the question of who owns her. But Vittoria doesn't need Bracciano's help. The trial is her element; she's spent a lifetime perfecting the arts she's called upon to use now. Don't let anyone know how you really feel, take a high moral tone when the opportunity arises, make yourself look like the injured party, imply that public sentiment is all on your side, and what can they do? It's a strategy that works elegantly: she scores point after point while her accusers are exhibiting the emptiness of their case, the shabbiness of their procedures, and the perversity of their motives. Bracciano doesn't say a word through all this because, I suspect, he can't believe his ears. A man who comes to court aching for a fight isn't going to like it when nobody needs him. Where's the submissive, helpless, wounded lapwing he thought he was here to defend? Suddenly she's armed with the power of an osprey, and he can only gaze in stupefied silence. Halfway through the trial, Bracciano swaggers out as conspicuously as he had come in.

This leaves Vittoria's defence in the most capable hands – her own. She knows how to make suspicion look like envy, morality like hypocrisy, vehemence like spleen. And in this case you can't blame her, because she's right:

> Sum up my faults I pray, and you shall find
> That beauty and gay clothes, a merry heart,
> And a good stomach to a feast, are all,
> All the poor crimes that you can charge me with:
> In faith my lord you might go pistol flies,
> The sport would be more noble.

> (3.2.207–12)

She's right when she alleges that her trial has been absurd, that the evidence against her is trivial, that what counts as normal in other people is held against her as a crime. She's also evasive – to a spectacular degree – if you take this speech as a statement about her inner life. As a self-portrait, it's remarkable for what it suppresses: her boredom with Camillo, her desire to 'rid him hence', her dream, her past, her infatuation with glamour, her ability to lead Bracciano from surmise to connivance with a mere toss of her curls. But disguising her feelings and evading accountability are a way of life for Vittoria. If her self-portrait is carefully manicured, it's because she's learned that evasion is the art of social survival.

The brilliance of her defence is the crime that hurts most. She's made a fool of Francisco de Medici, Duke of Florence; she's trapped Cardinal Monticelso into foaming with rage; and she hasn't made a single gesture of submission. These are faults men don't forgive if they're used to handling power. Something has to be done about Vittoria, not because of her alleged crimes, but because of what she is.[6] She's sentenced to 'A house / Of penitent whores' (3.2.266–7).

Flamineo, the satiric observer of other people's weaknesses, is like his sister Vittoria in at least one respect: his habit of revealing very little about himself. He's too preoccupied with climbing a very tricky corporate ladder to be able to afford emotion. So when Zanche throws herself at him, he screws her without relish and discards her without compunction. Love? Well, 'Lovers' oaths are like mariners' prayers, uttered in extremity; but when the tempest is o'er, and that the vessel leaves tumbling, they fall from protesting to drinking' (5.1.176–9). Flamineo has made his accommodations. If all women are whores at heart anyway, then you can pimp for your sister with impunity; and if all the world is composed of parasites and subparasites (to borrow Mosca's jargon), then you're no better and no worse than anyone else. On these cheerful assumptions Flamineo bases his conduct and his commentary. 'Women are caught as you take tortoises', he advises Bracciano; 'She must be turn'd on her back' (4.2.151–2). He's a student of 'policy' (1.2.353), an admirer of the 'quaint knave' who 'tickles you to death' (5.3.195–6); he knows that 'Flatterers are but the shadows of princes' bodies – the least thick cloud makes them invisible' (5.3.45–7). The perverse vitality of his language makes him a crowd pleaser in the theatre, but the code he lives by is pure cynicism: nasty, brutish, and sterile.

So Flamineo degrades his sister, insults his mother, and kills his brother in cold blood. When it's too late to salvage anything, he begins to develop an emotional life:

> I have a strange thing in me, to th'which
> I cannot give a name, without it be
> Compassion.
>
> (5.4.113–15)

Emotion makes him squirm; it's the first time he's been at a loss for words. He recovers his voice almost at once, and keeps it until the end, when death makes him feel he's 'caught / An everlasting cold' (5.6.270–1). While Francisco's henchmen are binding Flamineo to a pillar and killing him, they're also stabbing Vittoria. Flamineo watches, and says without shame, 'Th'art a noble sister – / I love thee now' (5.6.241–2). That is, now that she's impaled on Lodovico's sword. 'I love thee now.' Sorry this is late, but 'I love thee now.' In life as Flamineo has chosen to define it, the only space for love is what's left when everything else is annihilated.

Reading Act 5 of *The White Devil* is even more demanding than you'd expect from the rest of the play. Bracciano dies, Vittoria dies, Flamineo dies, but the riddles Webster built into their characters aren't resolved. The only way to prove this point would be to rehearse every incident, and quote every line of Act 5, giving just the right weight to each pause, calling just the right attention to each ambiguity, each change of mood, each failure of communication, each outburst of emotion, each silence. That is, the only proof is to read Act 5 and, for want of a seat in the Red Bull theatre, to read it with special alertness to its qualities as a theatrical script. All I can do here is mention the problems that Webster leaves unresolved.

First, the divergence between spectacle and sentiment. To say (simply) that Bracciano dies is to invoke solemnity. But try fleshing this out with some of the incidents that comprise his death. He puts on a poisoned helmet, can't remove it, calls for an armourer, calls for Vittoria, withdraws into privacy, and when he returns he's mad. When he *'seems...near his end'* (5.3.129.1), Lodovico and Gasparo perform a black mass over his helpless body, send everyone else offstage, revile him with insults, and strangle him. Before long Bracciano's ghost appears to Flamineo, *'in his leather cassock and breeches'*, carrying *'a pot of lily-flowers with a skull in't'* (5.4.123.1–3). To specify the tone of these scenes with any precision seems to me (at this remove) impossible; perhaps it was also impossible for the actors who mounted the first production. To say that Vittoria dies is to conflate the following events: having become Bracciano's widow, she enters *'with a book in her hand'* (5.6.0.1), refuses to reward Flamineo, shoots him with a pistol that isn't loaded, thinks she's killed him, stamps on his body, curses him, and watches in silence as he rises to his feet. Lodovico and Gasparo enter again; they butcher brother and sister with apparent relish, but without humbling the defiance of either. Do I need to add that the guards shoot Lodovico, on orders from the English Ambassador, as the first step in the mopping-up operation? Or that Vittoria (insincerely) makes a death-pact with Flamineo in order to gain access to the pistols that she (impotently) discharges at him? Violence isn't the point, or at least not the central point. It's the random, repetitive, misdirected, and foolishly ineffective quality of the violence that makes this final scene so unsettling. 'O my greatest sin lay in my blood', says Vittoria as she nears her end; 'Now my blood pays for't' (5.6.240–1). What do you make of a sentiment such as this when it's spoken by a woman who's just been romping on the body of the brother she thinks she's killed? Is it recognition of tragic error? Is it another evasive strategy (the fault wasn't really mine, it's all in the bad Corombona genes)? Or is it just what the boy actor has to say after he's squeezed the hidden bladder of theatrical blood hard enough to make an impressively dark stain on the bodice of his costume?

Theatrically, I think Webster miscalculated in Act 5 of *The White Devil*. It's not that he didn't care about plot and spectacle, but that he worked too hard at reaching the required bloody climax, and the strain shows. But there's a greater sense in which he succeeded, and it has to do with the relationship between Vittoria and Bracciano. Does Vittoria love Bracciano? Does Bracciano love Vittoria? Read Act 5 with those questions in mind, and the answers will still be riddles. When he knows he's dying, Bracciano says: 'Where's this good woman? had I infinite worlds / They were too little for thee. Must I leave thee?' (5.3.17–18). She comes to him. She bends over him. She listens to his pain. She wants to kiss him, but he warns her not to; he's covered with poison. She now speaks one line: 'I am lost for ever.' And he replies: 'How miserable a thing it is to die / 'Mongst women howling!' (5.3.34–6).

It looks like love, sometimes it sounds like love, but is it? When Vittoria knows that something has gone drastically wrong inside Bracciano's helmet, she turns to him with: 'O my loved lord, – poisoned?' (5.3.7). Surely this at least is unambiguous. It looks unambiguous until you realize it's the first time she's used any form of the word 'love'. She's a bit like her brother in this respect; 'love' is a word they don't use except in obituary notices. It looks unambiguous until you compare it with Hamlet's primal scream, 'I loved Ophelia' (5.1.259). Vittoria prefers the passive voice because it doesn't hold her accountable; she's never the subject of a sentence which has 'love' as its verb. And her line looks unambiguous until you start balancing 'loved' against 'poisoned?'; assertion against question; emotion against enquiry; the inclination to give against the will to survive. But by now it doesn't look unambiguous at all, and the same can be said of all the final steps they take. They love one another in the sense that they try to manufacture love. But the materials they work with are too vain, or selfish, or eager for dominance, or scarred with crime to produce what they desire. They have mastered the art of being lovers, without ever having been in love.

Since I want to approach *The Duchess of Malfi* by asking a question about audience response, I need a production to refer to. The first production has left interesting traces of itself – such as the cast list printed in the quarto of 1623 – but nothing more than traces. The production I need as a point of reference took place in 1945 at the Haymarket theatre, London. Edmund Wilson was in the audience. 'It seems to me', he wrote, 'one of the best productions that I have ever seen of anything anywhere.' Directed by George Rylands, the cast included Peggy Ashcroft (the Duchess), John Gielgud (Ferdinand), and Cecil Trouncer (Bosola). Wilson felt this interpretation to be 'so immensely imaginative and skillful and the acting at the same time so dynamic and so disciplined that it holds you from beginning to end'.[7] The reviewers, with some reservations, agreed. Peggy Ashcroft's Duchess was graceful, lyrical yet natural, beautifully sustained, the best thing she had done. Gielgud's Ferdinand was perversely thrilling, sinister, neurotic, passionately cold. But even among these giants, Cecil Trouncer stood out as Bosola. J.C. Trewin found Bosola to be 'the play's overmastering part';[8] Raymond Mortimer was equally impressed: 'I cannot imagine the part better played, and it is strange that he does not take the final curtain with Miss Ashcroft and Mr Gielgud.'[9]

Why should it be strange? What accounts for the unusual power – the mystique, if you like – of Bosola? The magic of the part seems to have been recognized from the first: John Lowin, who created the part of Bosola in 1614, stands at the top of the list of 'Actors' Names' in the first edition; Richard Burbage (the original Ferdinand) has to accept second billing. I don't think it's a matter of Bosola's special contact with the audience, or even the intelligence of his commentary or the wit of his language: nobody complains when Enobarbus, however well he's been played, fails to take the final call with Anthony and Cleopatra.

I'm going to suggest an answer to this question based largely on an intuitive hunch that comes about naturally enough if you look carefully at the relationship between Bosola and the Duchess. It's an answer that has something in common with a remark made by one of my students, who said (roughly) that she couldn't help feeling all of the degrading agony of Acts 3 and 4 might be prevented if only Bosola and the Duchess would walk out of Malfi, arm in arm, and spend the rest of their lives together in peaceful exile. That's not my answer, I should hasten to add, and it wasn't her final view of the matter either. But it's a step that needs to be taken – that is taken, I believe – in the imagination of the reader or spectator. But now I want to tread more cautiously, even if that means Bosola's problem with the Duchess will have to be deferred until Ferdinand's case has been heard, and Antonio's after that.

It's no longer necessary to argue that Ferdinand's attachment to the Duchess is incestuous. If it's not incest, what on earth is the matter with him?[10] Gielgud played Ferdinand's incest-wish in the Haymarket production, and if anything in Webster can rightly be described as theatrical tradition, following this lead would have to be it.[11] To argue that nobody in the play mentions incest is beside the point; it's not the sort of topic that comes up much in casual conversation, and I suspect the more fierce its hold on you, the less likely you are to feel comfortable about introducing it. So it comes out sounding like this:

> she's a young widow –
> I would not have her marry again....
> Do not you ask the reason: but be satisfied,
> I say I would not.
>
> (1.1.255–8)

Webster is too good a psychologist to be unaware of what Ferdinand is hiding, and too good a dramatist to settle for the convenience of a chance revelation or a telling aside. Ferdinand's impossible desire is implicit in every word he speaks about the Duchess, every gesture he makes in her direction, and Webster wisely decided that implicitness was exactly what he wanted.

Ferdinand's experience of his twin sister is, to begin, humourless. He can't stand hearing other people engage in sexual banter. When Silvio provokes Roderigo and Grisolan into laughing at a sexual pun, Ferdinand cuts them short with: 'Why do you laugh? Methinks you that are courtiers should be my touch-wood, take fire, when I give fire; that is, laugh when I laugh, were the subject never so witty' (1.1.122–5). But his own puns are so sick, that it must be hard for his courtiers to know their cues. After assaulting the Duchess with a tirade against widows who marry again, he amuses himself by adding, out of context, that 'women like that part which, like the lamprey, / Hath ne'er a bone in't'. The Duchess can't simply pretend she hasn't heard him, so she tries to brush it aside with 'Fie sir!' But he persists, with oily relish: 'Nay, / I mean the tongue' (1.1.336–8). If anybody laughs at this either on stage or in the audience, it's going to be with nervous confusion at having fallen into a trap. Ferdinand's joke is a small but perfect specimen of how he treats his sister: make her feel defensive, watch her squirm, and then slap her face because she misunderstood. Antonio is right about Ferdinand: 'What appears in him mirth, is merely outside' (1.1.170). The tension of living inside Ferdinand's head simply doesn't relax in anything like the normal way.

Any enjoyment the Duchess takes from life, especially sexual enjoyment, Ferdinand interprets as a betrayal of his claim to be her only lover. So his experience of his sister is possessive in the narrowest and most hostile senses of possession: you're mine and I'll make you do exactly what I want. He lays down the law: don't marry without my express approval, and don't let me catch you with another man. He threatens to invade her privacy: 'believ't, / Your darkest actions – nay, your privat'st thoughts – / Will come to light' (1.1.314–16). He supports his claim of ownership by selecting a husband for her: Count Malateste. When she dismisses this notion as preposterous – Malateste being 'a mere stick of sugar-candy' (3.1.42) – he decides to invade her bedroom to 'force confession from her' (3.1.79). Clearly he's far more interested in the thrill of invading than in collecting information; when he gets into her bedroom he knows that his dreadful rival is concealed somewhere within earshot, but instead of pulling down curtains and opening closet doors he curses and threatens and tries to degrade the value of what he fears he has found.

Since the Duchess doesn't allow herself to be browbeaten by such tactics, he can't help feeling the impotence of his will. He reacts the way you'd expect – with violence. What began as an ultimatum backed by a threat of invasion becomes a fantasy of dismembering her or burning her alive. It's a small step from emotional violence to the play-acting violence (sadism, that is) of the waxworks scene. In darkness he '*Gives her a dead man's hand*' (4.1.43.1), induces her to kiss it, waits until she shudders with revulsion, and then reveals '*the artificial figures of Antonio and his children, appearing as if they were dead*' (4.1.55.1–2). It's a slight variation of his formula: put her on the defensive, watch her cringe, and then slap her in the face with what you really had in mind.

To escalate violence from psychological warfare to physical brutality would be the next predictable step, and it's one that Ferdinand almost takes. Almost? Doesn't he arrange for the dance of madmen, the ceremonial entry of the executioners, the strangling of the Duchess, her youngest children, and her maid? Yes, he has all of these things done to her, by proxy, but he does nothing himself. His whole relationship to her has been surreptitious, underground, buried in layers of darkness or inhibition. He has made love to her only in his mind. He has entered her bedroom by stealth. The rudimentary facts of her sex life he has discovered second-hand, by employing a spy. The tortures he's put her through have either been protected by darkness or stage-managed by Bosola. He has killed her, but he hasn't touched her. His desire to the end is unacted, his life an appalling witness to the truth of Blake's claim that it's better to murder an infant than to nurse unacted desire. It needn't follow, either for Webster or for Blake, that all desires should be acted. Some desires should be acted; some shouldn't and (therefore) shouldn't be nursed. I don't think you could invent a more perfect word than 'nursing' for what Ferdinand does with his desires, or a more accurate judgement of his moral character than to say he'll conspire to commit infanticide (which he does) and won't stop there.

Everything in Ferdinand's behaviour points to the conclusion that his obsession with the Duchess is perversely and garishly sexual. He wants his sister's sexual being to be literally at his command but, failing that, he can at least make her the victim of his imagination. On learning that the Duchess has given birth to a boy, Ferdinand appeals to the Cardinal for what might – with some grotesque distortion – be called moral support: 'talk to me somewhat, quickly, / Or my imagination will carry me / To see her, in the shameful act of sin' (2.5.39–41). The Cardinal's talent for bringing out the worst in people is what prompts him now to ask, 'With whom?' Ferdinand takes it from there:

> Happily with some strong thigh'd bargeman;
> Or one o'th' wood-yard, that can quoit the sledge,
> Or toss the bar, or else some lovely squire
> That carries coals up to her privy lodgings.

> (2.5.42–5)

There's nothing the Duchess can do to resist these invented sexual partners. He's chosen them carefully, with a connoisseur's eye for physical vigour and an aristocrat's instinct for degrading associations. And of course she's loving every minute of it (the whore, as he defines her in the next lines) because she doesn't have any choice: he is at last in control.

There's a guilt-ridden quality in all of this, as there would have to be. 'I will never see thee more', he says as he leaves her bedroom (3.2.141); and when she lies dead at his feet he wants her face covered. Guilt is a great provoker of three things: inhibition, resentment, and madness. The last two of these are Ferdinand's destiny. The first he can overcome only now and again, and only when someone else decoys him into admitting his feelings. That's exactly what the Cardinal did by asking 'With whom?' Bosola does it again, by suggesting that Ferdinand stop the sequence of tortures and 'Send her a penitential garment to put on / Next to her delicate skin' (4.1.119–20). The tactile nuances of this image leap into Ferdinand's mind, and he comes as close as he ever will to complete honesty:

> Damn her! that body of hers,
> While that my blood ran pure in't, was more worth
> Than that which thou wouldst comfort, call'd a soul.
>
> (4.1.121–3)

Forget the soul: it's individual, uncontrollable, free. I value only what I claim (against her will, without her consent) as mine. Webster had the courage to make this kind of honesty as ugly as it ought to be.

To turn after this to Antonio's relationship with the Duchess is to bathe in relief. Theirs is a romantic relationship. There has been a jousting competition just before the play begins and, in one of those completely casual, underplayed bits of dialogue that Webster uses with a master's touch (1.1.88–9), Antonio is declared the winner. He's known as 'a good horseman' (1.1.140); having just returned from a trip to France – where, as Claudius remarks to Laertes, 'they can well on horseback' (4.7.72) – he's probably in peak form. So there's something chivalric and something athletic in Antonio's bearing, as there should be if he's going to live up to the Duchess's description of him as 'a complete man' (1.1.435). Yet he's not self-assertive, either as a courtier or as a lover; it's other people who comment on his achievements, and it's the Duchess who takes the initiative in bringing them together. After they're married, he still comes to her bedroom as a suitor – 'with cap and knee' (3.2.5) – hoping for a night's shelter and the joy of sleeping with 'the sprawling'st bedfellow' (3.2.13). They are married in an exchange of vows that both accept as binding, and that would be upheld by the law as Webster understood it; still, it's a private, personal, unofficial marriage, a wedding without public sanction or ceremony.[12] The dramatic effect of this ambivalent marriage is to preserve the romantic enchantment (and insecurity) of their relationship. Even as a husband, Antonio still has the duties and rituals of the knight-errant to perform; even as a wife, the Duchess remains the great lady of the castle, the damsel who is both the object and the guiding star of the knightly quest.

Webster understood intimacy in ways that few people (at least few men) before or since have been able to. There's an unstudied naturalness about the way the Duchess prepares for bed (3.2), an ease of manner and mood that only an artist who knows how to look and listen as well as write could have managed.[13] The rightness of the scene grows out of nuances: gentleness, confidence, courtesy, playfulness. Antonio watches Cariola combing the Duchess's hair. He takes a man's delight in being present at the unfolding of femaleness; he lets the Duchess know that he wants to sleep with her; he makes her feel that her bed is a haven of comfort and a place of privilege. She says no for excellent practical reasons (Ferdinand has just arrived at Malfi) and with a tone of voice that reassures: 'Alas, what pleasure can two lovers find in sleep?' (3.2.10). She can tease him because she understands his sense of humour (and he hers). There's wit in their conversation, but it's a wit that shares: it includes Cariola, it acknowledges need, it admits imperfections, it celebrates love. 'I prithee', says the Duchess, 'When were we so merry? – my hair tangles' (3.2.52–3). Only Webster could have done it this way. Marlowe had no casual moods at all, Jonson had too many important causes to fight for, Marston would have found a way of making human hair loathsome, and Fletcher was too anxious to reach a climax to lavish this kind of art on foreplay. Shakespeare? Well, if Shakespeare had anything like this in mind – even in the unpinning scene of *Othello* (4.3) – he left it for the actors to create.

True enough, Antonio starts out in a weak position (as steward to the Duchess) from which he never fully recovers. In their courtship scene he has to tread with extreme caution; she drops hints and invitations by the handful, but until he's sure he's got to pretend he doesn't see them. When emergencies arise (as they do repeatedly), Antonio doesn't have the power to deal with them. He can't blow his cover while Ferdinand is berating and insulting and threatening the Duchess in her bedroom; he admits he doesn't know what to do when she unexpectedly goes into labour; he's fearful when he thinks of the danger he's in, and with good reason. It's the Duchess who plans their escape to Ancona; it's she who decides that they must divide the children and go separate ways to double the chances of someone surviving. He understands his wife to perfection, but he never quite understands the perverse horror that surrounds her. Chivalry, good intentions, and even completeness aren't enough if where you live is Malfi. But in one sense Webster didn't care about Antonio's independent life, what absorbed him was the story of a relationship.

Do the Duchess and Antonio love one another? Of course they do. The question shouldn't even arise, and if it does, the best thing you can do is read the first two acts again and ask yourself if they'd make any sense as drama if the Duchess and Antonio weren't in love. The unfolding of their intimacy is all the more moving because of the danger which threatens them, as in the scene where the Duchess and Antonio say goodbye for the last time. 'I know not which is best', she says, 'To see you dead, or part with you' (3.5.66–7). In finding words for feeling, he is her equal:

> if I do never see thee more,
> Be a good mother to your little ones,
> And save them from the tiger: fare you well.
>
> (3.5.84–6)

What the two of them share has the range of a Beethoven symphony: it includes the frivolous, the elegiac, and almost anything in between. All this, without a single false note.

Bosola, in the social world of Malfi, is just a convenient extra who doesn't count: an intellectual with a criminal record, a malcontent with a talent for satire, a victim of chronic underemployment, a paradigm case of embittered idealism. But in the dramatic world of the play, he's a mover and shaker, a charismatic presence, 'an actor in the main of all' (5.5.85). What accounts for the field of force that Bosola carries with him wherever he goes? His intelligence? His intimate contact with the audience? His self-proclaimed honesty? His proficiency as a player of roles? His habit of presiding over the action? Yes, all of these. But most of Bosola's power comes from his relationship to the Duchess; he is in love with her from beginning to end.

He doesn't say he's in love with her, but he doesn't have to. This is Webster, not Thomas Kyd. He doesn't act as if he's in love with her. Or does he? He doesn't act the way a Jacobean courtier would act if he were in love. But if Bosola were in love – with a woman he knew to be unattainable, tantalizingly near yet socially unapproachable, sexually hungry but for somebody else – how would he act? Exactly as he does.

He agrees to work for her brothers because it's the only way for someone like him to get close enough to her to be noticed. Past experience should warn him to keep clear of the Cardinal: the last time he took this man's money – in a murder deal, rumour has it – he paid for it by doing time in the galleys. The nominal position he accepts – 'provisorship o'th' horse' (1.1.269) – isn't what you're likely to think you deserve if you once made a name for yourself as 'a speculative man' at the University of Padua (3.3.47). It's not loyalty to his employers that brings him back to Malfi, and it's not the dignity of work that keeps him there. Bosola cares more about the possible fringe benefits. His unofficial, real assignment is to spy on the Duchess, to make privacy difficult for her, to make marriage impossible. Those are Ferdinand's orders, but Bosola has unspoken reasons for making the mission his own.

If Bosola is as clever as everyone takes him to be, then why does he find out so little about the Duchess? And why does he seem so clumsy when he's being a spy? Does he really need the apricot test for pregnancy? Not after all the time he's spent looking at her, guessing the shape of her body by the cut of her clothes, noticing the changes in her health by the tone of her skin. When Antonio misplaces the astrological chart he's been drawing up for his new-born son, Bosola pounces on it as if it were the Rosetta stone. 'If one could find the father now!' he says with more caution than cleverness after he's read the whole document (2.3.71). He's been talking to the father not five minutes ago, and you'd think he might have seen why Antonio was veering and dodging and behaving like a skittish colt. But no, Bosola can't imagine who the father might be until the Duchess tells him. My guess is that Bosola doesn't want to know the truth. He wants the Duchess to be splendidly single, unattached, and therefore open to the suggestion of becoming attached to him. Failing that, if he loses her he wants to reassure himself that she wouldn't be worth having anyway: that sexual attachments for her are mere matters of class or convenience, as he knew all along, so he's better off without her condescension.

Bosola doesn't say anything like this himself because he's perfected the skilled reflex of defensive irony; 'he rails at those things which he wants' (1.1.25), and the things he rails at are mostly female. So he lists the signs of pregnancy with such precise loathing that you know he's a sensualist masquerading as an ascetic:

> I observe our duchess
> Is sick o' days, she pukes, her stomach seethes,
> The fins of her eyelids look most teeming blue,
> She wanes i'th' cheek, and waxes fat i'th' flank;
> And (contrary to our Italian fashion)
> Wears a loose-body'd gown.
>
> (2.1.63–8)

Be on guard against tenderness. Pretend that her sexual nature is nothing more wonderful than the inside of a furnace, and you'll stop feeling vulnerable. The pattern recurs in public a few minutes later, after he's given the Duchess the apricots and watched her eat them greedily, without ceremony, liking them all the better because 'they taste of musk' (2.1.136). She is all appetite here, as he perceives. He scolds her for not paring the apricots first, and tells her they were ripened 'in horse-dung' (2.1.140). But there's nothing dainty about her appetite: 'O you jest', she says, and with what could pass for the belief that, horse-dung or no horse-dung, these are the best apricots she's ever tasted, she offers one to Antonio. Having exposed and (as he thinks) devalued her appetite, Bosola can retreat into the haven that makes life bearable for him: irony.

If I'm right about Bosola's desire, then there are good reasons for presuming that he hates Antonio. Bosola believes that men should rise by merit, and it must be hard for him to swallow Antonio's spectacular promotion while he waits, as usual, in the limbo of neglect. When he's with the Duchess he can sing Antonio's praise, because he's able to see him through her eyes. But his heart isn't in it; there's a studied hyperbole about his claim that 'neglected poets' are about to confer immortality on 'this trophy of a man' (3.2.291–2). Jealousy works in odd ways: Antonio is both exactly what Bosola would like to be, and the person he despises most. And there's political malice at work too: having heard the Duchess confess that Antonio is her husband, Bosola takes his news at once to Ferdinand.

He brings back to the Duchess a letter from her brother which begins, '*Send Antonio to me; I want his head in a business*' (3.5.28). Ferdinand has to take credit for devising this ghoulish pun, but Bosola does his share. He uses the letter as a wedge to separate the couple. The Duchess gives her answer first. 'And what from you?' Bosola asks, turning to Antonio. Firmly, and for good reasons, Antonio tells him: 'I will not come' (3.5.47). You can feel Bosola holding back his tight-lipped scorn until Antonio has made his case, leaving him a perfect opening for what sounds like a prepared statement: 'This proclaims your breeding. / Every small thing draws a base mind to fear' (3.5.52–3). He's acting on Ferdinand's orders, to be sure. But why the insult – perfectly timed, intended for the Duchess's ears as much as for Antonio's – if not to appease Bosola's own view of where Antonio ranks in a real competition of merit.

In the last act, Bosola kills Antonio. He claims it's an accident, but it's the kind of accident that makes you wonder. If he had to answer a judicial enquiry, Bosola would have a lot of explaining to do. When the Cardinal says explicitly that he wants Antonio killed, Bosola gives tacit consent: 'But by what means shall I find him out?' (5.2.128). When Bosola tries to collect on the Cardinal's previous promises, all he gets is a reminder that there's another job to be finished: 'thou wilt kill Antonio?' And all he gives in return is 'Yes' (5.2.310–11). Not that he likes the work. In soliloquy it's 'poor Antonio' and 'good Antonio'; I'd like to pity you, but who can afford pity? The best I can do is 'put thee into safety from the reach / Of these most cruel biters' (5.2.330–41). Is this the beginning of a plan to rescue Antonio? Or is he thinking of a fine and private place, the safest place of all, the grave?

After midnight, in the mist of confusion and theatrical darkness, Bosola hears the Cardinal pronounce his name and the words 'He dies' (5.4.31). He sees the shape of a man. He stabs and kills him. 'Antonio! / The man I would have sav'd 'bove mine own life!' (5.4.52–3). Is this the truth at last? Or is it spoken for the benefit of Antonio's servant, who sees what's happened and keeps his distance only because Bosola tells him he's a dead man if he doesn't? If it's real compassion that Bosola feels now, then why does he whisper in Antonio's 'dying ear' the words he knows will crush all that remains of him? 'Thy fair duchess / And two sweet children', Bosola says, 'Are murder'd' (5.4.56–9). He claims he does it to help Antonio, to hasten death, to ease the pain. But by now there's a yawning gap between the reasons Bosola gives for his actions and the deeds themselves. You can say you're dishing out one last psychological torture out of sheer altruism, but even if you believe this yourself, the facts aren't going to change. Bosola kills Antonio. I'm not saying he wanted to kill Antonio all along, but I suspect him of taking satisfaction from the way it's turned out. The circumstances are confusing but the symbolic meaning is clear; Bosola has made his peace with Antonio.

As for the Duchess, she reserves for Bosola a trust and a deference that she gives to no other man. I'm not saying that she's in love with Bosola, only that she's responding to his feeling for her with something close to instinctive courtesy. With gentleness, in fact. She listens to his praise of Antonio with open-hearted joy: 'O, you render me excellent music' (3.2.274). It is genuinely wonderful to hear that the person you love is admired, valued, celebrated. With artless trust she places herself now into Bosola's power: 'This good one that you speak of, is my husband' (3.2.275). You can't blame her for wanting to tell someone, for feeling she'll burst if she keeps in her secret for another moment. Since Bosola does care for her, and knows how to charm her with words and attentions, you can't blame her for trusting him. You can only shudder as you anticipate how many ways she'll have to pay for this. Now she makes her confidence into a pact between them, by asking him to keep it a secret. And as if to prove she has no cause to doubt him, she asks that he 'take charge of all my coin and jewels' while she's busy planning her escape to Ancona (3.2.303). Bosola doesn't think Ancona is the wisest destination; he thinks they should travel as pilgrims to the shrine of Loretto instead. 'Sir', says the Duchess, 'your direction / Shall lead me by the hand' (3.2.312–13). This is the woman who won't bow to family pressure, because she knows what she wants: 'If all my royal kindred / Lay in my way unto this marriage, / I'd make them my low footsteps' (1.1.341–3). This is the woman who takes charge of domestic emergencies, who advises her husband about the politics of survival, and who quickly gains his consent and collaboration. But in Bosola's hands she's responsive, trusting, eager for him to be in control. 'Your direction / Shall lead me by the hand.' When a man and a woman are dancing in the old-fashioned way, this is how to begin.

As the Duchess approaches death, all of her most intimate scenes are played with Bosola at her side. Now a prisoner in her own palace, she is alone, at the mercy of her brothers, with only the dubious shelter of Bosola's presence to sustain her. 'All comfort to your grace!' Bosola says to his prisoner (4.1.18). But her faith has been betrayed, her nest blown apart; she no longer wants to follow where he leads. After the trick of the dead hand and the display of corpses in wax, Bosola points in the direction he wants her to go: 'Hereafter you may wisely cease to grieve / For that which cannot be recovered' (4.1.59–60). She will have none of this. 'Come, you must live', he says (4.1.69), as if trying to revive in her the old appetite for apricots. But she knows now that her desires won't be gratified any longer, and she's unwilling to endure a life of nothing but compromise. 'Come, be of comfort', he says with perfect sincerity; 'I will save your life' (4.1.86). He doesn't say how or why, but he offers to save her life. Does he want to save her? Of course he does, because this would bind her soul to his with stronger hoops than steel. Could he save her? If she gave him the smallest encouragement, I think he could. But she says, 'Indeed I have not leisure to tend so small a business' (4.1.87). I don't want to depend on you for anything, especially something so trivial as my life. Thanks all the same. He has his answer. There is nothing more he can offer, except pity. There is no place for him to retreat, except into irony. She curses the stars, and he says, 'Look you, the stars shine still' (4.1.100). If she's unwilling to place herself into his power, then he'll make sure that she pays by showing her how utterly powerless she is on her own.

Bosola's feeling for the Duchess only deepens when he sees her suffer: 'You may discern the shape of loveliness / More perfect in her tears, than in her smiles' (4.1.7–8). But as she resists him, as she dismisses the comfort he offers, he senses that his desire has become impossible. It's a dangerous combination, and he knows it. He tells Ferdinand he doesn't want to see her again. If he must he'll do it in disguise. He needs an impersonal mask to stand between what he feels for her and what he's going to do.

He comes to her *'like an old man'* after the dance of madmen (4.2.114.2). Old, as if to complement her prematurely silver hair. Old also in acknowledgement of an escaping past; everything used to seem possible, but not now. 'I am come to make thy tomb', he announces; and later, 'I am the common bellman' (4.2.116, 173). She doesn't see through his disguise, but she knows why he has come: to give her the only thing she has left to long for. To give her death.

He talks to her in metaphors of impossible desire: 'Didst thou ever see a lark in a cage? such is the soul in the body: this world is like her little turf of grass, and the heaven o'er our heads, like her looking-glass, only gives us a miserable knowledge of the small compass of our prison' (4.2.128–33). Confinement, constriction, and the mockery of mirrors. But you never really tame the bird, you never take away the flying instinct, you just make flight impossible. That's Bosola's indirect answer to the question, 'Who am I?' (4.2.123). Hers is simpler, less philosophical, richer in the confidence that comes from having lived: 'I am Duchess of Malfi still' (4.2.142). She doesn't allow his dividing intelligence to get its way; she doesn't bruise the body to pleasure soul; she is completely herself.

Hampered by his disguise, Bosola no longer dominates. The executioners don't frighten her. The 'manner' of death doesn't 'afflict' her; the 'cord' fails to 'terrify' (4.2.214–15). Try as he may, Bosola can't recover the initiative.

She's going to die exactly as she has lived: with perfect composure, effortless generosity, and a conviction that she's doing what's right for her. All he can do is watch her. 'I pray thee', she says to Cariola, 'look thou giv'st my little boy / Some syrup for his cold, and let the girl / Say her prayers, ere she sleep' (203–5). Yes, she's the same woman who worries about tangled strands of hair and likes apricots better if they smell of musk. Cariola has just volunteered her own life: 'I will die with her' (202). But no, says the Duchess. Let's have no false heroics. Life must go on, in the usual way, and don't forget the cough syrup.

She talks about death now, with a speculative turn of phrase that isn't often hers. Death has 'ten thousand several doors', she says; 'and 'tis found / They go on such strange geometrical hinges, / You may open them both ways' (4.2.219–22). G. Wilson Knight includes these geometrical hinges in a very long list of 'ordinary and rather uninteresting man-made objects' which clutter up the world of the play.[14] That's not a bad suggestion, in fact. At least it helps to define what the Duchess isn't doing. She's not pretending that death is a bridegroom, or a welcome guest, or a coronation. Impatient with ceremony to the last, she almost forgets to kneel. She knows it's going to be painful and ugly and ordinary, but she's made up her mind and she doesn't flinch. To Bosola she gives a last assignment: 'Go tell my brothers, when I am laid out, / They then may feed in quiet' (4.2.236–7). Now '*they strangle her*'.

It's a quiet death, as Ferdinand observes, but not a quick one. She has two more words to say, later. For the moment it's the spare, unromantic business of death that sinks in. Bosola takes over again, sounding like an administrator as he arranges the strangling of the children and the maid. He's beginning to settle into the state of moral numbness that's bound to come after what he's done. It's a condition of bitterness and self-hatred. 'I stand like one / That long hath ta'en a sweet and golden dream', he explains to Ferdinand; 'I am angry with myself, now that I wake' (4.2.323–5). And he'll never quite recover, no matter how strongly the Duchess continues to haunt him. He dies 'In a mist' (5.5.94), with a shrug of indifference about what he's leaving behind: 'Mine is another voyage' (5.5.105). When you've lost what matters most, it's not that important to cling to remnants.

The Duchess too has lost what matters most. But at least she made it her own in the first place. From the beginning she knew she was taking a risk, that her plan to marry Antonio was a 'dangerous venture', an 'Almost impossible' action (1.1.346–8). She knew how to act her desire, instead of just nursing it. So she created a life worth living, instead of a mess of inhibitions and compensations and half-hidden obsessions. Knowing how to live, in her case, includes knowing how and when to die.

Her two last words? 'Antonio!' and 'Mercy!' (4.2.350, 353). After the business of strangling is over, after Ferdinand has had his chance to worship the corpse, Bosola stays behind and looks at what he's done. Unlike the

Duchess, he can't accept the life he's created. If I could do it all over, he says to himself, it wouldn't be like this. Then, miraculously, he gets that impossible second chance. The Duchess begins breathing again, and speaks Antonio's name. What does Bosola do? He tells her it was all a joke, that Antonio is alive and well, that the bodies were nothing but waxwork dummies. And he expects *this* to comfort her? The news that she died for no reason at all is supposed to be a consolation? Bosola's love is infinitely harder to take than his cruelty. Strangling she could endure in silence; now she cries out for mercy. God save us all from the cruelty of impossible desire: from the pain of loving in this way, and from the greater pain of being loved as she is.

The difference between erotic pleasure as represented on stage and aesthetic pleasure as experienced by spectators is for the most part a very considerable gap in Webster's tragedies. First of all, there's almost nothing in the plays that would count as unqualified pleasure, and there's certainly a great deal of pain, almost all of it brought into being by the pursuit of or the desire for pleasure. The pleasure of mutual erotic attraction is certainly what animates Vittoria Corombona and Bracciano in *The White Devil*. But it is a pleasure inflected by danger, not only or even principally for the participants, but also for those people unlucky or foolish enough to be standing in its way. Because the lovers act with shocking expedition to bring about the deaths of Vittoria's husband and Bracciano's duchess, it becomes impossible for us as readers or spectators to interpret their shared experience as simply pleasure: insofar as this is a pleasure that transforms itself immediately into power (and the power to kill at that), theirs is a perverse pleasure. The aesthetic pleasures brought into being by *The White Devil* are therefore highly ambivalent: the admiration we feel for Vittoria as she defends herself against her hostile judges is qualified by our knowledge that she has been accessory to murder.

The Duchess of Malfi also releases ambivalent responses; indeed, since Bosola is so deeply involved in mediating the drama to us, our experience is likely to be neither pure nor simple. Still, we do have the joy of mutual intimacy between the Duchess and Antonio, created with such dexterity in their makeshift marriage and sustained with such playfulness in the bedroom scene, as a standard by which other pleasures are going to be measured. Even this pleasure is qualified, of course: by danger, by brevity, by irony. But here the qualifications only make the experience more valuable: moments of joy stolen from the certain eventual victory of hostile forces are bound to seem doubly precious, both to the characters who must grasp these fleeting opportunities, and to the spectators who must register vicariously both the value and the vulnerability of what they hear and see.

The aesthetic pleasures called into being by this play are of three different kinds. First, there is the pleasure of identification with the Duchess, of access to her circle of intimacy (however precarious), of admiration for the tenacity with which she fights (however hopelessly) to defend her private life. This first strand of aesthetic pleasure is a species of the pleasure of recognition: it arises from the spectators' intuitive understanding of the situation represented as emotionally meaningful. Yes, we are saying as readers or spectators, this is what intimacy feels like, and this is why we value it. On the other hand, a second strand of aesthetic pleasure is unleashed by the vicarious experience of horror: by the psychological harassment of the Cardinal and Ferdinand, by the theatrical tortures of the waxworks, by the physical brutality of the executioners. The thrill called into being by horror is a species of the pleasure of discovery: we are shocked into discovering that, given these perverse first principles, we should expect these ghoulish consequences. And although we shudder with revulsion, the pleasure encoded in this reaction is pleasure nonetheless. Finally, and largely because of the authority given to Bosola, there is the pleasure of irony. In a sense this pleasure is simply the interweaving of the two strands I've been describing separately. Bosola is there, both observing the private life of the Duchess with envy, and presiding over her destruction with compassion. He can see her both from Antonio's point of view and from Ferdinand's. But the pleasure of irony in this text is also large enough to include a vast and painful lamentation: at the smallness of human efforts in the face of inexorable fate, at the shortness of human life in the face of inevitable mortality, at the fragility of human love in the face of the cruelties invented to destroy it.

7
An Art That Has No Name: Thomas Middleton

I want to begin with three separate events in Middleton's life, the first of them a tangled, offhand, circumstantial anecdote. When Middleton was five his father died, leaving most of the assets compiled through his career as a bricklayer to Middleton's mother, Anne. Ten months later, when her son was six and her daughter (Avis) four, on 7 November 1586, Anne married a sailor, Thomas Harvey, who had returned to England earlier that year after failing to make his fortune in the West Indies. Harvey's actions and legal declarations show that he set out systematically to get his hands on as much of his new wife's property as he could. But she had protected herself and her children (before she ever met Harvey, it turns out), by arranging that her property be held in trust by three legal advisers. After eight or ten days of marriage the honeymoon was definitely over. Harvey was by this time demanding access to all of his wife's financial documents. She chose to reply, with melodramatic panache, by having herself arrested for failing to pay the orphans' portions. Harvey, now liable for his wife's debts, was forced to sell his own goods 'at An outcrye at his doore'[1] (presumably an informal auction) in order to get her released. The rest of this marriage has left a fourteen-year-long trail of legal wrangling in which, for example, he maintains that she has been defrauding him of his property while he's been away at sea, and she accuses him of trying to poison her.

I'm skipping over Middleton's youth – his residence at Queen's College, Oxford, his marriage to Mary (or Magdalen) Marback, his apprentice work for Henslowe – and picking him up at age 40 when, on 6 September 1620, he was appointed Chronologer to the City of London. This position carried a modest stipend (£6 13s 4d), which was raised (to £10) soon after Middleton's appointment, and fringe benefits considerably larger than salary. It looks like a sinecure or something close to it, but if it was, Middleton had earned it – by celebrating London as no one before him had done in his city comedies, and by writing the Lord Mayor's pageant, to mark the inauguration of the new mayor, on three separate occasions: for his namesake, Sir Thomas Myddleton (1613), for Sir George Bowles (1617), and for Sir William Cockaigne (1619). Though there's none of Middleton's wit in these productions, and by definition no irony at all, he wrote four more of them after he got the City Chronologer's job, and various other civic entertainments for special occasions. Middleton's favourite collaborator on these projects was Gerard Christmas (or Garret Crismas), whose regular job was wood-carving for the navy.

Only once in his life was Middleton a theatrical celebrity. At the age of 44 he wrote *A Game at Chess*, which opened at the Globe on 5 August 1624. It ran for nine successive performances – easily setting the record for longest-running play in history, up to that point – and closed when the king, acting through the privy council, put a stop to it. The public circumstances were exactly right for *A Game at Chess*, and the response was euphoric. The disgruntled Spanish ambassador had to report to his superiors 'that there were more than 3000 there on the day that the audience was smallest. There was such merriment, hubbub and applause that even if I had been many leagues away it would not have been possible for me not to have taken notice of it.' The Spanish establishment had been made the butt of a comprehensive satirical joke, as the ambassador clearly saw: 'The subject of the play is a game of chess, with white houses and black houses,...and the king of the blacks has easily been taken for our lord the King, because of his youth, dress and other details.' He alleges that the Spaniards are shown committing tasteless acts of sacrilege and debauchery, and of course he's dead right. He reports that his predecessor, Count Gondomar, was 'brought on to the stage in his litter almost to the life, and seated on his chair with a hole in it'.[2] These accusations, and many more like them, can be verified by looking at Middleton's text. The Black Knight, referred to as 'the fistula of Europe' (2.2.46), hectors his Pawn and preens himself with unctuous hypocrisy: then he asks for his 'chair of ease', which he settles into with extreme delicacy: 'O soft and gentle, sirrah! / There's a foul flaw in the bottom of my drum, Pawn' (4.2.3–7). To the Spanish this was a national insult. To King James an embarrassment big enough to require that his ministers reprimand the players (who were imprisoned and soon released after promising they'd never go near the play again) and summon the playwright (who promptly went into hiding). To the ordinary citizens of London, still breathing a collective sigh of relief over the news that Prince Charles wasn't going to marry the Spanish Catholic princess after all, it was a theatrical windfall.

I've chosen these three events not because they show Middleton at his best (which they don't) or even at his most typical, but because they point out how different he was from his famous contemporaries in temperament, connections, and circumstances. Eliot thought Middleton was a playwright without a point of view,[3] and this is a tempting refuge if you've come to him expecting Marlowe's titanic self-assurance or Jonson's bearish conviction or even Fletcher's voluptuous royalism. Middleton had none of these. But I think it's more likely that Middleton had a point of view which Eliot either didn't understand or perhaps didn't want to understand. If Margot Heinemann is right, and if Middleton really did see himself and his art as part of the opposition movement, as contributing to the cause of Parliamentary puritanism,[4] then his commitment would be outrageously hostile to the programme Eliot declared for himself: 'The general point of view may be described as classicist in literature, royalist in politics, and anglo-catholic in religion.'[5] But like most simple dichotomies, this one is too simple. Middleton would have wanted to resist being classified into either of the great seventeenth-century camps that the retrospective eye of history so easily distinguishes. He wouldn't have been comfortable in the presence of Lancelot Andrewes, but nor would he have called himself a puritan. Even Heinemann has to admit, nervously I think, that 'Middleton never uses the word "Puritan" in a favourable sense.'[6] He does use it, conspicuously in *A Chaste Maid in Cheapside*, with uninhibited satirical glee. But I don't think that puts him into the king's party or Buckingham's or Archbishop Laud's. Middleton was an ironist: sceptical of dogmas, uncomfortable with party-line loyalties, and keenly aware that a political stance which seemed cogent in 1605 might have become absurd by 1624. He had a well-trained ear for detecting whatever might sound sanctimonious on either side of the great divide. Where then did Middleton stand? Although at times he seems to be using strategic irony to disarm this very question, and although his position is never a simple one, the subtlety of his finest work would suggest that he was capable of standing quite stubbornly on his own ground.

In his attitude towards women, for example, he seems to have been liberated from many of the stereotypical vices and habits of his contemporaries. He did not believe that women are less intelligent than men, or that they deserve inferior education. I doubt if the passively decorative ideal of femininity could have survived the influence of a mother as enterprising as Middleton's appears to have been. In his comedies the female characters are just as clever and self-interested as the men; the middle-class women in particular don't think of themselves as chattels, and they rebel if their menfolk do. Thomasine, in *Michaelmas Term*, resents being married to a man so enraptured with the prospect of acquiring land that nothing else matters. 'Why am I wife to him that is not man?' she asks (2.3.206); her tone of voice makes it certain that she's not satisfied with being called 'sweet honey-thigh' (2.3.76) and then dismissed with a wave of her husband's hand. The women in Middleton's plays want to be taken seriously – as domestic, economic, conspiratorial, or sexual partners – and if they aren't they raise hell.

Middleton's view of society is a very messy picture on the whole. It includes woollen drapers (Quomodo in *Michaelmas Term*), tobacco sellers (Vapor in *A Fair Quarrel*), prostitutes (Frank Gullman in *A Mad World, My Masters*), distinguished criminals (Moll Cutpurse in *The Roaring Girl*), lawyers, country wenches, apothecaries, hairdressers, apprentices, scriveners, bailiffs, midwives, ruined gentlemen, discarded soldiers, merchant adventurers, moneylenders, and the odd wealthy aristocrat. This chaotic material isn't that much different from what Jonson was using in his comedies, but Middleton's way of organizing it is. He resists imposing a ready-made hierarchy onto the social fabric. Many of his characters are either sliding down the social scale or clawing their way up, but the integrity of the scale itself is in doubt; it seems to exist subjectively, in the minds of such middle-class overreachers as Quomodo or Walkadine Hoard (in *A Trick to Catch the Old One*), but it never has the status of divine truth or even social consensus. To call this a democratic attitude would be historically awkward but in many senses true. There's no stuffiness in his view of society – not even the snobbery of the self-made man – and the judgements he makes or wants others to make are the ones you can't evade by appealing to class prejudice or economic power. Jonson, after having established himself as a major playwright, began to earn big money by devising and writing scripts for the masques performed at court; Middleton, at a comparable point in his career, became the regular inventor of the Lord Mayors' shows. In middle age Jonson was granted a pension by the crown, Middleton became City Chronologer. The difference does imply something about what mattered to each of them.

And while Jonson couldn't stand the Italianate cleverness of his best scenographic collaborator, Middleton had no such problems with Gerard Christmas. To the printed text of *The Triumphs of Honour and Virtue*, the Lord Mayor's pageant for Sir Peter Proby (1622), Middleton appends this note: 'For the body of the whole triumph, with all the proper graces and ornaments of art and workmanship, the reputation of those rightly appertain to the deserts of Master Garret Crismas, an exquisite master in his art, and a performer above his promises.'[7] It's a generously worded acknowledgement. I've chosen this one (from among the half-dozen similar compliments Middleton paid Christmas) because it says something interesting about Middleton's concept of art. It seems to me exactly right that 'art' and 'workmanship' should be connected in Middleton's mind. To master an art is to acquire and perfect a particular skill. Used in this way, the term isn't veiled in darkness or overburdened with prestige. Unlike Jonson, Middleton doesn't have to argue about the relative status of pen and pencil (or in this case, the chisel), because for him status isn't the point. Nor does he have to renounce the metaphysical terrors he can't control, as Prospero does when he remembers the graves that have been opened 'By my so potent art' (5.1.50). Middleton's use of the term is more casual, closer to the ordinary usage of his day, and even less ponderous than a synonym such as 'craft' would be today. I don't think the difference between an artist and an artisan would have mattered much to him.

To demystify the term in this way needn't (and in Middleton's case doesn't) cleanse it of ambiguities. What counts as craftsmanship in one set of circumstances may be craftiness in another; the close association between 'art' and 'cunning' in Middleton's day would have ensured a permissive context for this ambiguity. In *The Changeling*, as Beatrice-Joanna pounces on the solution to her problem – to hire De Flores as her hit-man, that is – she's amazed that it's taken her so long to come up with the idea: 'Why, men of art make much of poison, / Keep one to expel another; where was my art?' (2.2.46–7). Knowledge, skill, craft, cunning, art: these are morally neutral, in the sense that they are instruments which men and women use for ends both foul and fair. In Middleton's world, it's perfectly right that a term such as 'art' should remain uncommitted. Verbally, he does want to have it both ways. And until you grant him this licence (and the responsibility that goes with it) you're unlikely to admire what he offers in his best plays: *A Chaste Maid in Cheapside* (1613), *Women Beware Women* (1621), and especially *The Changeling* (1622).

A Chaste Maid in Cheapside is a play about sexual management. Middleton takes the polymorphous perversity of his Londoners for granted, and poses a series of remarkable scenarios for dealing with it. The need for something more structured than just following your sexual inclinations arises most obviously in the Touchwood Senior plot. Touchwood Senior has a problem: fertility. His wife bears a child every year, and in some years two; his recreations with country wenches result in an epidemic of pregnancies serious enough to disable the labour-force in haymaking season. He's cursed with 'a fatal finger' (2.1.59), as he puts it, the instrument of domestic overpopulation.

Since money is in short supply, something has to be done. The illegitimate children aren't that much of a problem: Touchwood Senior is callous enough by now to disown his bastards and to offer their mothers nothing better than ridicule, threats, denials, or at most a handout of pretty small change. The big problem is the legitimate children, whom Touchwood Senior does undertake to support. He and Mrs Touchwood agree that it's best to live apart, at least until their economic crisis is over. So she's going to live with her uncle, and he (no doubt) will go back to making hay.

Both partners are content with this unequal resolution, and the husband in particular is gratified by his wife's ability to make the required adjustment:

> I hold that wife a most unmatched treasure
> That can unto her fortunes fix her pleasure
> And not unto her blood.
>
> (2.1.47–9)

I don't think Middleton is endorsing the double standard here, though if he means to be critical of it he hasn't made the most of a good opportunity. Maybe the exaggerated priapism of Touchwood Senior would have made it impossible to take the debate very far in any case. The point he does want to make is that uninhibited fertility is a social nuisance, and in this marriage something has to be done to prevent it. For a comically overstated problem there's a remedy both arbitrary and extreme.

But one man's meat is another man's poison. Sir Oliver Kix and his wife have the opposite problem: loads of money but no children.[8] Because both partners when provoked are in the habit of blaming their mates for infertility, their marriage is, after seven years, under plenty of emotional strain. And without direct heirs they fear that their property will eventually fall into the hands of Sir Walter Whorehound, the next legal claimant. So in this case too sexual management is needed. The laws of comic compensation require only that Lady Kix get access to Touchstone's famous finger, and the miracle unfolds: 'Ho, my wife's quicken'd', Sir Oliver chortles; 'I am a man for ever! / I think I have bestirr'd my stumps, i' faith' (5.3.1–2). And the fee Touchwood Senior earns as a fertility expert – £400 for administering a 'water that he useth' (2.1.175) – is going to rescue his marriage too from its double awkwardness of penury and abstinence.

Meanwhile, in what you might call the main plot if this were a more conventional play, the goldsmith Yellowhammer and his wife Maudline are trying to control the sexual choices of their children so as to ensure upward social mobility. For their son Tim they've picked out the Welsh Gentlewoman, a redhead whose relationship to Sir Walter Whorehound is decorously covered by the term 'niece', and whose dowry is said to include nineteen mountains in Wales. For their daughter Moll they've settled on Sir Walter Whorehound himself. Tim's Cambridge education has addled his brain to the point where he has no stamina to resist events; at the end of the play he is married to a whore whom he is trying to translate, by means of logic, into an honest woman. But Moll, whose domestic lessons in music, dancing, and deportment have all been directed to the end of making her 'fit for a knight's bed' (1.1.12), has survived this training with her will intact. Her true lover is Touchwood Junior, brother to Cheapside's pillar of potency. The lovers make repeated attempts to elope, each of which backfires and increases their misfortune; but in the final scene, where everyone except the Yellowhammers has gathered to mourn the death of this star-crossed pair, their coffins burst open at a signal from Touchwood Senior and the 'sweet, dear couple' (5.4.29) are united at last in a marriage ceremony that must have set the Jacobean record for brevity.

Bizarre as the rest of the play may be, it's the character of Allwit who makes everyone else look almost normal. Allwit's domestic life is perfectly tranquil: he has no quarrels with his wife, his children are models of cleverness and decency, his financial prospects are secure. The reason for all this bliss is the place the Allwits reserve in their family for the 'founder', Sir Walter Whorehound. Allwit celebrates his benefactor at length in a brilliant soliloquy:

The founder's come to town: I am like a man
Finding a table furnish'd to his hand,
As mine is still to me, prays for the founder,-
'Bless the right worshipful the good founder's life.'
I thank him, 'has maintain'd my house this ten years,
Not only keeps my wife, but a keeps me
And all my family: I am at his table;
He gets me all my children, and pays the nurse
Monthly or weekly; puts me to nothing....
                              I am as clear
From jealousy of a wife as from the charge:
O, two miraculous blessings! 'Tis the knight
Hath took that labour all out of my hands:
I may sit still and play; he's jealous for me,
Watches her steps, sets spies; I live at ease,
He has both the cost and torment: when the strings
Of his heart frets, I feed, laugh, or sing.

                                        (1.2.11–55)

At least he's not a hypocrite. Allwit understands his place in this ménage with such clarity, and outlines it with such disarming candidness, that you can't fault him for hiding anything. A cuckold he most certainly is: his name is the oral inversion of 'wittol', the term for a knowing and contented cuckold. What kind of response is Middleton setting in motion with this amazing creation? Not quite the scornful outrage that Jonson unleashes at Corvino's expense in *Volpone*. I think Allwit triggers a mixed response. It includes a grudging respect for someone who can carry his own system as far as this and way beyond what you thought possible: the kind of respect now reserved for the grasshopper-eating champion of the State of Oregon, or for parents who claim to have created a child prodigy through behaviour-modification therapy. But this kind of respect includes loathing as well: loathing of a discipline directed at no other end than proving what the human animal might be capable of if pushed and punished. Allwit is conducting an ugly experiment with human subjects, and it doesn't really exonerate him to say that the principal victim is himself.

The whole play is a send-up of sexual mismanagement, and in Allwit's case this takes the form of grotesque over-management. You can't really claim to be controlling your sexual nature if you engage in an act of repression so comprehensively deadening as this. The distortions are bound to show, as they do in Allwit's case.[9] There's a nasty streak of anti-feminism in his casual conversation, where it counts most: when he thinks of his wife awaiting labour he says 'she's even upon the point of grunting' (1.2.30); after the christening of his wife's new baby he winces at the atmosphere spread through his house by a female-dominated celebration: 'How hot they have made the rooms with their thick bums' (3.2.182). This is a man who secretly hates women – for obvious reasons – because the only alternative to doing so would be to hold himself in complete and utter contempt.[10] All this remains laughable, of course, or it should if the part of Allwit is played with the right cynical charm; but I think the laughter should include a nervous awareness that social construction of sexual roles and experimentation with alternate lifestyles do have their built-in limitations. How much can you achieve by sexual self-management and social engineering? If you're Allwit, almost everything, including complete annihilation of your claim to sexual being.

The setting of *Women Beware Women* is Renaissance Florence, but the forces that drive human action here are the same as they were in Cheapside: sex, money, and social status. Official and actual power are centred in the figure of the Duke of Florence, whose will is treated as if it were an absolute by the courtiers who surround him. But the presiding genius of the play-world is Livia, the woman who manages the sex lives of nearly everyone she encounters. A widow twice over, 39 years old (by her own account), and utterly bereft of ordinary inhibitions, Livia takes a professional pride in her ability to manipulate whoever passes through her 'shop in cunning', as she terms it (2.2.27). After one of her more spectacular matchmaking performances, she is admired by her brother Hippolito for practising 'Some art that has no name, sure, strange to me' (2.1.233). Livia's ability to bring otherwise reluctant women to the point of sexual compliance is treated as a kind of magic: "'Tis beyond sorcery this, drugs, or love-powders' (2.1.232). And she is in love with her own expertise above all; the game has become its own justification for her, the playing a greater joy than any object she might stand to win as a reward.

But I am not proposing to follow Livia's machinations through the structure of a very complicated play; instead, I want to focus on a particular scene, the sexual encounter between the Duke and Bianca (2.2), because in it are embedded some of the special perils and pleasures of interpreting Middleton's art. Bianca has recently arrived from Venice as the young wife of a possessive and doting husband, the 'factor' (roughly a salesperson or a marketing agent) Leantio. The Duke singles out her beautiful face from a crowd of onlookers at an outdoor procession and determines to make her his own. Word passes quickly along a discreet bureaucratic chain: the 'fawning' Guardiano (5.2.160) comes to inform Livia that the Duke has spoken twice of Bianca already. Livia springs into action: she flatters Bianca's mother-in-law with social invitations and attentions, she coaxes and cajoles the confused old woman into bringing Bianca with her, she makes Bianca feel important by insisting that Guardiano take her on a tour of the art collection, and while this is going on she distracts the mother-in-law by outsmarting her at chess. At the tactically right moment Guardiano slips noiselessly away, and Bianca is left alone with a surprise visitor – the Duke.

He now approaches her with a sexual rhetoric that combines flattery, intimidation, reassurance, suggestiveness, and bribery: 'There's nothing but respect and honour near thee', he croons (2.2.324). He finds her as beautiful as 'figures that are drawn for goddesses' (342). He likes her resistance, in fact it's a sure sign that she knows how to please him. But she mustn't take it too far: 'I can command, / Think upon that' (362–3). All she needs to do is 'trust in our love' and she'll get whatever she wants, including 'peace' (385–6). Does she really want to spend years of her life in marginal econcomic circumstances and social isolation? 'Come play the wise wench, and provide for ever' (382). She's roughly 16; he's 55. She knows it's a trap, but it's been baited so well that she melts into silent compliance.

Or does she? Up to this point, and for reasons that will soon be apparent, I have deliberately avoided taking a firm position on what has become the most controversial question in the interpretation of *Women Beware Women*. I defer the matter once more in order to present, in chronological sequence (with dates added in parentheses) a series of nine twentieth-century comments on the scene I have been describing:

This scene [2.1] is immediately followed by the masterly seduction of Bianca. (1935)[11]

The two older women remain to play a curious game of chess – a game which provides an ironic commentary on the seduction about to take place above. (1955)[12]

The game of seduction is played out like the chess game in a beautifully organised scene. (1979)[13]

She is deliberately confronted with the Duke in a lonely part of the house; and he is quite prepared to rape her if she will not take him willingly.... The seduction is inescapable. (1980)[14]

Critics who have treated Bianca's fall as a seduction are wrong.... If this is not a rape, it is certainly sexual mastery rather than sexual persuasion. (1984)[15]

Let's first rid ourselves of the idea that the Duke's action constitutes a seduction (which is what virtually every critic calls it) rather than a rape. Middleton is very explicit about this. (1987)[16]

It is true that the Duke does not enter the stage, rip Bianca's clothes off, and rape her onstage, but I think his rhetoric of persuasion and Bianca's reaction after the event allow for a reading that lies closer to rape than to seduction. (1991)[17]

> Middleton balances the interaction between the Duke and Bianca in II.ii somewhere between rape and seduction. (1997)[18]

> To me the most rape-like aspect of the offstage encounter is its duration .... I find it hard to believe that intercourse between strangers which takes the woman by surprise and lasts less than three minutes could amount to anything short of violation. (1998)[19]

Clearly there's a great deal more at stake here than simply getting the right reading of a particular scene. Let's begin by noticing that, before 1980, the Duke *seduces* Bianca; after 1980 he *rapes* her. The quotation from 1980 uses both words, positing rape as a threat used by the Duke to achieve his real goal of seduction. The change in vocabulary couldn't be accounted for without reference to twentieth-century feminism; after the polemical avant-garde of feminist discourse had done its work in the 1970s, what had not been thinkable to earlier generations became suddenly available in the 1980s. At the same time, and for many of the same reasons, the semantic field to which the word 'rape' could refer was greatly expanded. As a result, the burden of proof shifted from those who wanted to claim (as a novelty) that rape had occurred to those who wanted to resist this claim (despite the growing consensus). Notice too how quickly the tentative hypothesis about rape rewrote itself as a roundly dogmatic insistence that no other view should be tolerated. The more polemical proponents of the rape theory were eager to discredit earlier critics who had spoken of seduction, implying in their critique that to describe the Duke as a seducer is tantamount to exoneration. No allowance was made for an earlier rhetoric in which the act of seduction was held to be reprehensible – in which 'seduction' no doubt covered a great deal of the semantic territory now taken over by 'rape'. The history of critical responses to this scene, if thoroughly analysed, would appear to lead to a fairly comprehensive unpacking of twentieth-century cultural presuppositions. It would turn out, as it so often does, that the critics who read the text are in turn being read by it.

But getting the scene right *is* important, and I believe the first step on this journey would be to acknowledge that what Middleton gives us is something far more subtle than either of the two heralded labels would imply. Indeed, several of the critics I have quoted are making exactly this point, either implicitly or explicitly. Middleton gives us a carefully orchestrated sexual performance by a man who is accustomed to getting his own way. He also gives us some signs of resistance on the part of the young woman who knows she has become the target of his sexual advances. 'O treachery to honour!' Bianca says when she realizes that she's been left to fend for herself. Apparently she trembles, because the Duke tries to put her at ease: 'Prithee tremble not. / I feel thy breast shake like a turtle panting / Under a loving hand that makes much on't' (2.2.320–2). It's almost impossible to read these lines without imagining some form of physical contact between the Duke and Bianca, though of course Middleton doesn't tell us how much. And it's impossible to read the Duke's line, 'Strive not to seek / Thy liberty' (329–30), without inferring that Bianca is making some effort to escape what she recognizes as a 'danger' (326) to her. But she says very little in this crucial scene, and almost all of her lines are capable of being read either as resistance or as compliance. 'Oh my extremity!' she says; 'My lord, what seek you?' (345–6). If this is resistance, it is surely not resolute enough to protect her. Indeed, she may well be wondering whether resistance is futile; she is surely at a terrible disadvantage in terms of power, experience, access to meaningful assistance, and even (perhaps) knowledge of what it is she wants. As soon as she has entered the sphere of sexual negotiation, it's clear that she can't win; and it is becoming less and less likely that she has even the power to withdraw. As soon as she believes she has passed the point of no return, she has in fact done so.

A great deal more could be said about the nuances of this scene, especially as they relate to the image of Bianca as a bride with which the play begins, and to the unfolding of her eventual corruption in the rest of the tragic action. But no amount of commentary, however detailed or precise, would settle the question once and for all. Does Bianca give her consent to what is happening to her? In a sense she appears to: her strategies of resistance seem less forceful than what the situation calls for. In a sense she appears not to: the efforts she does make to draw back from the edge of danger are quickly rendered meaningless by a strategist far more powerful than she is. Middleton's technique, like Livia's, is also an art without a name: try to describe it one way, and an equally plausible and quite antithetical description will suggest itself. What Middleton offers his readers and spectators, then, is the very considerable pleasure of ambiguity, of doubleness, of irony. So his art does have a name after all, or at least a series of putative names, all of them provisional in the sense that they imply not only a single point of view but its obverse as well.

In *The Changeling* Middleton was able to reach something deeper and more primitive than the sexual networking of *A Chaste Maid in Cheapside* and *Women Beware Women*. What happens between Beatrice-Joanna and De Flores is enough to confer on their relationship a charismatic energy that makes *The Changeling* a disturbing play, even today. You can't explain this power, but you can identify it easily enough: they are a couple apart, both the achievement and the violation of everything their society values, Patti Hearst and her Symbionese Liberation Army captor. They dominate the play because every audience – no matter how timid, ordinary, or sane – will want them to.

Though nobody doubts its pre-eminent place in the Middleton canon, *The Changeling* is a work of joint authorship. Middleton's collaborator was William Rowley, journeyman playwright, veteran comic actor, specialist in playing the role of the boorish clown.[20] I'm tempted to say no more about this question, other than quoting Northrop Frye: 'It has been proved all through the history of drama that the word "collaborator" does not have to be used in its wartime sense of traitor, and that collaboration often, in fact usually, creates a distinct and unified personality.'[21] But a few particulars need to be added. By the time they set out to write *The Changeling*, both Middleton and Rowley had plenty of experience in the craft of collective authorship. Having worked in partnership before, most notably on *A Fair Quarrel*, they knew one another's talents, idiosyncrasies, and work habits; and they knew how to get a job done quickly.[22] Still, no matter how plausible the routine of writing in this way may sound, the result is what stands out as spectacular; as a team, Middleton and Rowley could work wonders that eluded them as individuals. And in this sense their shared artistic power is just as mysterious as the charisma of the theatrically dominant pair they created.

By herself Beatrice-Joanna is wilful, vain, self-absorbed, manipulative, conventional, and (of course) beautiful. She's the Jacobean female stereotype: her most trifling whims and most terrifying impulses are directed towards the single goal of gaining endorsement (or at least preventing disapproval) from the men she sees as socially important. She's been trained to think of her social preferences as if they were sacred truth, so the appearance of a prospective lover, even more attractive and ingratiating than anyone heretofore, means that 'This was the man was meant me' (1.1.85). Since the romance she's creating has to be pure, there's no room in it for annoyance, ambivalence, complication, or ugliness; when De Flores interrupts her fantasy of securing a new suitor (Alsemero) with unwelcome news about the return of the old one (Alonzo de Piracquo), she insults and abuses him as if his mere existence were more than she ought to condone. And as soon as she's rid of De Flores' immediate attentions she consoles herself by remembering that, when there's a flaw in the script she's writing, she can always ask Daddy to fix it:

> I never see this fellow, but I think
> Of some harm towards me, danger's in my mind still;
> I scarce leave trembling of an hour after.
> The next good mood I find my father in,
> I'll get him quite discarded.

> (2.1.89–93)

The only thing in her mind is a vague and unspecified sense of 'danger'; this is of course a psychologically pregnant admission for the audience, because a woman who feels an intuitive sense of danger in the presence of a man should pause to interpret her feelings. But this is exactly what Beatrice-Joanna won't or can't do. For her, De Flores isn't a sexually eligible man at all; he's just 'this fellow', he doesn't even live on her social planet, and

besides he's ugly. Having dismissed what annoys her in this euphemistic
way, she turns her attention at once to the only thing that matters: what she
perceives as her real love life.

De Flores in isolation is at first glance even less impressive than she is. He
operates by a combination of cynicism and opportunism that ought to be
known as the injured merit syndrome. Outwardly obsequious, he's as much
of a snob as anyone. So he can endure abuse by telling himself that some
fine day it'll be his turn. 'I must confess my face is bad enough', he says
(2.1.37). But not to worry. He's known sexually pampered men who were
downright repulsive, with 'Wrinkles like troughs' and other signs of 'swine-
deformity' (2.1.43). If you dismiss the merits of other people as unreal and
their happiness as unearned, then the best thing you can do is wait for an
opening and make the most of it, by whatever means. There may be an
implicit critique of shallow social values in this attitude, but there's a fair bit
of self-hatred as well. De Flores concedes his personal ugliness and then
justifies it by condemning the social ugliness of everyone else.

But no matter how flawed or shallow they may be as individuals, as a
couple these two are compelling. Sometimes they communicate in body
language alone. At the end of the opening scene, in which Beatrice-Joanna
is busily promoting her social agenda and De Flores is just watching, she
carelessly drops a glove on her way out. He picks it up, offers to return it,
and says: 'Here, lady' (1.1.226). She rebukes him, rejects the glove as if it's
now polluted, and to complete her contempt she tosses her other glove at
him: 'Take 'em and draw thine own skin off with 'em' (230). It's a short
moment, but it's not innocent. Body language is never innocent, at least not
when a woman is removing something she wears and giving it to a man. But
I'm not going to linger over a single gesture, because what's urgently compelling about this relationship happens when they meet face-to-face.

The first brilliant scene of *The Changeling* is the encounter between
Beatrice-Joanna and De Flores which ensures that everything else will follow: she engages his help to dispose of her unwanted suitor, and to liberate
her in this way for the pleasure of true romance. Having decided that she
needs De Flores, she approaches him in four precisely choreographed steps:
she addresses him by name, 'De Flores' (2.2.70); she tells him he's looking
good lately; she invites him to 'Come hither; nearer, man!' (78); and she
touches him. Since she's never been so much as civil to him before, De Flores
is understandably (and greedily) amazed. He's been watching her for what
seems like forever on the off chance that she might throw a favour his way,
and so far the closest he's come is the privilege of handling her discarded
gloves. He's not about to miss any signs of improvement, and although he's
got to be guarded in his responses to her, in a string of asides he lets the
spectators know exactly what's on his mind. When she addresses him cour-
teously he's overjoyed; instead of slinging insults 'She call'd me fairly by my
name De Flores' (71). When she flatters him by praising his improved good

looks, he brushes the compliment aside because he doesn't believe her: ''Tis the same physnomy, to a hair and pimple, / Which she call'd scurvy scarce an hour ago' (76–7). When she calls him closer he's 'up to the chin in heaven' (79). And when she caresses him, he's ready to be swept away: 'Her fingers touch'd me! / She smells all amber' (81–2). He's not about to spoil everything by losing his wits or his composure, mind you; this is a come-on, as anyone who's sexually literate can see, and he's not about to lose the opportunity being promised by doing anything impulsive. As always, De Flores can make himself wait.

Does Beatrice-Joanna understand what she's doing to him? Of course she does. She's young and she's inexperienced, but she's not a fool. Manipulating men is the one thing she's equipped by nature and training to be good at. You can make excuses for her (she will soon be making them herself) by bringing in the narrowness of her education or her feelings of powerless isolation, but you can't take away her conscious decision to act the way she does – by using 'my art' (2.2.47) as she calls it. Just before their interview begins she tells herself that no matter how strong her aversion to De Flores, she can suppress it for strategic reasons: 'Must I needs show it? Cannot I keep that secret, / And serve my turn upon him?' (68–9). She alters her behaviour at once, by design, and is gratified to notice that he's also altering his.

She continues to stroke him by reappraising the 'Hardness' of his face as evidence of 'manhood' (2.2.92–3). She begins to sigh: 'Oh my De Flores!' (98). She lets him know she needs special help; if only I'd been born a man, she tells him, then I'd be able to solve my own problems, 'to oppose my loathings', as she puts it, 'nay remove 'em / For ever from my sight' (112–13). He comes to her rescue with chivalric poise; he kneels to her and says, 'Claim so much man in me' (115). They are striking a bargain, these two; the man is undertaking to serve the woman, and she is offering to reward him.

The service he's required to perform is murder, as both of them clearly understand. Beatrice-Joanna never calls it by such a distasteful name; but then she sees it as an action which simply annihilates the unlucky person who happens to be obstructing her scenario of happiness. She warns De Flores that for him there will be 'blood and danger' (119), but he treats these as further inducements. There's no doubt in her mind about what she wants from him, and no hesitation in his about what he will do for her. By the end of the scene their conversation has become an exchange of energies; they are moving together like two extremely skilful dancers who know each other just well enough to become uninhibited. She: 'Then take him to thy fury'. He: 'I thirst for him'. She: 'Alonzo de Piracquo'. He: 'His end's upon him; / He shall be seen no more' (133–5). With frightening speed these two have reached perfect accord.

They have reached a perfect misunderstanding, too, on the question of how she is going to reward him. In Beatrice-Joanna's mind there's a flawless map of her own self-interest, but there are only the vaguest hints of what might satisfy him. The mere privilege of being useful to her is a powerful motive in itself, by her calculations, but she doesn't assume that will be enough in this case. As she watches him beg for his service she imagines that money is what he's after; so she gives him some as if to whet his appetite for more. 'As thou art forward and thy service dangerous', she says, 'Thy reward shall be precious' (2.2.129–30). 'That have I thought on', he replies; 'I have assur'd myself of that beforehand, / And know it will be precious, the thought ravishes' (130–2). He leaves her just enough room to misinterpret his intentions, if she wants to, and she leaps into it. Every statement about the reward has an ironic doubleness that allows her to retreat into the trap of not knowing what he will demand.

De Flores knows exactly how and why their relationship has changed. As soon as Beatrice-Joanna leaves, her mission accomplished, he talks explicitly, to himself and to the audience, about his expectations:

> Methinks I feel her in mine arms already,
> Her wanton fingers combing out this beard, ·
> And being pleased, praising this bad face.
> Hunger and pleasure, they'll commend sometimes
> Slovenly dishes, and feed heartily on 'em,
> Nay, which is stranger, refuse daintier for 'em.
> Some women are odd feeders.
>
> (2.2.147–53)

He's still unsure about his own attractiveness, but he now has a precise feeling for how she will touch him (because she has) and a confident awareness of how he will please her (because he has). Some of what he says is crude, but, to judge by subsequent events, all of it is true. De Flores knows this woman better than she knows herself.

Beatrice-Joanna thinks she knows exactly what it is she wants. When she looks at Alsemero she can say, 'I have within mine eye all my desires' (2.2.8). And since there can be no greater good than this, she won't be fussy about how she goes about getting it. Yes, she misunderstands her bargain with De Flores by underestimating his demands. But she misinterprets the whole encounter with De Flores by pretending it never happened to her. She can't touch De Flores and remain untouched; she can't seduce him and remain unseduced. After the new bond between them has been created and acknowledged, she looks at De Flores again: 'How lovely now / Dost thou appear to me!' (135–6). These are words of greater emotional weight and authority than anything she says to Alsemero. She's already begun to reward De Flores in exactly the way he wants, though of course she doesn't know it. Not yet.

De Flores carries out the murder with chilling efficiency and returns, when Beatrice-Joanna is again alone, to claim his reward. This time he has the initiative and he knows it. He makes her wait – a little – until she asks: 'Is it done then?' (3.4.24). There should be a pause now, I think, before he answers: 'Piraquo is no more' (25). She weeps with joy at the news but he brings her back to him by announcing he's got a 'token' for her; he produces from a pocket in his costume the piece of flesh he cut from his victim's body and presents it to her by remarking that it came 'unwillingly' (26–7): 'I could not get the ring without the finger' (28). She's shocked by this, as he knows she will be and as he wants her to be. The code of good mental grooming has not prepared her for this: 'Bless me! What hast thou done?' (29). And when he sees that she's on the defensive he rushes forward, easily making her delicacy seem false and foolish. What's all this fuss about a finger when the real deed has been murder? 'A greedy hand thrust in a dish at court, / In a mistake hath had as much as this' (31–2). He refuses to let her retreat into the self-serving euphemistic dream in which blood and all of its attendant ugliness is somebody else's business.

This tactic of shocking her with sensory overload, and thus shattering the decorum by which she conducts her social life, he will use repeatedly until she is ready to submit. Concurrently, he uses two other strategies: holding his ground and offering comfort. Holding your ground is particularly effective when the other person is improvising a dance from one precarious alternative to another, as it is when Henry Bolingbroke uses this ploy on the king in the deposition scene of *Richard II*. Extending the gratifications of comfort over a history of antagonism or alienation will be possible only when the injured person feels weakest and most exposed, as in Cordelia's treatment of her father near the end of *King Lear*. In both Shakespearean instances, and in *The Changeling*, the result is complete abdication, passive surrender.

De Flores holds his ground without wavering while she offers him 3000 florins, then doubles the amount, and at last raises the bid to every penny she's worth. He can do so because he's got a carefully arranged scale of values, and as he's already said, he's thought about it 'beforehand' (2.2.131). While she rummages through her social handbag to find something that will suffice, he merely sticks to his one position; either I get you, he tells her without flinching, or we both get nothing:

> For I place wealth after the heels of pleasure,
> And were I not resolv'd in my belief
> That thy virginity were perfect in thee,
> I should but take my recompense with grudging,
> As if I had but half my hopes I agreed for.
>
> (3.4.115–19)

While he's sure of himself, 'resolv'd' in his 'belief', intuitively right in every assumption he makes about her, she's coasting without an anchor.

'I understand thee not', she says when he refuses her money (68); 'I'm in a labyrinth' (71). She realizes she's getting out of her depth, and urges him to leave at once; then he can 'send' his 'demand in writing' (80). It's an oddly bureaucratic straw for her to be grasping at; all he needs to do is repeat that he won't go anywhere without her. And again she's at a loss: 'What's your meaning?' (82). She tries wagging a prudent finger at him (when he claims the right to kiss her); she tries moral outrage; she tries pulling rank; she tries appealing to his pity. In each case he has a perfectly plausible refutation based on a single principle: 'The wealth of all Valencia shall not buy / My pleasure from me' (160–1).

When he sees her adrift in confusion, he offers her the solace of shared guilt: 'we should stick together', he argues (3.4.84). Without me here to protect you, there are going to be questions that you can't answer, suspicions that you can't put to rest. 'Nor is it fit we two, engag'd so jointly, / Should part and live asunder' (88–9). Repeatedly he invites her with the half-cajoling, half-soothing imperative, 'Come' (85, 92). As each line of defence melts away, her confusion builds into desperation. By the end of the scene she is kneeling to him, begging for mercy. 'I make thee master', she says with greater verbal adroitness than she realizes:

> Of all the wealth I have in gold and jewels:
> Let me go poor unto my bed with honour
> And I am rich in all things.
>
> (156–9)

He is unrelenting, and she knows he has won. Now he can lift her out of this humiliating mess and into his arms: 'Come, rise, and shroud your blushes in my bosom' (167). She will never resist him again.

This is a wonderful scene for many reasons, most of which have been amply celebrated. Its emotional undertow is both threatening and irresistible; its dramatic unfolding is both logically compelling and ironically satisfying; its language both tersely appropriate and loaded with ambiguities that reach into every corner of the play.[23] I think it is also the most frightening exposure in drama of how and why the game of sexual coercion is played. To praise the scene in this way is to emphasize what is psychologically horrible about it, and I think that emphasis is warranted. It is a scene in which one person gains absolute control over another through strategies that exploit and degrade. 'Though thou writ'st maid', De Flores says to Beatrice-Joanna, 'thou whore in thy affection!' (3.4.142). He now has the power to make her swallow anything, and he knows it. But even if the relationship is disgusting, it's also in some curious and amazing way exactly right, for both of them. When Beatrice-Joanna defends herself by appealing to the social 'distance' between them (130), to the privilege of caste that ought to, she thinks, make her invulnerable, De Flores makes a counter-statement that both shatters and liberates her:

> Look but into your conscience, read me there,
> 'Tis a true book you'll find me there your equal:
> Push, fly not to your birth, but settle you
> In what the act has made you, y'are no more now;
> You must forget your parentage to me:
> Y'are the deed's creature.
>
> (132–7)

He is, as always, right about her. They are equal partners in action, in guilt, in desire. The cause of her humiliation is the pain of relinquishing a superior position. I find myself backing De Flores here in the same way as I'm backing Jane Eyre when she challenges Rochester: 'I am not talking to you now through the medium of custom, conventionalities, nor even of mortal flesh: it is my spirit that addresses your spirit; just as if both had passed through the grave, and we stood at God's feet, equal – as we are!'[24] And what I find most disturbing about the bond between De Flores and Beatrice-Joanna is not its degrading ugliness but the shock of being forced to acknowledge how perfectly they belong to each other.

In both of the meetings I've been describing De Flores and Beatrice-Joanna are working towards separate, indeed mutually antagonistic, goals. By the time we see them next they are a couple, not only instinctively but also by design. Paula Johnson points out, in a splendid essay, that after their second meeting they have a secret to hide that nobody else knows; the bond of shared knowledge unites them with one another and in opposition to the rest of their society.[25] I'm sure she is right, and I would want to add only that the knowledge they want to protect is both criminal and carnal. Beatrice-Joanna makes the explicit equation between knowledge and sexual experience while she's inducing her maid Diaphanta to take her place in Alsemero's bed on her wedding-night. She needs a virgin to stand in for her, and as soon as she believes Diaphanta's credentials she looks no further. The reason she gives Diaphanta for proposing such a plan is her own sexual timidity: 'if I'd thought upon the fear at first, / Man should have been unknown' (4.1.72–3). The literal meaning here is: had I kept clearly in mind how afraid I am of sex, I wouldn't have agreed to get married. In Beatrice-Joanna's phrasing, to be a virgin is not to know. And less obviously the same equation lies behind much of the sexual bargaining between her and De Flores. While she's resisting him she says, 'I understand thee not' (3.4.68). He will answer this by pointing out that 'Justice invites your blood to understand me' (3.4.100). What happens between them in the rest of the play is a sign of how deeply they do know each other now.

When she's back in society Beatrice-Joanna still doesn't realize that her true partner is De Flores. She goes through the hasty charade of marriage to Alsemero (presented in the 'Dumb Show' which opens Act 4), and when she's alone she talks about her new predicament:

> This fellow has undone me endlessly,
> Never was bride so fearfully distress'd....

(4.1.1–2)

She's gone back to pretending that De Flores doesn't mean a thing to her; he's once again 'This fellow', a damned nuisance he is too, because the man she's married is 'So clear in understanding' (6) that he'll know at once she's not a virgin. So she does what she did before: she improvises a solution in which a servant (this time Diaphanta) is entrusted with the mission of setting everything right. She even repeats the mistake of assuming (as she did with De Flores) that a mere servant isn't going to develop inconvenient self-interest that might compete with her own.[26] When she's by herself, Beatrice-Joanna thinks and acts in ways that would imply she hasn't changed all that much.

The difference comes out when she's with De Flores again, now capable of proving she's his partner in more than a sexual sense. It's past one a.m. and she's waiting nervously for Diaphanta to give up her place in Alsemero's bed:

> This strumpet serves her own ends, 'tis apparent now,
> Devours the pleasure with a greedy appetite,
> And never minds my honour or my peace,
> Makes havoc of my right.

(5.1.2–5)

Maybe she shouldn't be surprised, by now, to find that a woman she's never thought of as more than a servant is turning out to be her sexual equal. But if you've always thought of yourself as queen of the castle I can see that it might be annoying. In the savage resolve to make Diaphanta pay with her life there's at least a gangster-like honesty, and I suppose that's preferable to euphemistic wishes about having your 'loathings' removed. As the clock strikes two she hears De Flores whisper for her attention, and soon they are making hasty arrangements.

He has a plan: start a fire in Diaphanta's chamber; she's bound to hurry back, where he'll be waiting 'with a piece high-charg'd, / As twere to cleanse the chimney' (5.1.45–6). It will all seem plausible, natural, and in the confusion following the alarm nobody will be curious enough about Diaphanta's charred body to wonder how the gun was actually used. Beatrice-Joanna is impressed: 'I'm forc'd to love thee now, / 'Cause thou provid'st so carefully for my honour' (5.1.47–8). He quickly corrects her: "'Slid, it concerns the safety of us both, / Our pleasure and continuance' (49–50). His statement of the case is more precise, more accurate than hers, but I think hers is more deeply revealing. She doesn't say she's forced to yield to him again; she's forced to *love* him. So she is no longer trapped by circumstance or blackmail or somebody else's intransigent will. She's trapped by something within herself, that she identified when she first spoke of her trembling aversion to De Flores, but which she is only learning to acknowledge now. When she hears shouts of fire offstage, she admits she admires him:

> Already? How rare is that man's speed!
> How heartily he serves me! His face loathes one,
> But look upon his care, who would not love him?
> The east is not more beauteous than his service.
>
> (69–72)

And when he returns as foreman of the bucket brigade, barking out orders, and running off again with a gun in his hand, she's moved: 'Here's a man worth loving' (76). You can't win Beatrice-Joanna's love with good manners and pleasing eloquence; these she secretly despises because she knows how to manipulate them so well herself. You can win her with action – rough and violent action – because she needs to feel that she's being *forced* to love.

I'm not saying that she chose De Flores for her lover from the beginning. But she clearly chose him as her collaborator – as the one person who would know what she knew about the murder of Piracquo. And from the moment she chose him she also chose to treat him as lovers want to be treated: with gentleness, courtesy, trust. Now she has what she wants, but she still wants to believe it was forced on her. Why? Because she wants the best of both worlds: she wants to follow her desires wherever they lead without accepting blame for the consequences. Or, in Paula Johnson's words, she wants 'pleasure without blame because without consent'.[27]

All that remains of this relationship is their death scene, and I will deal with it briefly while raising some of the larger questions that need to be asked about *The Changeling*. The first is an explicitly social question, namely, what kind of society were Middleton and Rowley setting out to create in this play? This question is important because the way you answer it has a bearing on everything I've said so far: on De Flores' conviction that his is a case of injured merit, on Beatrice-Joanna's belief that she's trapped by circumstances, on their shared status as outlaws. If that's indeed what they are, then what are the social forces by virtue of which they are exiled?

Let's begin with a powerful symbol of social stability – the castle in which the entire action of the main plot takes place.[28] When you're inside it, the castle is a labyrinth; when you're outside it's a fortress. Vermandero takes a great deal of pride in this dignified monument of his. When he meets Alsemero he's eager to show off his ancestral home, provided that the visitor has the right pedigree. When Alsemero identifies himself as a Valencian, the son of John de Alsemero, no courtesy can be denied him: 'You must see my castle, / And her best entertainment, ere we part' (1.1.201–2). The whole set-up is a museum in which the obsolete manners of a chivalric past are on display. It's a conservative environment: genealogical connections do make all the difference here, rituals of initiation do open doors, hospitality is generous and free. The aristocratic ease of all this is what rankles with De Flores, who knows he will never be a part of it no matter how he presents his credentials. 'Though my hard fate has thrust me into servitude', he says, 'I tumbled into th'world a gentleman' (2.1.48–9). That's all anyone says about his birthright. It could be fabricated, it could be true. The point is that De Flores builds his resentful case against society out of a feeling of being disinherited.[29]

The nostalgic separateness of the castle world is especially remarkable when you notice that it excludes, both physically and culturally, all of the competitive jostling of middle-class life. For Middleton, addicted as he was by a lifetime of observation and art to the city of London, this is a spectacular exclusion. This isn't a city comedy, of course, so you can't expect the Yellowhammers and Puritans and assorted entrepreneurs of *A Chaste Maid*; but even in *Women Beware Women* there's a strong sense of a city at work, a city that needs its merchants (like Leantio) and turns out for a parade (like the Duke's). In *The Changeling* the city is Alicant, a port on the southeastern coast of Spain; but aside from their occasional use of its name and its harbour, there's no sign that the castle people have any connection with it. Diaphanta refers to it, as a servant might be expected to; she twits Jasperino for his jocular madness by pointing out that 'we have a doctor in the city that undertakes the cure of such' (1.1.138–9). On the evidence of *The Changeling* you'd think the city was that place where they have the madhouse and little more.

There are few women in the castle – two, to be precise – and only one woman who counts. This again is a major surprise, if you take the rest of Middleton's work into account. Why should Beatrice-Joanna stand so strikingly alone in a world where men are permitted a variety of tastes and alliances among members of their own sex? Why should her mother, once 'her fellow' by Vermandero's reckoning, be conveniently 'married…to joys eternal' (3.4.4–5)? Why should Beatrice-Joanna fail so conspicuously to develop any feeling of sisterhood with the one woman she does meet in her day-to-day life, Diaphanta?

I'm sure that the authors set out to create a patriarchal society, regardless of how they might have explained (or not explained) this concept to each other. Without this hypothesis I don't think you can account for the obsessive frequency with which Beatrice-Joanna worries about pleasing her father, especially when you notice how easy Vermandero is to please and how malleably ready to be pleased by damn near anything she desires. In a conservative patriarchy, virginity is the measure of absolute worth in a woman, and this is a premise on which the action of *The Changeling* turns. Alsemero takes a laughably technical attitude towards the purity of his bride: he's got the right apparatus, the beakers filled with milky liquid, the secret code for infallibly detecting sin or pregnancy. It's not all that impressive when you find out that in bed he can't tell one woman from another, but for him it's all serious stuff, an unbreakable rule in the code he lives by. And he's not the only one. Beatrice-Joanna herself asks for a deferment of her marriage by appealing to 'the dear companion of my soul, / Virginity, whom I thus long have liv'd with' (1.1.193–4). And De Flores believes that her virginity doubles the value of his recompense. The point is not that any of these claims is true, but that they are believed. And in this social environment, once Beatrice-Joanna has internalized the values of the male community, management of her sexual resources (of her irreplaceable sexual resource, to be precise) is all she has to work with. That doesn't excuse her for the way she mismanages things, but it does help to explain why she does it. When defending your virginity becomes an absolute imperative, I suppose murdering a prospective husband can be made to look like self-defence.[30]

But to admit that Beatrice-Joanna's position is precarious isn't the same thing as claiming it's hopeless. To the question, what else could she do, the answer is always going to be: plenty. She could go to her father and admit she doesn't really want a short reprieve, but a different man altogether. She could elope with Alsemero and pay the consequences. She could let Alsemero fight a duel for the right to her hand in marriage, as he proposes to do. Each alternative entails some measure of embarrassment or risk, and these 'loathings' Beatrice-Joanna will not tolerate. She'll annihilate Alonzo rather than suffer the indignity of weaseling her way out of a bad commitment. She'll execute Diaphanta in a trice rather than risk exposure. There's an imperious insistence on the sanctity of her own desires in all of this that has led L.G. Salingar to compare her story with that of Frances Howard,[31] the undisputed female star of the famous Jacobean sex-scandal in which Thomas Overbury was murdered for objecting to Howard's plan to divorce the Earl of Essex and marry her lover, Robert Carr. The connection is a good one, whether Middleton and Rowley were making it or not. It stands behind Salingar's precisely argued evaluation of Beatrice-Joanna's failures: 'Beatrice makes her own hell; but she does so with the unconscious complicity of the men of her own rank around her, by blindly trusting in their prejudices and beliefs. Her mind is a mirror of social certitudes.'[32]

Unlike most of the great tragedies of Middleton and Rowley's day, *The Changeling* takes place in a completely secular environment. The castle people go to church, of course, but I can't believe they're doing so out of devotion to anything more elevated than the status quo. The one event that happens in the house of worship is a sexual awakening: ' 'Twas in the temple where I first beheld her', says Alsemero (1.1.1), and he proves his allegiance to the castle world at once by taking this as a sign of the holiness of his infatuation. Nobody prays in *The Changeling*. It wouldn't occur to anyone to do so. No matter how bizarre or how basic their moral conundrums or choices, people don't look to religion for help. They don't even use theological terms or concepts when they're arguing. There's a vaguely spiritual climate at times. During the marriage ceremony, 'ALONZO's *ghost appears to*

DE FLORES...*showing him the hand whose finger he had cut off'* (4.1.0.7–9). And when the lovers are arranging Diaphanta's murder, the Ghost appears again, so dimly this time that neither of them can be sure what's happening. De Flores does speak to it; 'I dread thee not', he says, and while the Ghost 'slides by' he explains to Beatrice-Joanna that it's 'but a mist of conscience' (5.1.59–61). It's a remarkably subservient Ghost, this faint echo of a spiritual past in the minds of two people who don't want anything to do with it. All Beatrice-Joanna needs to do is mop away the 'shivering sweat' it leaves behind (63) and they can both get on with the serious business of murder as if nothing had happened.

So in a sense *The Changeling* is a critique of what happens when you make pleasure into an absolute standard and abandon the formulas of an obsolete tradition: the aristocratic, patriarchal, nostalgic formulas of life in the castle. This is most obviously the path taken by De Flores, who appeals repeatedly to pleasure as the one good he will not relinquish: 'For I place wealth after the heels of pleasure' (3.4.115); 'The wealth of all Valencia shall not buy my pleasure from me' (3.4.160–1). In these assertions he is addressing Beatrice-Joanna as the object of pleasure, which indeed she is. But there is a sense in which she too treats pleasure as an absolute: the scenario of her own gratification is what motivates the murder of Alonzo to begin with. So it is rhetorically telling when De Flores, having established the bond of sexual and criminal teamwork between himself and Beatrice-Joanna, should identify the good he strives for as 'Our pleasure and continuance' (5.1.50). *My* pleasure has become *our* pleasure, as Beatrice-Joanna moves from being the object of a quest to being the subject of a collaborative destiny. The energy with which both of these partners pursue their pleasure has the effect of pushing traditional voices of restraint into the margins: moral questions are no longer settled by appealing to the judgement of God (who is absent) or even to the wisdom of the patriarch (who is present but ineffectual). So the pursuit of pleasure rages out of control, with no external authority and no self-critical awareness capable of containing it. If the excessive mismanagement of pleasure led to absurdity in *A Chaste Maid in Cheapside*, here the obsessive unfurling of pleasure leads to its tragic equivalent, anarchy. When the world is changing faster than might be comfortable for most human beings, when old values are under attack and new ones uncertain, resorting to pleasure as the only thing of value is a real and a dangerous temptation.

Now for my last question about *The Changeling*: the one everybody asks, since William Empson made it famous,[33] about the relationship between the main plot and the subplot. As the castle is the exclusive setting for the main plot, so the madhouse contains the comic scenes. It too is a fortress and a labyrinth, a world of naked power (authorized by Dr Alibius, enforced by Lollio) and subterfuge (insofar as Antonio pretends to be a fool and

Franciscus a madman). There are dozens of similarities in plot, situation, character, and language – so many in fact that it's possible to pile up a pretty mechanical list of parallels if what you want to do is demonstrate the coherence of the play. You could begin with Lollio's advice about cuckoldry. Alibius wants to keep his young wife to himself – 'I would wear my ring on my own finger', as he puts it (1.2.27) – to which Lollio quips: 'You must keep it on still then; if it but lie by, one or other will be thrusting into't' (30–1). This comes just moments after De Flores, while fondling Beatrice-Joanna's gloves, imagines her revulsion if he were to 'thrust' his 'fingers / Into her sockets here' (1.1.233–4). Not all of the parallelisms are as gross or as inescapable as this one, though there are enough persuasive examples to make the case for an interlocking design. But I think this case can be (and has been) made too laboriously. What stands out in a reading or a production of *The Changeling* is the radical divergence in tone between the two plots. And this gap doesn't really get any narrower, even when you add up dramatic and verbal similarities.

One of the problems, let's face it, is the inferior writing in the subplot. Rowley wasn't nearly the artist that Middleton was, and in scenes where he was pretty much on his own the difference shows. Does that mean the subplot can be cut out with little or no damage to the text or performance? Not for a moment. The idea of the madhouse is a metaphor of such consequence that to lose it is to miss the experience of the play.

It's helpful to approach the madhouse scenes in ways suggested by Foucault in *Madness and Civilization*. 'Confinement was an institutional creation peculiar to the seventeenth century', Foucault points out. 'A sensibility was born which had drawn a line and laid a cornerstone, and which chose – only to banish.'[34] In short, the madhouse was taking on the vast and ultimately hopeless task of repression. Nominally supervised by a wing of the medical profession, it was in fact organized and run like a prison; its mission was not to heal but to control. Its tactics were police tactics, and its inhabitants were misfits of every shape and size: 'a population without resources, without social moorings, a class rejected or rendered mobile by new economic developments'; 'the unemployed, the idle, and vagabonds'.[35] The madhouse in *The Changeling* is an early stage in what Foucault calls 'The Great Confinement'. The fool and madman have lost the quasi-magical powers they enjoyed in *King Lear*; they have certainly lost their independence.

Lollio's task is therefore the one conferred on him by society: he must keep the mess and ugliness which threaten conservative society under control, inside boundaries, out of sight. He's entitled to do this by whatever means he finds effective. So the whip is the symbol of his kind of authority; he assures his employer, Alibius, that there's nothing to fear from the rowdy behaviour of the inmates 'so long as we are there with our commanding pizzles' (4.3.61–2). The instrument of repression in this case is the cock of a dead animal, probably a bull. Is it just a vulgar joke that Lollio can't resist? Or is it an allusion to the patriarchal character of the Great Confinement as it operates in this play? It might be both.

The humour of the subplot is always gross, and most of it is sexual. A great deal of it has to do with cuckoldry, and therefore with challenges to the authority of the patriarch. When Lollio introduces his master's young wife Isabella to the newest inmate, Antonio, he reassures her with what has to be an obscene leer: 'Fear him not, mistress, 'tis a gentle nigget; you may play with him, as safely with him as with his bauble' (3.3.102–3). Punning of this kind is the subversive language of the madhouse, the verbal code that promises a way of circumventing the rules of official confinement. But it's a false promise, at least when Lollio makes it, because he's as much a tool of the system as anyone. The best he can hope for is to have his 'share' (3.3.245), to 'put in' for his 'thirds' (4.3.36) if he gets the chance. Like De Flores he's not interested in changing the system but in exploiting it if he can.

The pressure of confinement is what allows the two plots, unequal as they are, to work together. A social system that celebrates its own courtliness, defensively and nostalgically, will have little room for freaks and oddballs, so they have to be shut up elsewhere and beaten into submission. The decorum of the castle and the whip in Lollio's hand are both instruments of repression.

So the closing scene is not only the end of a bizarre love story but also a ritual of exclusion. The secret knowledge of De Flores and Beatrice-Joanna is a secret no longer. Alsemero has found out the truth, so he calls his wife a whore and locks her up in his cabinet. De Flores, when challenged, has at least the decency to admit he got exactly what he wanted; and though he too calls his partner a whore, he follows her into the cabinet of confinement. He knows they are meant for each other, even now. He wounds her fatally offstage, and brings her back in his arms. 'Here we are', he says (5.3.143).

Beatrice-Joanna still belongs to the castle world in a way that De Flores never will. The outrage of her husband only made her impudent, but her father's face melts her into shame and capitulation:

> Oh come not near me, sir, I shall defile you:
> I am that of your blood was taken from you
> For your better health; look no more upon't,
> But cast it to the ground regardlessly:
> Let the common sewer take it from distinction.
>
> (5.3.149–53)

This is about as perfect a summing-up as anyone in the castle world would want to hear: the threat of something deeper and more violent than conforming courtesy has to be bled away, especially if the threat is female. Alsemero recovers from his loss with remarkable alacrity; excluding the bad blood satisfies him because it sets off his own spotless immunity. Vermandero has a harder time coming to terms with the blot on his honour, but lets Alsemero cheer him up with the observation that 'justice hath so right / The guilty hit, that innocence is quit / By proclamation, and may joy again' (185–7). The men who were once so eager to pamper Beatrice-Joanna are now just as anxious to rearrange their world so as to pretend she never existed. It's their turn to rid themselves of their loathings.

But not De Flores. He stands his ground as always, this time with Beatrice-Joanna's body in his arms:

> I lov'd this woman in spite of her heart;
> Her love I earn'd out of Piracquo's murder.
>
> (165–6)

It's the scornful declaration of the self-made man to the rivals he sees as more privileged and less deserving. He knows it's a suicidal declaration. Before the castle people can direct their judgemental malice to its target, he pulls out his 'penknife', stabs himself, and dies (173–7).

The play doesn't offer you a choice between good and evil, but something closer to a choice between hypocrisy and corruption. The secretive criminal obsessions of Beatrice-Joanna and De Flores are held up not against a standard of unimpeachable virtue but against a background of unbearable smugness. It's not an easy choice to make, and that's how Middleton wants it to be.

The distinctive aesthetic pleasure yielded by Middleton's drama, as I implied at the outset, is the pleasure of irony. In a sense this is a version of the pleasure of discovery. We watch in amazement as Allwit follows his self-avowed principles of sexual management to the point of self-cancellation, or as Beatrice-Joanna begins the chain reaction that will lead from the inscription of her sexual desire as sacred truth to its reinterpretation as corrupted blood, or as De Flores calculates his own advantage to the point of suicidal immolation. And the watching includes a kind of voyeuristic pleasure: the ironic trajectory followed by the pleasure-seekers in Middleton's drama allows us to be both taken in by the relentless single-mindedness of their pursuit, and yet curiously detached, aware that we are watching as events unfold for our gratification as readers and spectators. The doubleness I am describing here is of course available in a great deal of the drama of the time, as my observations about Jonson or Marston or Webster have already implied. But in Middleton the doubleness character-istic of irony becomes more than a technique, and therefore more than one pleasure among many. His grasp of the degree to which service is also mastery, purity also degradation, and repression also indulgence seems to me unfalteringly subtle. There are certain pleasures that lie outside Middleton's artistic range, among them the kinds of magnificence that arise from univocal admiration or abhorrence. Middleton's art frees itself from both of these through the exercise of irony, and in doing so achieves a greatness of its own.

8
Endless Dreams: John Ford

Ford's plays are both old-fashioned, for their time, and strikingly innovative. The clearest example of this oddly paradoxical effect in Ford's writing is *The Chronicle History of Perkin Warbeck* (*c*.1633), a play which continues the story of the Tudor dynasty at a point where Shakespeare had abandoned it in the 1590s, at the accession of Henry VII to be precise; even the title has the quaintness of the deliberately outmoded about it, and if that isn't enough, Ford goes out of his way in the Prologue to admit that he's writing in a genre now 'So out of fashion' (l. 2) that it's likely to be misunderstood. But while all this is true, it would be absurd to claim that Ford is simply reviving the obsolete, because his history play reads like something quite different from any of its predecessors. This has a great deal to do with Ford's angle of vision, which enables him to confer authority on characters not authorized by history.

Perkin Warbeck is not a king or a duke but a pretender: a man who lives out the fantasy of apparently believing and certainly claiming that he's Richard Duke of York (one of the little princes reputedly murdered in the Tower by Richard III) and that by virtue of his miraculous preservation he has a better title to the throne than the reigning monarch. I choose the word 'fantasy' with malice aforethought, because it suits both this particular instance and a general tendency in Ford's writing as well. It would be fair to say that Perkin's delusion – the authenticity which he creates for it and the integrity which others confer upon it – is at the centre of this eccentric play. And it wouldn't be stretching things much to say that there's always a fantasy of some especially problematic kind in Ford's drama. Ford's earliest independent play, *The Lover's Melancholy* (1628), is a somewhat bookish dramatization, written under the acknowledged influence of Burton's *Anatomy*, of the mental distortions brought on by erotic fantasy. And elsewhere in Ford's plays the compelling actions and the decisive conflicts happen not on the battlefield or even in the bedroom, but in the mind.

Take the case of *Love's Sacrifice* (*c*.1631), for example, not Ford's best or most famous play, but in many ways his most typical. The plot is on one level a rewriting of *Othello*; Philippo Caraffa, Duke of Pavy, murders his beautiful young wife Bianca because he suspects her of sexual infidelity with Fernando, his best friend and favourite courtier. The recollections of *Othello* are inescapable partly because of the presence of Roderico D'Avolos, a sinister malcontent who plants and nurtures the idea of jealousy in Caraffa's mind. But if Shakespeare's play conjures up the 'green-eyed monster' (3.3.168) of jealousy in order to display it as a superstition and a blasphemy against true love, in Ford there are powerful dramatic endorsements of the delusion.

These come in the form of several scenes in which Bianca and Fernando converse in private and reveal their emotional intimacy. In the first of these Fernando approaches Bianca with the furtive humility of a lover who hopes for a gentle reception though he knows he's entitled to nothing. Bianca takes the high road of moral outrage, and threatens him with exposure if he speaks again. But before long they are back at it. They are playing chess together when he interrupts the game, kneels, declares his love, and she counters with another variant of 'how dare you' and another empty threat. We know it's empty because she can't stay away from this man any more than he can resist her.

She comes to his bedroom '*in her night-mantle*', '*draws a curtain*' to reveal Fernando '*in bed, sleeping*' (2.4.0.1–3), places a candle near his bedside, and wakens him with artful whispers. He thinks, understandably, that the big moment has arrived, and she now admits that she's been yearning for his love all along:

> Fernando, in short words, how e'er my tongue
> Did often chide thy love, each word thou spak'st
> Was music to my ear.

> (2.4.23–5)

But Bianca is no shallow libertine. She will yield, if Fernando tempts her, but she adds the proviso that, if Fernando makes love to her (which she wants as much as he does), 'Ere yet the morning shall new-christen day, / I'll kill myself' (2.4.55–6). This is both a brilliant and an infuriating moment in Ford's text. It is brilliant in its representation of Bianca's mental cul de sac; she's a woman who has come to acknowledge the truth about herself as a sexual being with desires of her own, but her social choices are still rigidly prescribed by a patriarchal structure which she has in fact completely internalized. She is free to choose the grand passion of her life at last, but she recognizes that such a choice equals annihilation.

It's an infuriating moment because it raises to the alarm level the degree of sexual frustration. Fernando is paralysed by this redefinition of their courtship because he's sensitive enough to realize that she means what she says. The scene ends with both of them swearing love and allegiance to one another, in this life and beyond, but without the satisfaction their bodies are craving. They will never make love in the physical sense, either here or during the rest of the play. And in giving them the power to resist what they both want above all else, Ford has created frustration not only for them but for the audience. Theatrically and psychologically he has aroused expectations that he resolutely refuses to satisfy; in Swinburne's colourful if dismissive phrase, he has constructed a love relationship out of 'obscene abstinence'.[1] It's impossible to read this play without wishing, either overtly or in some obscure corner of one's mind, that Bianca and Fernando would put an end to the paralysis of inhibition and become what they really are: lovers. I would argue that this wish is present regardless of how it interacts with the moral stance of the reader: the Victorians who lash out against Bianca for being an adulteress in her heart and the moderns who accuse her of lacking the courage of her convictions are both requiring the satisfaction that the play prepares them for but denies.

Although they never in fact make love, Bianca and Fernando do create for themselves and for each other a relationship that is above all erotic. Whenever they are on stage together, their mutual attraction threatens to leap over the restraints required by their social situation. Their behaviour isn't openly erotic, but in Ford's plays sex is always a mental experience above all else. You can restrain the body's energies, as these two people do, but the mind is free. Bianca and Fernando are enmeshed in a mutually created fantasy; to borrow language more congenial to the social sciences, they are engaged in interpersonal sexual scripting.[2] Sex is a fantasy for them, but a fantasy they share, value, and promote through mutual corroboration. The language and the semiology of their relationship reflects the erotic intimacy they've achieved in a mental universe not subject to social constraints.

So it's not all that surprising to find Caraffa and his allies piecing together a circumstantial case against these lovers. Nor is it surprising that, when they know they're in trouble, they should retreat to the intimate space of a bed-chamber where Bianca is '*discovered...in her night attire, leaning on a cushion at a table, holding* FERNANDO *by the hand*' (5.1.4.1–3). There is a surprise in the last act of the play, and this occurs when Bianca is called upon to defend herself against her husband's accusations. She's in the perfect position to return outrage for outrage, to protest her innocence, to dismiss his evidence as hearsay and fabrication. What does she do instead? She admits her guilt; indeed, she positively relishes it. What drove her on to betray her husband, besmirch her honour, and break her marriage vows? Simple, really. 'I held Fernando much the properer man' (5.1.70). How can she be so impudent as to brazenly exult in her guilt when accused by the very man she has wronged? She explains to Caraffa with breathtaking precision that, just as he found in her 'A spark of beauty more than you had seen', so she has chosen Fernando for the same reason: 'The selfsame appetite which led you on / To marry me, led me to love your friend' (5.1.93–6). This declaration is a wonderful moment in a variety of ways, most but not all of them rhetorical. It's a suicidal moment, in the sense that it provokes the duke into the state of despairing fury that he will call upon when he kills her. It shocks the duke by calling into question his cherished beliefs about patriarchal power and privilege. It's unsettling for the audience too; the double standard is exposed for the shabby thing it is in Bianca's declaration, whether she realizes it or not. She might paraphrase her own utterance as 'Yes, you're right Caraffa, I'm no better than a common slut', but she's created a rhetorical position which can also be read as 'So you see, once you grant that women have desires of their own, quite independent of men's prescriptions for them, you have no means other than tyranny to deny them the right of choice, of autonomy, of agency.' But if her words act in these various rhetorical ways, they also express something that is fundamentally true. Bianca has chosen Fernando, as he has chosen her, and together they have constructed a fantasy of love that neither of them will deny though it costs them their lives.

I've been making a claim for *Love's Sacrifice* as Ford's most typical play; T.S. Eliot was making a similar point when he described it as 'disfigured by all the faults of which Ford was capable'.[3] This acerbic and unsupported remark, though it contains a germ of truth, has also done a disservice to Ford criticism by ensuring that *Love's Sacrifice* will survive – if at all – as a marginal text.[4] It is not a great play, but it is a fertile one in that it shows Ford's imagination posing the questions that make his art distinctive. 'Why should the laws, / The iron laws of ceremony, bar / Mutual embraces? What's a vow?... / Can there be sin in unity?' (5.1.5–8). These are Bianca's questions, but they are also Ford's. Without raising questions like these he could not have written *The Broken Heart* (c.1629) and *'Tis Pity She's a Whore* (c.1630).[5]

> Thou cheat'st us *Ford*, mak'st one seeme two by Art.
> What is *Love's Sacrifice*, but *the broken Heart*?[6]

These enigmatic lines by Richard Crashaw can be read in at least two ways. If you assume that the writing (or the reading) of *The Broken Heart* happened first, then Crashaw could be saying: *Love's Sacrifice* is nothing more than *The Broken Heart* all over again; there's really only one idea, doubled by the feigning power of the artist. If you make the opposite assumption – that *Love's Sacrifice* came first – then Crashaw could be pointing out that the yearning or the need to make a sacrifice (of the self) for the sake of love is completed by the icon of the broken heart; the apparent differences between the two plays disguise the sense in which both of them raise the same questions about erotic desires that can't be acted out. The linkage between the two texts is critically suggestive because *The Broken Heart* is Ford's most comprehensive statement about repression.[7]

Sex, in *The Broken Heart*, is again a mental phenomenon. The overt behaviour of the characters is governed by a code of restraint which borders on the ceremonial, and lapses from the norm are quickly identified as aberrant. The sense of a code governing everyone is greatly enhanced by Ford's unusual setting for this play: ancient Sparta. (All of his other plays, with the necessary exception of *Perkin Warbeck*, have Italian settings.) What Sparta gave to Ford wasn't really another culture that he could bring to life, but an excuse for highlighting a particular ethos. To borrow from the play's language, the Spartan ethic designates virtues like 'steadiness', 'courage', and 'toughness' as distinctively 'masculine'. All of these words come together in the climactic scene (5.2) of Calantha's dance and Orgilus' self-inflicted execution. Calantha's restraint during the dance has been especially remarkable in view of her gender, observes one of the courtiers: ''Tis strange, these tragedies should never touch on / Her female pity' (5.2.94–5). To which Bassanes, a recent convert to the code of restraint, replies:

> She has a masculine spirit.
> And wherefore should I pule, and, like a girl,
> Put finger in the eye? Let's be all toughness,
> Without distinction betwixt sex and sex.
>
> (95–8)

The ideal is not androgyny, but the imposition of the masculine code on both sexes. Calantha admits as much when, having become queen, she identifies her own gender as a major political problem. Will her subjects, she wonders, be able to accept 'the sceptre of a virgin' when they've been accustomed to 'princes / Of masculine and stirring composition?' (5.3.5–7). The ethos of Sparta is demonstrably and rigidly patriarchal; the qualities held up as desirable are designated as 'masculine', and those shunned as symptoms of weakness are attributed to girls and women.

The social authority vested in this code controls behaviour, but fails to extinguish desire. Thrasus, the patriarchal head of the family to which both Ithocles and Penthea belong, is now dead; but while he lived he agreed to the marriage of his daughter to Orgilus, the son of his old political enemy, Crotolon. Both fathers assented to this plan as a way of healing old wounds, and both children were eager for it because they had fallen in love. The relationship between Penthea and Orgilus had progressed as far as betrothal when Thrasus died, before the lovers could taste 'The sweets our vows expected' (1.1.33). Authority over Penthea's sexual being passed not to Orgilus, but to Ithocles, the new patriarchal head. He had ideas of his own, among them the ambition to add to his political weight by marrying his sister to the wealthy nobleman Bassanes. This he succeeded in doing, while he was still too young to realize that the marriage would be a disaster.

It's a disaster from Orgilus' point of view because he never gets the woman he wants, of course. But the marriage is a disaster for Bassanes too. He is, in a sense, proud of having Penthea as his wife. But the high esteem in which he holds Penthea only adds to his misery, because he knows he doesn't interest or deserve her. He's mocked by his own desire, since he can never expect it to be returned. Sensing quite correctly the coldness of Penthea's response to him, he's tormented with jealousy. He knows about her previous attachment to Orgilus, but his fear of betrayal doesn't limit itself to a single rival. The whole world swarms with opportunities for cuckoldry, so it becomes his impossible task to ensure that Penthea lives a completely guarded life. 'I'll have that window next the street dammed up', he says (2.1.1), echoing the sentiments and borrowing the strategies of Jonson's Corvino. Repression of this kind only increases terror, and ensures that Bassanes isn't really getting much out of the experience of marriage.

I doubt that he's getting any sex, at least by this late stage in the relationship. I draw this inference in part from his outburst of jealous rage at the suggestion that Penthea might become pregnant (2.1.122); were this to happen, the one thing Bassanes *won't* think is that the child is his own. More pathetically, he virtually admits his sexual inadequacy while speaking to Penthea herself. Trying to apologize for his ill-mannered jealousy, he flatters her with submissive adulation and wishes he could offer more: 'O that I could preserve thee in fruition / As in devotion' (3.2.165–6). To the modern ear the word 'fruition' may suggest that Bassanes is here lamenting the childlessness of their marriage. He may indeed be doing this. But Ford's audience would have taken 'fruition' to mean pleasure, and in this context explicitly sexual pleasure. Readers who aren't convinced might have a look at Suckling's two poems 'Against Fruition', Cowley's poem on the same theme, and Aphra Behn's 'To *Alexis* in Answer to his Poem against Fruition'.[8] So I think Bassanes is saying either that he's sexually impotent (he may have become sexually impotent since their marriage) or that he's incapable of arousing any sexual response in her. Both of these interpretations would be consistent with his earlier assumption that her pregnancy would equal his cuckoldry. Either interpretation places Bassanes in the unhappy position of being a sexual failure with the very woman he would most like to please.

For Penthea herself, the woman whom everyone admires and many desire, the present state of affairs is – if anything – worse than for either of the two men. Suspended between two marriages, the unconsummated betrothal to the man she loves and the official but forced alliance with a man she can only pity, she now speaks a language in which paradox is the norm:

> There is no peace left for a ravished wife
> Widowed by lawless marriage.
>
> (4.2.146–7)

The source of her ambivalence isn't all that mysterious; it consists of her belief that betrothal to Orgilus has the validity of a genuine marriage, and that her present relationship is therefore tarnished, however lawful it may be. Her view could of course be supported with good legal arguments drawn from the culture in which Ford lived. As various scholars have shown, the vows of betrothal between Juliet and Claudio in *Measure for Measure*, like those between the Duchess and Antonio in *The Duchess of Malfi*, were treated as legal marriages in all ways that mattered, and could not be dissolved once sexual intercourse had occurred.[9] What has passed between Orgilus and Penthea is by these standards a true marriage, awaiting only consummation in the flesh. And even if Penthea were to find legal arguments to absolve her of her prior commitment to Orgilus, she would still be left with an emotional attachment she can't dissolve: she agrees with Orgilus that she is by every moral criterion *his* wife. So the state of being which she now occupies is a travesty of what she might have become. Her marriage to Bassanes is variously represented (by Penthea herself) as a 'rape' (2.3.79), a 'divorce' (2.3.57), a protracted, open-eyed sleep (4.2.74–5), and a journey to the grave (4.2.78–9). A sense of worthlessness and a conviction of guilt are conflated in her self-image as 'a faith-breaker, / A spotted whore' (3.2.69–70). That's what you've made me, she tells her brother Ithocles, and she explains the image with a precision he cannot ignore:

> For she that's wife to Orgilus and lives
> In known adultery with Bassanes,
> Is at the best a whore.
>
> (3.2.73–5)

Convinced of her own degradation, and of the impossibility of significant change for the better, Penthea looks forward to only one further event: death.

Penthea's death-wish is apparent in everything she says and does; it follows her through the play like an invisible halo. In one scene, the only intimate encounter between Penthea and Calantha, it is the centre of attention. Penthea has made her will, and she interprets it to Calantha, whom she asks to serve as 'executrix' (3.5.36), in three separate stages corresponding to the 'three poor jewels' she is able to 'bequeath' (49). The first of these is her youth, which she leaves 'To virgin wives, such as abuse not wedlock / By freedom of desires' (52–3) and 'To married maids, such as prefer the number / Of honourable issue in their virtues, / Before the flattery of delights by marriage' (56–8). She honours these two groups of women with the gift of perpetual youth: 'May those be ever young' (59). What, precisely, is she saying here? She is inventing two paradoxical classes of women ('virgin wives' and 'married maids') to represent something about the ambivalence of her own experience. Both groups are simultaneously married and not married, like the 'still unravished bride' of Keats's 'Ode on a Grecian Urn'. Both belong to the world of pre-sexual marriage, which in Penthea's experience corresponds to the period of betrothal to Orgilus when she was his wife (by virtue of the vows they had exchanged) but not yet his wife (in the sense that the marriage wasn't consummated). To confer eternal youth upon 'virgin wives' and 'married maids' is Penthea's way of expressing a wish to return to her own life of pre-sexual happiness as the betrothed mistress of Orgilus, to a state of being, that is, before the shame of marriage to Bassanes turned her into the whore she now imagines herself to be. Implicitly, Penthea has invented for herself the category of *virgin whore*: she is both the bride still awaiting the consummation of her marriage, and the degraded partner in adultery. Her own paradoxical situation is therefore both like and unlike that of the women to whom she offers her bequest; like them she has been arrested in a state of being that cannot flourish, but unlike them she occupies a position of perpetual disgrace.

The second jewel in Penthea's will is her 'fame', which she gives 'To Memory, and Time's old daughter, Truth' (60–2). This is an altogether less cryptic bequest. Having given up any hope of a personal future, Penthea is concerned about how she will be remembered; she wants to be vindicated by her own death, as I suppose all suicides do; she wants to convince her husband, her brother, and her lover that the life she has left was indeed unbearable, and that her resolution to end it has been an honourable action. Her third bequest is her brother Ithocles, whom she gives to Calantha. She has learned, from Ithocles himself, that he loves Calantha; she knows that he cannot express his love. So she does it for him. Much as she resents her brother for damaging her own life beyond recall, she doesn't want him to suffer the same lingering torment that she has endured:

> I must leave the world
> To revel in Elysium, and 'tis just
> To wish my brother some advantage here.
>
> (95–7)

Not that she's able to conquer her resentment completely. She will soon be urging Orgilus to direct his anger at Ithocles, and in doing so she is releasing her understandable desire for revenge. But her own way out of the labyrinth of ambivalence is clear: she will starve herself to death.

Ford situates Penthea in a social context that is narrowly masculine and blatantly patriarchal, and then allows her to achieve, subversively, the most powerful voice in the play. The authority of her eloquence can be crudely measured by noticing its impact on the people who surround her. Penthea is like Hamlet in one respect: she has the ability to make other people feel acutely uncomfortable. Bassanes, in response to the vexing combination of Penthea's apparent passivity and her uncompromising withdrawal from him, is driven back and forth between the compulsion of jealousy and the conviction that he's got to mend his ways. Ithocles, just now savouring the taste of his newly won prominence as a military leader, has to swallow the bitterness of guilt as he acknowledges that his reputation has been built at Penthea's expense. Orgilus, who never gives up thinking of himself as Penthea's lover and husband, is confined by her voice to a prison of sexual frustration. All of these tensions meet most memorably in the scene which represents Penthea having gone mad at last, entering with '*her hair about her ears*' (4.2.57.1), and speaking in the most cryptic range of her paradoxical register. Orgilus kisses her hand, and she comments on the coldness of his lips:

> every drop
> Of blood is turnèd to an amethyst,
> Which married bachelors hang in their ears.
>
> (129–31)

She recognizes that Orgilus too has been the victim of repression, that he now belongs as securely as she does to the class of people who can't emerge from pre-sexual marriage. Bassanes can't contain his humiliation during this scene, and Ithocles turns his guilt into pity, but Orgilus finds a new clarity in what appears bizarre: 'If this be madness, madness is an oracle' (133). He will now provoke the catastrophe by killing Ithocles in a mood of serene male rivalry, and by killing himself in the Senecan way – by letting his own blood – as if to complete the repressive design that has haunted him from the start.

Although Ford ensures that Penthea speaks with a voice of her own, no matter who may try to smother it, he does imprison her in a fantasy of past happiness that prevents her from achieving or even wanting personal autonomy. When she imagines alternatives to the unbearable present, she always puts in grammatical signals (like the past conditional) to confer on her thoughts the explicit status of opportunities forever lost. That, for instance, is how the notion of motherhood is stored. 'I might have been / Mother to many prattling babes', she says (4.2.87–8); but Penthea knows that she's 'past child-bearing' (4.2.94), not literally of course, not biologically, but in every other meaningful sense of the phrase. So she isolates Orgilus in the mirage of an unreachable past, deliberately excluding him from the future, even if her circumstances were to change. Were Bassanes to die, for example, she would still refuse Orgilus on the grounds that

> My true love
> Abhors to think that Orgilus deserved
> No better favours than a second bed.
>
> (2.3.100–2)

Surprising and cruel though this thought may seem, it's entirely of a piece with her belief that the past can't be recovered, that she's been degraded by the present, and that the future is hopeless. Penthea's voice, designated as 'Complaint' by Ford's allegorical tag in the dramatis personae, has the power to change the behaviour of others but is helpless in relation to herself.

A final word on Calantha, the Spartan princess whose fate is the nominal reason for the title of the play. She is in most observable respects the direct foil to Penthea. As heiress to the throne she has access to political power. As the daughter of the sometimes foolish but tolerant and well-meaning patriarch, Amyclas, she has the power to choose her own husband and the promise of her father that he won't interfere. She shows this power in action by discouraging the attentions of Nearchus, Prince of Argos, and expressing a preference for Ithocles. She manages all of this in a style quite unlike Penthea's: with very few words, in fact, and several well-timed symbolic gestures. She has the world at her beck and call until very near the end, having taken the trouble to plan intelligently for her political and domestic future. Then comes the celebrated dance in which she learns, from three different messengers, of the death of her father, the starvation of Penthea, and the murder of Ithocles. She resumes dancing as if nothing of consequence had happened following each of these reports. In this way she earns the tribute to her 'masculine spirit' (5.2.95) which I quoted at the start of this discussion.

But something of great moment is being repressed by this behaviour. So much is evident from the behaviour itself, which is represented theatrically as a way of warding off for a time the pain she now has to endure. So much is evident also by the deliberately ceremonial way in which Calantha now goes about her business: she claims the throne as her inheritance, she judges and sentences Orgilus, she prepares for her coronation. And the ceremonial feeling is augmented in the final scene of the play, which opens with one of Ford's most elaborate stage directions. The scene requires '*an altar covered with white*', '*two lights of virgin wax*', and the '*music of recorders*' (5.3.0.1–2). Attendants must carry in the body of Ithocles, crowned, and place his coffin near the altar. After this Calantha leads in a procession of women, all in white, and '*kneels before the altar*' (5.3.0.8), thus taking her place beside the body of her lover. Now silence, prayers, and '*soft music*' (5.3.0.9) while the attendants stand apart, leaving Calantha and her dead bridegroom alone at centre stage. I say bridegroom because all of this is preparatory to the moment when Calantha, with great dignity, will place her 'mother's wedding ring' on the finger of Ithocles, with the declaration: 'Thus I new-marry him whose wife I am. / Death shall not separate us' (5.3.64–7). With one deft stroke Ford has placed Calantha into exactly the position occupied by Penthea throughout the play; she too is a virgin wife, a married maid, a woman suspended between desire and gratification.

It's as if the lingering sorrows of Penthea are compressed into the last few minutes of Calantha's life. She admits now that the extraordinary restraint with which she danced through the messages of death was a deception, a display of courage hiding grief too raw for expression. But 'griefs will have their vent', as Orgilus has observed (4.1.116). Repression is only a temporary refuge, even for Calantha. 'They are the silent griefs which cut the heart-strings', she says; 'Let me die smiling' (5.3.75–6).

When Calantha dies, after kissing the cold lips of the corpse she has married, she fulfils the prediction of the Oracle that *'The lifeless trunk shall wed the broken heart'* (4.1.134). She also completes the tragic circle which brings all of these characters together as victims of a social code too rigid to nourish the human heart. What haunts Bassanes, what gnaws at Ithocles, what torments Penthea, and what kills Calantha is the return of the repressed. And it should be possible now to read Crashaw's couplet in a third sense, perhaps intended, perhaps not. 'What is *Love's Sacrifice*, but *the broken Heart?*' It's not merely the similarity of two texts that's being asserted here, but the link between two experiences. To sacrifice love, for whatever reasons, is an act of violence against the heart. Crashaw may not have written his epigram with this meaning in mind, but I have no doubt that Ford would have read it this way.

'Tis Pity She's a Whore is Ford's most disturbing play. As in *The Broken Heart*, Ford is working with a system of repression that offers to contain and control desire. As in *Love's Sacrifice*, he represents a pair of lovers constructing a mutually sustaining fantasy which removes them from society. The system of repression in this case is the incest taboo, and the shared fantasy is the idea of oneness carried to its absolute perfection. It's the beauty of this fantasy that disturbs.[10] To dramatize incest is enough in itself to create a certain shock-value, as Ford may have learned from Webster's *The Duchess of Malfi* or Beaumont and Fletcher's *A King and No King*. But both of these plays provide spectators with a way out: Ferdinand's desire for his sister is a species of derangement that reduces itself to the wolvish howlings of lycanthropy; Arbaces' desire for Panthea isn't really incest at all, as we learn to our relief when Panthea's true identity is restored by the magic of the tragicomic plot. But in *'Tis Pity* incest is both wonderful and real; that's what takes this play beyond the superficially shocking and into a mental space where the nature of desire itself is at stake.

The rhetorical strategy which allows Ford to get away with his outrageous project might with some justice be described as the process of disarming. Ford knows that most of his readers and spectators will come to the experience of the play with plenty of hostile preparation. They will be saying to themselves and to one another that incest is simply wrong. Whether they describe it as sinful or sordid or mutually destructive or exploitative will depend upon their local circumstances and preferred moral vocabularies. But there will be no real disagreement about the judgement most people will be making from the moment they discover that Giovanni and Annabella are entering into a sexual partnership in defiance of the most widely respected human prohibition.

But even while formulating a judgement such as this, the audience will notice that their expectations aren't being met. Giovanni and Annabella don't behave like moral monsters.[11] They speak to one another with great gentleness, warmth, respect, and intuitive sympathy. Giovanni declares his love in conceits he might have learned from the Petrarchan sonnet, but in his blank verse they sound authentic rather than ornate:

> I have too long suppressed the hidden flames
> That almost have consumed me; I have spent
> Many a silent night in sighs and groans,
> Ran over all my thoughts, despised my fate,
> Reasoned against the reasons of my love,
> Done all that smoothed-cheek Virtue could advise,
> But found all bootless: 'tis my destiny
> That you must either love, or I must die.
>
> (1.2.222–9)

In a skilfully contrived poem, the claim to have endured long nights of inarticulate agony may sound forced (because of the apparent ease with which artistry conquers silence), and the appeal to death as the only alternative to love may seem jejune (how many Astrophils commit suicide in the long run anyway?). But Giovanni *has* been struggling to no avail against a force which overpowers him. He *has* confided in his spiritual counsellor, Friar Bonaventura, but the moral advice he's been given hasn't changed his mind. He stands on genuinely dangerous ground; if Annabella accepts his proposal, then he must hold himself responsible for driving both of them into a whirlpool of passion which can never be openly acknowledged or socially endorsed; if she rejects him, on the other hand, he can't simply make a graceful retreat and carry on as if nothing had happened. The rhetoric of absolutes, so glibly applied to other contexts, seems to have been invented to serve the extremity of his case.

Annabella's response, after a series of questions designed explictly to find out if he means what he says, is to match his reckless proposal with unconditional acceptance:

> Live; thou hast won
> The field, and never fought; what thou hast urged,
> My captive heart had long ago resolved.
> I blush to tell thee – but I'll tell thee now –
> For every sigh that thou hast spent for me,
> I have sighed ten; for every tear shed twenty:
> And not so much for that I loved, as that
> I durst not say I loved; nor scarcely think it.
>
> (1.2.244–51)

Though Annabella blushes, there's nothing coquettish in her behaviour. She too is aware that the rituals, displays, and indirections of courtship are beside the point in a situation where only an absolute answer (either way) will suffice. So she speaks openly of her own desire, and within minutes the two of them are kneeling to exchange vows: 'Love me, or kill me, brother' (256); 'Love me, or kill me, sister' (259).

The beauty of this moment depends on the honesty, the courage, and the perfect agreement between the two partners. Simply put, it depends on the purity of their desire, the singleness of a compulsion that refuses complication or contingency.[12] In the mundane world of Parma, lovers' actions and words are enmeshed within a network of convention, compromise, and intrigue. Only Giovanni and Annabella can approach one another with the language of pure desire, because they have decided, mutually and soberly, to step outside the system altogether.[13]

So the process of disarming expectations cuts both ways. If you thought that partners in incest were by definition monstrous and degraded people, well, here are Giovanni and Annabella, yearning for one another with a tenderness that virtually turns into music. And if you're now thinking that, however wonderful this exclusive passion may be in itself, it would nonetheless be better if it could be nourished within a social context, Ford supplies an implicit critique of that objection too. The play shows you what happens when love is nourished by society; it does this at some length and in ways that are worth exploring.

The place to begin is with Annabella's legitimate suitors: Bergetto, Grimaldi, and Soranzo. Bergetto is by far the most likeable of the three, but as a prospective husband he's not much of a prize. He's not attracted to Annabella; he's just following the advice of his rich uncle Donado when he poses as a suitor. This is what the prospect of courtship sounds like when Bergetto describes it to his servant Poggio: 'But sirrah, I have another purchase in hand, I shall have the wench mine uncle says; I will but wash my face, and shift socks, and then have at her i'faith' (1.2.116–19). When Donado asks for a progress report, Bergetto preens himself with this: 'O, the wench: Ud's sa'me, uncle, I tickled her with a rare speech, that I made her almost burst her belly with laughing' (1.3.55–7). Bergetto reminds me of Jonson's Bartholomew Cokes. He's immune to the various acquisitive urges that motivate his peers; what moves him is the rumour, reported by his barber, that someone has arrived in Parma with 'a strange horse... whose head, to the wonder of all Christian people, stands just behind where his tail is' (1.3.37–40). The experience of desire, for Bergetto, is like a child's thrill of expectation on entering a fairground. He craves satisfaction too, not in the purity of oneness, but in the multiplicity of created pleasures that Jonson described as the 'enormities' of Bartholomew Fair.

Grimaldi, the Roman nobleman who presents himself as a suitor in Parma, seems if anything less interested in Annabella than Bergetto is. Worried about his status and reputation to the point of narcissism, Grimaldi impresses no one. Putana, Annabella's sexually knowing and outspoken governess, is witheringly dismissive in her portrait of Grimaldi: he's 'a very well-timbered fellow', she acknowledges, but 'I do not like him'. Soldiers of his kind, she says, are likely to have 'some privy maim or other that mars their standing upright. I like him the worse he crinkles so much in the hams' (1.2.76–83). Grimaldi doesn't establish himself as more than a stereotype, so judgements like this are left unchallenged. Courtship, for him, is a chivalric adventure which he hopes will enhance his reputation; that it makes him look nasty and ridiculous is a sufficient comment on the shallowness of his quest.

Soranzo is the suitor who wins, technically at least, in the sense that he becomes Annabella's husband. Superficially Soranzo has a great deal to recommend him. Putana likes him because he's young, rich, upper-class, good-looking, and sexually experienced: he's just now in the process of extricating himself from an adulterous affair with Hippolita. Annabella's father Florio likes him because he believes that Soranzo is a man with prospects. Soranzo's interest in Annabella may be pretty conventional, but at least it exists. He goes to the trouble of quoting snippets of erotic poetry and rewriting them with Annabella in mind. He speaks to her in words that lovers delight to hear:

> I have loved you long, and loved you truly;
> Not hope of what you have, but what you are
> Have drawn me on: then let me not in vain
> Still feel the rigour of your chaste disdain.
> I'm sick, and sick to th' heart.
>
> (3.2.31–5)

The big problem is that Annabella doesn't like him at all. To his confession of love-sickness she responds by calling out: 'Help, aqua-vitae!' He knows he's being mocked, and for a moment it appears that their courtship will go no further. But Annabella knows that she's already pregnant with Giovanni's child. She needs a husband of convenience – someone she doesn't respect and whom she can manipulate. She holds out just enough encouragement to ensure that Soranzo will come back for more, and, once she's taken this initial step in his direction, social pressures will carry her forward until eventually she agrees to marry him.

It's not illicit passion that comes across as sordid in *'Tis Pity She's a Whore*. It's conventional, socially-sanctioned desire that is shown to be corrupt, dishonest, self-seeking, loathsome. This principle applies with special precision to the wedding feast which celebrates the union of Soranzo and Annabella. The marriage itself is dishonest on two counts: Annabella has neglected to tell Soranzo that she's pregnant with another man's child, and Soranzo hasn't mentioned his prior commitment to another woman. Annabella's pregnancy will soon become a major issue, but at the moment it's Soranzo's sex life which holds centre stage. Hippolita is the woman who's recently been Soranzo's lover. To judge by her account, she has a promise from Soranzo to marry her; more than that, he has conspired with her in the attempt to murder her husband Richardetto so as to make a new marriage possible. Morally, it doesn't really matter that Richardetto has escaped the attempt on his life and is now observing these events protected by his disguise as a medical doctor. Both Hippolita and Soranzo think he is dead, so there's good reason for Hippolita to resent her once ardent lover's hasty alliance to another woman. Hippolita attends the wedding feast in disguise, as the leader of a masque of ladies dressed in white and bearing willow garlands. After the dance she reveals her identity and proposes a toast to the newlyweds. The cup of wine she intends for Soranzo has – of course – been laced with poison. But Vasques, Soranzo's loyal if cynical servant, exchanges the cups so that Hippolita dies, poisoned through her own contrivance, and with curses of hatred still on her lips: 'may thy bed / Of marriage be a rack unto thy heart', she says to Soranzo; 'May'st thou live / To father bastards' (4.1.94–8). The citizens of Parma don't see how close to the mark these darts of malice are coming; they join in celebrating the 'Wonderful justice' which removes the unwelcome intruder from their midst.

All of this is crude, conventional, and overstated – not only in my retelling, but in the text itself. Unlike Webster in *The White Devil*, Ford isn't at this point interested in giving a crime of passion the authority of emotional plausibility. The crudeness of Hippolita's retaliation is part of the dramatic technique. It will be matched a scene or two later by Soranzo's reaction to the discovery that the woman he's married is pregnant. 'Come strumpet, famous whore', he cries as he drags a resisting and defiant Annabella onstage; 'could none but I / Be picked out to be cloak to your close tricks, / Your belly-sports?' (4.3.1–12). The strident self-justifying moralism is by now a familiar note; Soranzo has used it before in announcing to Hippolita that she's nothing more than a slut and therefore not worth his further attention. The combination of moral self-righteousness and vulgarity is an ugly one; it ensures that the legitimate relationship between husband and wife seems degraded by comparison with the purity and wholeness of incest.

The integrity of the love between Giovanni and Annabella is represented as a perfect congruence between mind and body. Giovanni makes this point himself in refuting Friar Bonaventura's objections to incest:

> It is a principle, which you have taught
> When I was yet your scholar, that the frame
> And composition of the mind doth follow
> The frame and composition of the body;
> So where the body's furniture is beauty,
> The mind's must needs be virtue; which allowed,

Virtue itself is reason but refined,
And love the quintessence of that; this proves
My sister's beauty, being rarely fair,
Is rarely virtuous; chiefly in her love,
And chiefly in that love, her love to me.

(2.5.14–24)

The friar is understandably shocked at this appropriation of his own teaching; he appeals to the authority of religion, which won't permit incestuous love no matter how attractive it may seem when judged 'By Nature's light' alone (31). A more sceptical challenge might call into question Giovanni's starting assumption: experience of the world would suggest no necessary connection between physical beauty and spiritual worth. But there's a sense in which both of these challenges are beside the point. Giovanni and Annabella have discovered in their own relationship that perfect correspondence between mind and body which is always known as love. They have discovered it while other people, in their flawed and partial ways, are unable to heal the disjunction between the ghost and the machine. Bergetto may boast of his physical aggression as a lover, but his mind is elsewhere – following the first available hobbyhorse. Soranzo may appeal to the limitless value he places on Annabella, but his body language is the old rhetoric of possession by violence. Giovanni and Annabella, with far more reason than most lovers for fearing the intervention of a hostile world, have only their mutual constancy to rely on. Having become lovers, they create reassurances built on trust and fidelity. 'Go where thou wilt', says Annabella to her brother as he prepares to leave; 'in mind I'll keep thee here' (2.1.39). And in spite of the circumstantial pressures that separate them, she remains true to her word.

For as long as she can, that is. The play creates a fantasy of mutual constancy – a fantasy to which both of the lovers contribute. Their goal is 'to be ever one, / One soul, one flesh, one love, one heart, one *all*' (1.1.33–4). But the fantasy can't prevent contingency, multiplicity, change. The presence of Annabella's suitors is, from the outset, a signal of social pressure moving against the lovers. Then comes her pregnancy, described by Putana in language that won't conform to erotic fantasy: 'Am I at these years ignorant what the meanings of qualms and water-pangs be? of changing of colours, queasiness of stomachs, pukings, and another thing that I could name?' (3.3.10–13). Now it becomes imperative that Annabella have a husband; so after hearing Friar Bonaventura counsel her to leave her wicked life, she agrees to marry Soranzo. This only provokes more trouble, as soon as Soranzo discovers the nature of the bargain. In response to his furious accusations she tells him that the man who impregnated her was so wonderful that any mortal woman 'Would have kneeled to him, and have begged for love' (4.3.39); that she'll never reveal the identity of her lover; and that he

(Soranzo) should consider himself lucky to be inheriting a child with such a splendid paternity. Here Annabella is confirming the fantasy against the assault of the contingent world. But it can't last, and she knows it. When she next appears she's sending a letter to Giovanni, and promising the friar to mend her ways:

> here I sadly vow
> Repentance, and a leaving of that life
> I long have died in.
>
> (5.1.35–7)

The fantasy of complete oneness has been unsustainable, except for the brief and stolen moments at the beginning of the play in which the lovers create it.

The bizarre ending of the play is a spectacular demonstration of the self-destructive nature of the play's momentum. From Giovanni's point of view, the catastrophe is a vindication of his fantasy against the forces which have conspired to overthrow it. Another social ritual is in progress – not a marriage this time, but Soranzo's birthday celebration. The guests are taking their places at the banquet table; then '*Enter* GIOVANNI *with a heart upon his dagger*' (5.6.9.1). It's the most outrageous moment in Ford's drama, and from Giovanni's perspective, it's also a moment of unambiguous triumph. 'The glory of my deed / Darkened the mid-day sun', he alleges; as for the bloody object he holds, ''tis a heart, / A heart my lords, in which is mine entombed' (21–7). The fantasy of perfect oneness is now complete, not in the mind only but in the flesh. I am the one who holds her heart, forever, don't you see? It's blindingly clear to him.

It's not at all clear to the others, who are reacting not to a sexual script they haven't been writing in the first place, but to a piece of raw meat being waved in their faces at the beginning of a banquet. So there's understandable confusion, consternation, disbelief. 'What means this?' asks the Cardinal (14), and as Giovanni makes his explanation, Florio interjects with the painful incredulity of a parent who can't bear to hear the truth. Eagerly, with obsessive gloating and suicidal recklessness, Giovanni tells all:

> Here I swear
> By all that you call sacred, by the love
> I bore my Annabella whilst she lived,
> These hands have from her bosom ripped this heart.
>
> (5.6.56–9)

Vasques, who's been sent offstage to find the body, now enters to declare that Giovanni's account is 'most strangely true' (60). Florio promptly dies, and the remaining acts of violence uncoil without restraint: Giovanni stabs

Soranzo and is murdered by Soranzo's hired bandits. The brutality of this doesn't deprive Giovanni of his dying fantasy:

> Where'er I go, let me enjoy this grace,
> Freely to view my Annabella's face.
>
> (106–7)

I've been stressing the single-minded, terrifying purity of Giovanni's position because this, as much as the viscerally alarming stage direction, is what accounts for the spectacular impact of the final scene. But I should add that the mutually constructed fantasy of Act 1 is no longer a genuinely shared experience by Act 5. Ford makes this point with great subtlety in the scenes which lead up to the catastrophe. Annabella, now a creature of contingency herself, says a weary farewell to the 'false joys' of the past (5.1.2). She resents being held a virtual prisoner by her jealous husband, without access to friends or even servants; she feels guilt about the duplicity of her conduct; she feels the need for forgiveness; she knows that the consequences of her exposure are going to be fatal. While Annabella is working out a mental position that will allow her to face death, Giovanni is claiming that nothing has changed. He might have 'thought all taste of love would die' after Annabella's marriage, but he was wrong: 'I find no change / Of pleasure in this formal law of sports' (5.3.5–7). Society is just a silly schoolmaster who thinks intimidation will control desire. Annabella has lived through the changes of marriage, pregnancy, and confinement; she can't disregard contingency, as her brother does, with an impetuous wave of the hand.

So when they meet for the last time, in Annabella's bedroom, their attitudes towards the disaster they both see coming have become sharply differentiated. Annabella is full of warnings and forebodings; she wants to devise an escape for Giovanni. He speaks with exaggerated confidence of his ability to master fate. Annabella claims she's sure that heaven and hell exist; for him they're just 'a dream' (5.5.36). She is tentative, responsive, yielding, while he is assertive and bold. He tells her to pray, and she prays; he asks for a kiss and she grants it – once, twice, three times. He begs forgiveness, and she forgives. Then, 'To save thy fame, and kill thee in a kiss', he *Stabs her* (5.5.84). There is an undertone of protest in her last line – 'Brother, unkind, unkind' (93) – a coloration made stronger by the historical overlapping of the words *unkind* and *unnatural*. The lovers are still agreed on one thing in this final scene together: both are prepared to 'welcome' death (29). But hers is a submissive welcome to a fate that he believes he can control. In death he claims her one last time as his own. In defiance of morality, custom, religion, decency, he can now call her heart his own and prove that it is by impaling it on his dagger. The purity of his desire for union has obliterated the difference between self and other. There is a grotesque horror in this that provokes revulsion, but there is also an attraction far more disturbing.

Giovanni has acted out the naked logic of desire – the logic which yearns for oneness, 'One soul, one flesh, one love, one heart, one *all*' (1.1.34).

The zealous yearning for purity is a special articulation of the pleasure of escape. If the lovers can become truly one, as Giovanni believes, they will be able to leave the world of contingency behind. And although this fantasy is particularly compelling in *'Tis Pity*, partly because the inhibition it offers to overcome is so powerful, the pleasure of escape is a recurring feature of Ford's theatrical landscape. In *Love's Sacrifice* the rapturous devotion of Bianca and Fernando to one another amounts to a shared emotional escape from the 'iron laws of ceremony' (5.1.6) and from the vicissitudes of ordinary living. By means of a kind of dramaturgical pun, Ford creates a defining instance of pure desire: pure in the sense that it resists all compromise, and pure also in the sense that it never yields to contamination in the flesh. This pattern is repeated in *The Broken Heart*, where Penthea's allegiance to the past is both the recollection of a lost purity that can never be recovered in substance, and an escape into the fantasy of wholeness after death. 'I must leave the world', she says, 'To revel in Elysium' (3.5.95–6). The song which accompanies her offstage death celebrates a life 'Pure as are unwritten papers' and mourns the loss of a love that might have been in terms that suggest an escape into pure subjectivity:

> Love is dead. Let lovers' eyes,
> Locked in endless dreams,
> Th' extremes of all extremes,
> Ope no more; for now Love dies,
> Now love dies, implying
> Love's martyrs must be ever, ever dying.
>
> (4.3.148–53)

In *'Tis Pity* the fantasy of oneness is played out against the objections of pragmatists, moralists, and all other spokespersons for decency, order, and common sense. Such liberation of forbidden pleasures is both exhilarating and threatening. It unleashes a rhetoric of pure devotion, an escape from the scrutiny of rational enquiry and moral objection. Unquestioned allegiance is in Ford's drama either a sign of madness or an act of love. *'Tis Pity* compresses these alternatives into a single passion, a single-minded pursuit of singleness itself.

Where then does this leave the reader or spectator of Ford's drama? Is our aesthetic response also characterized by the pleasure of escape? I would argue that it is, but only in a limited sense that is difficult though not impossible to describe. By a curious reversal of the usual pattern, the protagonist's pleasure in Ford's drama is the spectator's pain. When Giovanni confronts us with Annabella's heart impaled on his dagger, we recognize this gesture as the sign of a terrible pleasure that he has created in collaboration with his sister, but we recoil from it too. The shock value of this moment, and of many other less extreme situations in Ford's drama, comes with our recognition that what has been made most beautiful for us is precisely what we have to renounce. We have shared in the pleasure of escape, by means of the mimetic invitation offered us by the drama, but for us as spectators and readers, this pleasure cannot be absolute and must be vicarious. The aesthetic pleasure offered by Ford is therefore not escapist: there is nothing here that caters to the taste for having your own fantasies blandly reinforced. The pleasure offered by Ford's theatre is closer to that of an adventure known to be both dangerous and destructive. It is therefore also a pleasure of discovery, because it invites us into regions of subjectivity that we cannot explore except through the practice of art.

9
Conclusion

At the age of 26 the Italian humanist Lorenzo Valla wrote a treatise on pleasure, *De voluptate* (1431), a document he would be rewriting and revising under various titles (*De vero bono, De vero falsque bono*) during the two remaining decades of his life. The argument is cast in the form of a dialogue, with the biggest parts assigned to Catone Sacco of Pavia (a lawyer), Maffeo Veggio (a poet), and Antonio da Rho, also known as Raudensius (a Franciscan monk). In very general terms these speakers are entrusted with representing the Stoic, Epicurean, and Christian positions on pleasure.

Catone is given the first long speech, a defence of virtue as the sole good, and a denigration of pleasure as both a source and a side-effect of the human propensity to choose evil over good: 'Nature has engendered in us a certain calamitous love of delighting in our own sickness, and the vices that are the plagues of our minds are a source of our pleasure.'[1] Although Nature is given credit for authorizing pleasure, Catone implies that the design is radically flawed, that the pursuit of pleasure is exactly what lies behind the perversity of human behaviour.

In response to this opening gambit, Maffeo Veggio accuses the Stoics of inflexibility and argues that the promptings of Nature must be good, since they are indistinguishable from the handiwork of God. 'Nature has offered a multitude of goods to mortals', Veggio observes; 'It is up to us to know how to enjoy them properly' (85). These goods he then divides into goods of the body (health, beauty, strength, the operation of the five senses) and goods of the soul (nobility, loyalty, public service, and so on), in order to maintain that pleasure, properly defined, 'is a good, from whatever source, located in a sense of delight felt by the soul and the body' (89). This definition gives him a vantage point from which to refute the notion that pleasure is what we share with the lower orders of creation, the animals in particular. It is precisely the culture of pleasure, in Veggio's view, that sets human beings apart: 'In a cursory sense, men are superior to all other animals on two counts: we can express what we feel, and we can drink wine' (105). This is of course a whimsical defence of the humanist agenda, but it makes an important point. At the conclusion of his speech, Veggio shows that he's willing to practise what he preaches by inviting all of the members of the assembled company to his house for dinner, an invitation everyone, even Catone, gratefully accepts.

After dinner the conversation resumes in Veggio's gardens, where Raudensius is given the task of adjudicating between the two positions already advanced. Raudensius allows that both virtue and pleasure are 'excellent things', but insists that 'they should be understood differently from the ways that your arguments intended' (235). This rhetorical step prepares for a decisive turn to the Christian God, who for Raudensius is not only the author but the true object of pleasure. This of course leads to an entirely conventional polarization into a twofold valuation of pleasure: 'one pleasure now on earth, the other hereafter in the heavens' (267). There is no doubt in Raudensius' mind that the here-and-now pleasures are hollow and inadequate shadows of the eternal pleasures of heaven. Raudensius gives a rhapsodic account of such eternal pleasures, after which various auditors offer glowing praise for his consummate speech, and the members of the party disperse in the directions of their domiciles. It would appear that the whole book has been a set-up from the beginning: the dialogue has been structured in such a way that, regardless of the intervening arguments, eternal pleasure can be made to seem infinitely more valuable than any good we could experience on earth.

That Valla's dialogue should end in this way isn't all that surprising, given the inheritance of a long Christian tradition and the direct patronage of the author by the papal court. What I do find surprising is the degree to which Valla managed, even under these circumstances, to open a *debate* on pleasure in which three quite irreconcilable positions are forcefully maintained: that human beings ought to renounce pleasure in order to achieve virtue; that the proper enjoyment of physical and spiritual pleasures is the goal of human culture; and that earthly pleasure is merely a dim reflection of the eternal pleasure promised to the faithful Christian in the life after death. The intellectual daring required to open the question in this way is exactly what identifies Valla as a harbinger of Renaissance thought: the traditional answers are still important to him, but they now have to contend with the challenge that arises, almost of necessity, when human culture is resituated at the centre of the created universe.

The great secular institution of the English theatre wasn't simply the continuation of an academic debate, but it was nonetheless a forum in which competing interpretations of pleasure could be and were played out with remarkable energy and freedom. In one sense this might have been inevitable: the theatre companies were in the business of creating pleasure for their spectators, and insofar as playwrights reflected on the status and value of their own profession, they were implicitly engaged in the interpretation of aesthetic pleasure. But much more comprehensively, the playwrights I've selected for analysis in this book were prepared to represent the pursuit of pleasure (even forbidden pleasures, dangerous pleasures, and destructive pleasures) as a distinctive and defining aspect of the culture they inhabited. This did not mean, of course, that all or any of them were simply proposing pleasure as the absolute good. But I think it did mean that pleasure and the interpretation of pleasure were at the centre of the art they practised.

There are plenty of opportunities in the drama from Marlowe to Ford for the Stoic and Christian positions on pleasure to speak for themselves. Marston's drama, with its powerful revulsion against the temptations of the body, is perhaps the most obvious call for a renunciation of pleasure in the interests of achieving virtue. Both Malevole in *The Malcontent* and Freevill in *The Dutch Courtesan* are proponents of this position, and Malheureux is a would-be proponent who learns that he's vulnerable to temptation no matter how strenuously he tries to deny it. The clearest advocate of the Christian viewpoint is the Good Angel in *Doctor Faustus*, who reminds the protagonist of a doctrine he knows all too well: 'for the vain pleasure of four and twenty years hath Faustus lost eternal joy and felicity' (5.2.36–8). In more complicated ways both Stoic renunciation and Christian deferral of pleasure inflect the language and the behaviour of characters like Frankford in *A Woman Killed with Kindness*, Bosola in *The Duchess of Malfi*, and Penthea in *The Broken Heart*.

But by far the most striking feature of the representation of pleasure in English Renaissance drama is the willingness of playwrights to explore the position that Valla assigns to the poet Mattheo Veggio, namely, that the cultivation of pleasure is an opportunity that human beings should energetically pursue. By the end of Doctor Faustus' first speech we know that he is driven to explore the 'world of profit and delight' (1.1.54) that magic appears to make available. The same phrase could apply almost as well to Volpone's objectives, if due allowance is made for the degree to which the competitive instinct defines what is pleasurable in Jonson's Venice. In *Bartholomew Fair* the pursuit of pleasure has become a circus, and a hotbed of 'enormities' (2.1.37), but it is indeed pleasure that draws Jonson's Londoners to the fair, just as surely as it draws spectators to the theatre. In *A Chaste Maid in Cheapside* the mismanagement of sexual pleasure leads to a series of deceptions and compromises that would be merely risible if they weren't also in some sense disturbing. Just how threatening the pursuit of pleasure can become is a question Middleton repeatedly poses, nowhere more adroitly than in *The Changeling*. De Flores has narrowed Doctor Faustus' quest down to one quite specific objective: 'For I place wealth after the heels of pleasure' (3.4.115), he explains to Beatrice-Joanna, and in the subsequent unravelling of his intentions, he narrows the target even further until it is unmistakably Beatrice-Joanna herself. This would be simply horrible if it weren't equally true that Beatrice-Joanna pursues her own gratification with similar ruthless disregard for her victims, and therefore quickly becomes De Flores' partner in more ways than one. Webster too is sensitive to the ironies arising from the narrowly selfish pursuit of pleasure, but in *The Duchess of Malfi* he represents intimate pleasure as a refuge from the ravenous corruption of the world at large. It is of course sexual pleasure that the Duchess shares with Antonio: 'Alas, what pleasure can two lovers find in sleep?' (3.2.10) she says to him (teasingly) as she prepares for bed. But the pleasures of the Duchess are generous, inclusive, and frivolous as well as sexual: she can relish the taste of an apricot even if it was ripened in horse-dung without for a moment forgetting that she is the Duchess of Malfi still. It is the Duchess's unassuming openness to pleasure as a good, both for herself and for others, that sets her apart from the depravity which surrounds her.

What stands out even in a brief panoramic account of the kind I have just given is not a consensus about pleasure on the part of English Renaissance dramatists, but rather a remarkable variety of artistic hypotheses, intuitions, explorations. And this indeed is the best reason for thinking of each playwright, as I have done in most of the preceding chapters, as an individual author with a particular vision, a distinctive repertoire of artistic strategies, and hence an orientation towards the question of pleasure that might be highly idiosyncratic. It has been my objective throughout this book to capture something of this diversity of attitudes and approaches, and I have no intention of rounding off edges or flattening textured surfaces now in order to reach closure. Rather, I would argue that the diversity of stances, voices, and visions is one of the principal reasons why English Renaissance drama is still worth reading and performing today.

The diversity I have been demonstrating and by implication valuing is simply not available when Renaissance drama is presented, either in the theatre or in the academic curriculum, as the production of a single dominant figure (namely Shakespeare) who may have learned a little from and taught a great deal to his contemporaries and successors. True, Shakespeare has been the locus of aesthetic pleasure for many generations of actors, audiences, students, and scholars. But for this very reason his plays have become a virtual requirement for citizenship in the literary world. Under these circumstances, it is almost impossible to recover some of the pleasures – surprise, for example – that his first readers and spectators doubtless felt. And it is only too easy to superimpose a constricting uniformity on the whole enterprise of Renaissance drama by expecting other playwrights, directly or indirectly, explicitly or implicitly, quietly or polemically, to conform to the Shakespearean model, whatever that is taken to be. It is my conviction that the pleasures offered by most Renaissance playwrights will always elude us if we are unwilling to see the plays in their own brightness, not always overshadowed by, compared with, or made supplementary to the plays of Shakespeare. This conviction, as I stated at the outset, has in part shaped my methodology; it has also been a strategy for promoting an attitude of critical pluralism in which different plays and playwrights can be known by and admired for what makes them distinctive.

But I do want to end with a synoptic view of the drama from Marlowe to Ford, partly in order to draw some inferences about the relationship between pleasure and agency. Let's begin with the intuitively satisfying notion that a pleasure freely chosen is bound to be more gratifying than one prescribed in advance. This principle underlies a great many crucial choices enacted in Renaissance drama. It helps to account for the ravishment Doctor Faustus feels on turning to his necromantic books after setting aside the prescribed curriculum that has governed his academic life. It offers an explanation for the alacrity with which he indulges in the pranks and projections which magic places within his reach: these crude demonstrations may seem in some sense unworthy of him, but they are what he has chosen to do. The same principle makes plausible the joy expressed by Batholomew Cokes as he bargains for his basket of gingerbread men, or even the perverse relish that Allwit takes in managing the affair between his wife and Sir Walter Whorehound. It would be difficult to argue that any of these is the right choice for the character in question to make, but it is easy to recognize nonetheless that the choice is connected to the character's pleasure. Making this recognition is among the aesthetic pleasures that accompanies the act of reading or watching these choices unfold.

With respect to erotic choices, the paradigm I've outlined needs to be complicated in significant ways, though the connection between pleasure and agency remains unbroken. One of the great strengths of Renaissance drama is the subtlety with which it is able to represent how erotic choices happen, even when they are tightly monitored by social institutions and pressures. As anyone conversant with the social history of the period (or indeed with *Romeo and Juliet* or *The Two Gentlemen of Verona*) is likely to know, the right to choose a sexual partner for yourself was by no means a secure assumption. A prospective husband might have to engage in a long series of diplomatic manoeuvres simply to ensure that it would be he (and not his parents) who would do the final choosing. It's doubtful that prospective brides had even the same degree of autonomy as their male counterparts. Young women might be extremely reluctant to disobey openly the wishes of their fathers, but even where this was the case, the written evidence would suggest that the woman's consent to any arrangements was increasingly treated as a prerequisite. The right to decide was clearly moving away from the family (as represented by its patriarchal head) and towards the prospective partners themselves.[2]

What happens in the drama is at one level a mimetic staging of the very same conflict between social pressures and personal choices that social historians describe. I am not proposing that the drama reflects, in a more or less passive way, the social and ideological tensions in the culture that surrounds it. On the issue of consent prior to marriage, the drama would seem to be if anything ahead of its time, insofar as playwrights tend to confer authority upon freely chosen sexual relationships, and to treat arranged or dynastic marriages with scorn. The most obvious example would be *The Broken Heart*, in which the marriage that might have been (between Orgilus and Penthea) is represented as fully authentic because willingly chosen, while the marriage that in fact occurs (between Bassanes and Penthea) is a protracted exercise in bad faith because it was made against Penthea's will. The Duchess of Malfi, conversely, is able to stand up against the virulent opposition of her brothers in order to assert her choice of Antonio, fearful all the while of the terrible price she will be made to pay. As the net of surveillance tightens around her, she wishes for a state of being in which the freedom to choose would be natural: the birds who live in nature, she argues, are happier than mortals, 'for they may choose their mates, / And carol their sweet pleasures to the spring' (3.5.20–1). Here the rhetoric of pleasure freely chosen draws us as spectators into a sympathetic awareness of the value of what is threatened. The list of authentically chosen sexual partners could be extended almost at will: think of Edward and Gaveston, of Moll Yellowhammer and Touchwood Junior, of the King of Rhodes and Evadne, of Vittorio and Bracciano, of Fernando and Bianca, of Giovanni and Annabella. The point is not that these couples are either admirable or wicked, but only that the exercise of choice confers upon their sexual partnerships a dramatic authority that they couldn't earn in any other way. Such authority, moreover, depends on our recognition that the choices being made are genuine; however carefully we qualify and historicize such notions as consent, such rituals as courtship, the difference between choosing a sexual partner and being assigned to one is a gap that won't close. The difference was as real to the authors of Renaissance plays as it is for spectators in the theatre today.

I don't mean to imply that we make sexual choices as individuals, in the cold light of day, by dispassionately considering all of the options. When we speak of falling in love, after all, we are advancing a quite different view of how erotic choices are made – a view that implies the suspension of direct volition and that hints at the hand of fate as a player in human affairs. One persuasive reason for this recurring sentiment is the knowledge that in sexual decision-making each of us is not only choosing but is being chosen (or not chosen) by someone else. Almost any comedy by Shakespeare will show, sometimes with great ingenuity, how fate or magic needs to intervene before couples can be sorted into mutually attracting pairs at the end. In Jonsonian comedy, where there is no magical assistance, erotic choices are likely to be both crude and inept: Morose's ponderously justified selection of Epicoene is an extreme example. In most of the plays I have chosen to discuss, the only magic available to potential lovers is the interplay of psychological forces that either brings them together or keeps them suspended in ungratified attraction. The Duchess of Malfi chooses Antonio for her husband not by a naked act of will, but in a series of hints, gestures, invitations, and insinuations that he picks up and returns, with greater and greater confidence as he realizes the joy of choosing and being chosen at the same time. If I am right about Bosola, then his bitterness includes the pain of knowing that he will never be chosen by the partner he would gladly choose.

Between the symmetry of a completely mutual decision and the isolation of complete rejection there's an ambiguous territory in which negotiation occurs but the terms of any settlement are unclear. This is Middleton's favourite predicament. Both Bianca in *Women Beware Women* and Beatrice-Joanna in *The Changeling* have, if only tacitly and naively, given their consent to something; but it's by no means sure that they've agreed to what the men in both instances expect of them. Both women are quickly crossing into situations from which they will be unable to retreat; both are dealing with men who will do what they can to remove the option of saying no. This process too can feel like a fatal attraction, because volition has been subverted by design. The vulnerability which Bianca and Beatrice-Joanna now experience is easily confused with love, and it is therefore easily transformed into erotic pleasure. But there is a difference. To be in love, after all, is to have made a choice – a choice that includes but is not quite identical with the willingness to be chosen.

The notion of consent, though crucial to most of the sexual interactions in the drama, is seldom invoked in its narrowest and most legalistic level of meaning. In the situations I have just described we are, in more ways than one, watching a drama unfold: giving consent is therefore a certain kind of performance, withholding consent another. The scenes in which these actions occur are likely to be interactive scenarios, in which the signals offered by one participant are interpreted (or misinterpreted) by another, and in which the result of the interaction is therefore bound to be more complicated than a simple yes or no. Playwrights by the very nature of their craft tend to be artists capable of representing more than one point of view, and dramatically complicated scenes are therefore often capable of being read from more than one perspective. It is for these reasons that my analysis has in general highlighted not individual characters in isolation, but two characters (and sometimes more than two) engaged in constructing a choice through collaboration. Erotic pleasure on stage, like aesthetic pleasure for the spectator, is almost by definition an interactive event.

When viewed in chronological sequence, the plays and playwrights I've been discussing appear to be participating in a process of historical change. At the beginning of the sequence, in Marlowe for example, making a choice is a largely solitary action, and even sexual choosing is likely to be represented only from a single point of view. When Tamburlaine captures

Zenocrate, he simply decides at once that she will be his sexual partner, and all she can do is adjust (rapidly) to this new state of affairs. Here it is the man who does the choosing, while the woman is merely chosen: a pattern that repeats itself, with some variation, in Jonson and Marston. In *The Dutch Courtesan*, for example, the act of choosing between a courtesan and a wife is virtually assigned to Freevill by his name; only in the cleverness of Crispenella's handling of unwanted suitors does Marston include the recognition that women are engaged in making choices too. This recognition is more fully articulated in Webster, where Vittoria Corombona collaborates with Bracciano in the construction of their sexual affair, and where the Duchess of Malfi is given the initiative (by virtue of her superior social rank) in creating the marriage with Antonio. And it is explored at length by Middleton, whose comic wives (such as Mistress Allwit) and tragic mistresses (such as Beatrice-Joanna) are as actively engaged in the pursuit of sexual pleasure as the men who exploit them. The relationship between Giovanni and Annabella, freely and knowingly chosen by both partners, is a reduction of this pattern not quite to the absurd but rather beyond the pale of what most readers or spectators can condone. It is certainly pleasure that Giovanni and Annabella jointly choose, but it is a pleasure that in a sense empties out the otherness of the person chosen, and in doing so annihilates itself.

The change from a single male-authored erotic choice to a complicated psychological negotiation in which both genders participate is doubtless the sign of a cultural shift in which old-fashioned aristocratic values were losing out against emergent middle-class energies. This is a change that has been noticed by other scholars, and given various names depending on the critical perspective being taken. For feminist critics in particular, the change has been a welcome sign of the willingness to revisit and revise long-standing prejudices. Thus, in Linda Woodbridge's words, though the drama of the early seventeenth century had been characterized by 'unprecedented misogyny', in the later work of Webster and Middleton 'the image of women in the drama changed startlingly for the better'.[3] This is a judgement I am happy to endorse, as the readings of individual plays I have offered would suggest. But I would add that something more is at stake here, both ideologically and artistically, than the image of women by itself. The contest between unilateral male choice and negotiated choosing by both sexes was being played out in the political, religious, and domestic arrangements of the time, and it should not be surprising to find that playwrights and theatres were engaged in the process of rethinking the conventions and values of their culture. What stands out in the drama, however, is the degree to which cultural change implied the possibility of a redistribution of pleasure: creative agency in the pursuit of erotic pleasure had become thinkable as a conversation in which both male and female voices could be heard.

In various ways the Renaissance playwrights and their audiences were engaged in constructing a world in which it would be possible for human beings to treat one another as consenting adults. Such an environment does not guarantee a lifetime of pleasure, or even the removal of pain. On the contrary, it introduces people to a world of shared responsibility without guarantees; it offers them the opportunity to engage, as partners, in the cultivation of pleasure for themselves and others. This is a world we are still only learning to inhabit, an opportunity we are still only learning to explore.

Notes

1. Interpreting pleasure

1. Immanuel Kant, *The Critique of Judgement*, trans. James Creed Meredith (Oxford: Clarendon, 1952) 31.
2. *Classical Literary Criticism*, trans. T.S. Dorsch (Harmondsworth: Penguin, 1965) 31, 38.
3. *Republic* 10, trans. Paul Shorey, in *The Collected Dialogues of Plato*, ed. Edith Hamilton and Huntington Cairns (Princeton, NJ: Princeton University Press, 1961) 827. Subsequent references to Plato are from this edition.
4. Aristotle speaks eloquently of the pleasures of mimesis: 'inborn in all of us is the instinct to enjoy works of imitation. What happens in actual experience is evidence of this; for we enjoy looking at the most accurate representations of things which in themselves we find painful to see, such as the forms of the lowest animals and of corpses' (*Classical Literary Criticism* 35).
5. See A.D. Nuttal, *Why Does Tragedy Give Pleasure?* (Oxford: Clarendon, 1996) 85.
6. 'Art as Technique', in *Russian Formalist Criticism: Four Essays*, ed. and trans. Lee T. Lemon and Marion J. Reis (Lincoln: University of Nebraska Press, 1965) 12.
7. *Jokes and their Relation to the Unconscious*, in *The Standard Edition of the Complete Psychological Works of Sigmund Freud*, trans. James Strachey and Anna Freud et al. (London: Hogarth, 1953–74) 8: 96. Subsequent references to Freud are from this edition.
8. James Joyce, *A Portrait of the Artist as a Young Man* (New York: Viking, 1964) 205.
9. See Laura Levine, *Men in Women's Clothing: Anti-Theatricality and Effeminization, 1579–1642* (Cambridge: Cambridge University Press, 1994) 10–25; and Stephen Orgel, *Impersonations: the Performance of Gender in Shakespeare's England* (Cambridge: Cambridge University Press, 1996) 26–30.
10. See the account of the development of Plato's thinking in this regard in J.C.B. Gosling and C.C.W. Taylor, *The Greeks on Pleasure* (Oxford: Clarendon, 1982) 97–8, 103–6.
11. Steven Connor, 'Aesthetics, Pleasure and Value', in *The Politics of Pleasure: Aesthetics and Cultural Theory*, ed. Stephen Regan (Buckingham: Open University Press, 1992) 204.
12. See Carol Thomas Neely, 'Constructing the Subject: Feminist Practice and the New Renaissance Discourses', *English Literary Renaissance* 18 (1988): 7.
13. Stephen Greenblatt, 'Friction and Fiction', in *Shakespearean Negotiations: the Circulation of Social Energy in Renaissance England* (Oxford: Clarendon, 1988) 83–4.
14. See Joan Kelly-Gadol, 'Did Women Have a Renaissance?', in *Becoming Visible: Women in European History*, ed. Renate Bridenthal and Claudia Koonz (Boston: Houghton Mifflin, 1977) 137–64.
15. Catherine Belsey, *The Subject of Tragedy: Identity and Difference in Renaissance Drama* (London: Methuen, 1985) 218.
16. Catherine Belsey, *Desire: Love Stories in Western Culture* (Oxford: Blackwell, 1994) 136, 61.
17. *Shakespeare and the Loss of Eden: the Construction of Family Values in Early Modern Culture* (Basingstoke: Macmillan Press – now Palgrave Macmillan, 1999) 35.

18. See Greenblatt's reference to the shaping influence of Foucault's thought in *Learning to Curse: Essays in Early Modern Culture* (New York: Routledge, 1990) 3; Lacan's thinking is discussed at some length in Belsey's *Desire* 55–64, and his influence is acknowledged in *Shakespeare and the Loss of Eden* 51, 82 *et passim*.

19. Michel Foucault, *The History of Sexuality*, vol. 1: Introduction, trans. Robert Hurley (New York: Random House, 1978) 45. For a subtle analysis of this passage, see Suzanne Gearhart, 'The Taming of Michel Foucault: New Historicism, Psychoanalysis, and the Subversion of Power', *New Literary History* 28 (1997): 462–3.

20. See Edward Pechter, 'The New Historicism and its Discontents', *PMLA* 102 (1987): 296–8, 301–2.

21. See his comments on 'artistic imitation' in *Beyond the Pleasure Principle* 18: 17 and his more fully articulated statement about artistic creation in 'Formulations on the Two Principles of Mental Functioning' 12: 224.

22. *The Four Fundamental Concepts of Psycho-Analysis*, ed. Jacques-Alain Miller, trans. Alan Sheridan (Harmondsworth: Penguin, 1994) 31.

23. *Desire* 61.

24. Jean E. Howard, *The Stage and Social Struggle in Early Modern England* (London: Routledge, 1994) 18.

25. Thomas Cartelli, *Marlowe, Shakespeare, and the Economy of Theatrical Experience* (Philadelphia: University of Pennsylvania Press, 1991) 36–7.

26. Celia R. Daileader, *Eroticism on the Renaissance Stage: Transcendence, Desire, and the Limits of the Visible* (Cambridge: Cambridge University Press, 1998) 49.

27. Roland Barthes, *The Pleasure of the Text*, trans. Richard Miller (New York: Hill and Wang, 1975) 57–8.

28. See Richard Howard's 'Note on the Text', in *The Pleasure of the Text* v–vi.

29. Fredric Jameson, 'Pleasure: a Political Issue', in *The Ideologies of Theory: Essays 1971–1986* (Minneapolis: University of Minnesota Press, 1988) 2: 65.

30. Wendy Steiner, *The Scandal of Pleasure: Art in an Age of Fundamentalism* (Chicago: University of Chicago Press, 1995) 207.

31. Stanley Corngold, *Complex Pleasure: Forms of Feeling in German Literature* (Stanford: Stanford University Press, 1998) 2.

32. Roger Kuin, *Chamber Music: Elizabethan Sonnet Sequences and the Pleasure of Criticism* (Toronto: University of Toronto Press, 1998) 13.

33. See, for example, Elizabeth Hansen, 'Against a Synechdochic Shakespeare', in *Discontinuities: New Essays on Renaissance Literature and Criticism*, ed. Viviana Comensoli and Paul Stevens (Toronto: University of Toronto Press, 1998) 75.

34. James Shapiro, 'Recent Studies in Tudor and Stuart Drama', *Studies in English Literature, 1500–1900* 36 (1996): 517–18.

35. Valerie Traub's *Desire and Anxiety: Circulations of Sexuality in Shakespearean Drama* (London: Routledge, 1992) is a book exclusively about Shakespeare; it offers detailed critical discussions of nine plays by Shakespeare, and nothing (beyond a passing reference) on any other dramatist. Jean E. Howard's *The Stage and Social Struggle* includes discussion of ten plays by Shakespeare, five (in total) by other playwrights.

36. Michel Foucault, 'What Is an Author?', trans. Josué V. Harari, *The Foucault Reader*, ed. Paul Rainbow (New York: Pantheon, 1984) 108.

37. Roland Barthes, 'The Death of the Author', in *Images/Music/Text*, trans. Stephen Heath (New York: Farrar, Straus and Giroux, 1977) 142–8.

38. Jeffrey Masten, *Textual Intercourse: Collaboration, Authorship, and Sexualities in Renaissance Drama* (Cambridge: Cambridge University Press, 1997) 13.

39. Scott McMillan and Sally-Beth MacLean, *The Queen's Men and their Plays*
    (Cambridge: Cambridge University Press, 1998) 7.
40. *The Duchess of Malfi*, ed. John Russell Brown, The Revels Plays (London: Methuen,
    1964) 3, 5.
41. *A Line of Life: Pointing at the Immortalitie of a Vertuous Name* (London, 1620) A2ᵛ.

2. Tobacco and boys: Christopher Marlowe

1. The testimony of Baines, made shortly before Marlowe's death on 30 May 1593,
   is printed in full by C.F. Tucker Brooke in *The Life of Marlowe and the Tragedy of
   Dido Queen of Carthage* (London: Methuen, 1930) 98–100. R.B. Wernham points
   out, citing documentary evidence in 'Christopher Marlowe at Flushing in 1592',
   English Historical Review 91 (1976): 344–5, that Baines and Marlowe had known and
   disliked one another at least as early as January 1591/92, when Baines provided
   information leading to Marlowe's arrest for 'coining' a single counterfeit shilling
   of pewter.
2. The term 'homosexual' of course didn't exist in the early modern period, and its
   absence is used by Foucault to argue that the phenomenon of a distinct homosexual identity (as opposed to homoerotic actions and attractions of various
   kinds) is a nineteenth-century invention. 'As defined by the ancient civil or
   canonical codes', Foucault writes, 'sodomy was a category of forbidden acts; their
   perpetrator was nothing more than the juridicial subject of them.' But in the
   nineteenth century, the medical discourse of sexuality changed all that:
   'Homosexuality appeared as one of the forms of sexuality when it was transposed
   from the practice of sodomy onto a kind of interior androgyny, a hermaphrodism
   of the soul. The sodomite had been a temporary aberration; the homosexual was
   now a species'. See *The History of Sexuality*, vol. 1: Introduction, trans. Robert
   Hurley (New York: Random House, 1978) 43. Foucault's extreme nominalism has
   led many subsequent scholars to use 'sodomy' as the general term for same-sex
   attraction in the early modern period, on the grounds that 'homosexuality' is
   anachronistic. But even scholars who recognize the difficulty of treating 'homosexuality' as a trans-historical category find it impossible to do without it; see
   Alan Bray, *Homosexuality in Renaissance England* (London: Gay Men's Press, 1982)
   13–32, and Bruce R. Smith, *Homosexual Desire in Shakespeare's England: a Cultural
   Poetics* (Chicago: University of Chicago Press, 1991) 14. For a persuasive critique
   of the view that homosexuality is a relatively recent (that is, nineteenth-century)
   invention, see Joseph Cady, '"Masculine Love", Renaissance Writing, and the
   "New Invention" of Homosexuality', *Homosexuality in Renaissance and Enlightenment
   England: Literary Representations in Historical Context*, ed. Claude J. Summers (New
   York: Haworth, 1992) 9–40. For an intelligent summary of the controversy, see
   Michael B. Young, *James VI and I and the History of Homosexuality* (Basingstoke:
   Macmillan Press – now Palgrave Macmillan, 2000) 3–6, 36–50.
3. See Havelock Ellis, *Sexual Inversion, Studies in the Psychology of Sex* 2, 3rd edn.
   (1901; Philadelphia: F.A. Davis, 1928) 43.
4. See Mario Praz, 'Christopher Marlowe', *English Studies* 13 (1931): 209–23; Harry
   Levin, *The Overreacher: a Study of Christopher Marlowe* (Cambridge, MA: Harvard
   University Press, 1952) 158–9, and 'Marlowe Today', *Tulane Drama Review* 8
   (Summer 1964): 26–7; L.C. Knights, 'The Strange Case of Christopher Marlowe',
   in *Further Explorations* (Stanford: Stanford University Press, 1965) 85–7; Brian

Morris, 'Comic Method in Marlowe's *Hero and Leander*', in *Christopher Marlowe: Mermaid Critical Commentaries*, ed. Brian Morris (London: Ernest Benn, 1968) 123–9; Stephen Greenblatt, 'Marlowe and the Will to Absolute Play', in *Renaissance Self-Fashioning: from More to Shakespeare* (Chicago: University of Chicago Press, 1980) 220; Jonathan Goldberg, 'Sodomy and Society: the Case of Christopher Marlowe', *Southwest Review* 69 (1984): 371–8; Joseph A. Porter, 'Marlowe, Shakespeare, and the Canonization of Heterosexuality', *South Atlantic Quarterly* 88 (1989): 127–30; Thomas Cartelli, *Marlowe, Shakespeare, and the Economy of Theatrical Experience* (Philadelphia: University of Pennsylvania Press, 1991) 126–7, 131; Gregory Woods, 'Body, Costume, and Desire in Christopher Marlowe', in *Homosexuality in Renaissance and Enlightenment England: Literary Representations in Historical Context*, ed. Claude J. Summers (New York: Haworth, 1992) 69–84; Michael Hattaway, 'Christopher Marlowe: Ideology and Subversion', in *Christopher Marlowe and English Renaissance Culture*, ed. Darryll Grantley and Peter Roberts (Aldershot: Scolar Press, 1996) 210–11; and Ian McAdam, *The Irony of Identity: Self and Imagination in the Drama of Christopher Marlowe* (Newark: University of Delaware Press, 1999) 33–41. See also the particular studies of *Edward II* cited in note 10 below.

5. Constance Brown Kuriyama, *Hammer or Anvil: Psychological Patterns in Christopher Marlowe's Plays* (New Brunswick, NJ: Rutgers University Press, 1980).

6. Fred B. Tromly, *Playing with Desire: Christopher Marlowe and the Art of Tantalization* (Toronto: University of Toronto Press, 1998) 16–17. The source of both images is Geffrey Whitney's *A Choice of Emblems* (1586).

7. For a highly intelligent reading of the structures of authority in this text, and of Barabas' problematic location in relation to them, see Emily C. Bartels, *Spectacles of Strangeness: Imperialism, Alienation, and Marlowe* (Philadelphia: University of Pennsylvania Press, 1993) 87–96.

8. Lawrence Stone, *The Family, Sex and Marriage in England, 1500–1800* (New York: Harper, 1977) 492.

9. See Bray, *Homosexuality in Renaissance England* 71–80.

10. L.G. Mills read the relationship as one of pure friendship in 'The Meaning of *Edward II*', *Modern Philology* 32 (1934–35): 11–31; given the date of this essay, it is difficult to know whether Mills meant friendship and nothing more, or whether the discourse of his time didn't allow him to name the sexual aspect of friendship in a scholarly context. In more permissive decades, the relationship has been read as principally sexual; see Leonora Leet Brodwin, '*Edward II*: Marlowe's Culminating Treatment of Love', *ELH* 31 (1964): 139–55; Purvis E. Boyette, 'Wanton Humour and Wanton Poets: Homosexuality in Marlowe's *Edward II*', *Tulane Studies in English* 32 (1977): 33–50; Claude J. Summers, 'Sex, Politics, and Self-Realization in *Edward II*', in *'A Poet and a Filthy Play-Maker': New Essays on Christopher Marlowe*, ed. Kenneth Friedenreich et al. (New York: AMS Press, 1988) 221–40; Jennifer Brady, 'Fear and Loathing in Marlowe's *Edward II*', in *Sexuality and Politics in Renaissance Drama*, ed. Carole Levin and Karen Robertson, Studies in Renaissance Literature 10 (Lewiston, NY: Edwin Mellen, 1991) 175–91; Stephen Guy-Bray, 'Homophobia and the Depoliticising of *Edward II*', *English Studies in Canada* 17 (1991): 125–33; Derek Jarman, *Queer Edward II* (London: British Film Institute, 1991); Gregory W. Bredbeck, *Sodomy and Interpretation: Marlowe to Milton* (Ithaca, NY: Cornell University Press, 1991) 57–60; Jonathan Goldberg, *Sodometries: Renaissance Texts, Modern Sexualities* (Stanford: Stanford University Press, 1992) 105–26; Catherine Belsey, 'Desire's Excess and the English

Renaissance Theatre: *Edward II, Troilus and Cressida, Othello'*, in *Erotic Politics: Desire on the Renaissance Stage*, ed. Susan Zimmerman (London: Routledge, 1992) 84–8; Viviana Comensoli, 'Homophobia and the Regulation of Desire: a Psychoanalytic Reading of Marlowe's *Edward II'*, *Journal of the History of Sexuality* 4 (1993–94): 175–200; Mario DiGangi, 'Marlowe, Queer Studies, and Renaissance Homoeroticism', in *Marlowe, History, and Sexuality: New Critical Essays on Christopher Marlowe*, ed. Paul Whitefield White (New York: AMS Press, 1998) 195–212; and McAdam, *The Irony of Identity* 198–231. Jarman's book is the screen-play for his movie adaptation of *Edward II*; it includes personal commentary by Jarman and some of his associates, much of it motivated by a belief that homo-sexuality should be openly celebrated. For an intelligent critique of Jarman's interpretation (in print and on screen), see Thomas Cartelli, 'Queer Edward II: Postmodern Sexualities and the Early Modern Subject', *Marlowe, History, and Sexuality* 213–23.

11. Toby Robertson (interviewed by John Russell Brown), 'Directing *Edward II'*, *Tulane Drama Review* 8 (Summer 1964): 177–8.
12. See Germaine Greer, *The Female Eunuch* (New York: McGraw-Hill, 1971) 50–2.
13. For intelligent commentary on this scene see Nicholas Brooke, 'Marlowe the Dramatist', in *Elizabethan Theatre*, ed. John Russell Brown and Bernard Harris, Stratford-upon-Avon Studies 9 (London: Edward Arnold, 1966) 103–5, and Boyette, 'Wanton Humour' 47–9.
14. 'Directing *Edward II'* 179.
15. Edward A. Snow, 'Marlowe's *Doctor Faustus* and the Ends of Desire', in *Two Renaissance Mythmakers: Christopher Marlowe and Ben Jonson*, ed. Alvin Kernan, Selected Papers from the English Institute ns 1 (Baltimore: Johns Hopkins University Press, 1977) 70–110.
16. All references are to Michael Keefer's edition of the A version (1604). The rela-tionship between the two early texts of *Doctor Faustus* (A 1604 and B 1616) is a complicated question in textual history that impinges on many other concerns: the authorship of the play, its theatrical history, its governing theatrical assump-tions, and so on. Recent scholarship has shown that the arguments advanced by Greg (in *Doctor Faustus: 1604–1616*, ed. W.W. Greg [Oxford: Clarendon, 1950]), to the effect that B is the more authoritative text and that A is a faulty memorial reconstruction of B, are no longer tenable. The relevant evidence is cited by Keefer (Introduction xi–xxi, lx–lxix) and discussed at great length by Eric Rasmussen (in *A Textual Companion to* Doctor Faustus [Manchester: Manchester University Press, 1993]), who concludes that A is 'the text with primary author-ity' while B 'appears to be at many removes from Marlowe's hand' (93). For an ingenious interpretation of the doctrinal and cultural differences between the two versions, see Leah S. Marcus, *Unediting the Renaissance: Shakespeare, Marlowe, Milton* (London: Routledge, 1996) 38–62.

3. A shrew yet honest: Ben Jonson

1. *Ben Jonson*, ed. C.H. Herford, Percy Simpson, and Evelyn Simpson (Oxford: Clarendon, 1925–52) 1: 139–40. This edition is identified as *Jonson* in further citations.
2. See Appendix A in *The Plays and Poems of William Cartwright*, ed. G. Blakemore Evans (Madison: University of Wisconsin Press, 1951) 831.

3. *Jonson* 8: 592–3. This passage, like many others in *Discoveries*, is a free translation from Seneca the elder (see *Jonson* 11: 244). But here and elsewhere I'm assuming that an idea didn't matter less to Jonson just because he found it in an author he admired.
4. For a brief and witty account of Jonson's invention of his public self, see Edward B. Partridge, 'Jonson's Large and Unique View of Life', *The Elizabethan Theatre* 4 (1972): 145–50; for a subtle and persuasive account on an extended scale, see Richard Helgerson, *Self-Crowned Laureates: Spenser, Jonson, Milton, and the Literary System* (Berkeley: University of California Press, 1983) 101–84.
5. See the Conversations with Drummond, in *Jonson* 1: 138, 140, 136.
6. *Jonson* 1: 138–9.
7. For a portrait of Jonson which takes into account both kinds of competitiveness, see W. David Kay, *Ben Jonson: a Literary Life* (Basingstoke: Macmillan Press – now Palgrave Macmillan, 1995): on the one hand, Jonson approached classical authors in a 'spirit of emulous rivalry', Kay writes; and his attitude towards his contemporaries was 'complicated by his strong sense of rivalry, which issued in ridicule of those whose works he thought inferior or in jealousy of those whose accomplishments he admired' (98).
8. *Jonson* 8: 609–10. For a full discussion of the matters of principle which separated Jonson and Jones, see D.J. Gordon, 'Poet and Architect: the Intellectual Setting of the Quarrel between Ben Jonson and Inigo Jones', *Journal of the Warburg and Courtauld Institutes* 12 (1949): 152–78.
9. Ben Jonson, *Poems*, ed. Ian Donaldson (London: Oxford University Press, 1975) 321, 326, 67. Further citations from the non-dramatic verse refer to this edition.
10. Jonas Barish, 'Jonson and the Loathèd Stage', in *A Celebration of Ben Jonson*, ed. William Blissett et al. (Toronto: University of Toronto Press, 1973) 27–53. The essay reappears, slightly modified, in Barish's *The Antitheatrical Prejudice* (Berkeley: University of California Press, 1981) 132–54.
11. Recently scholars have addressed the question of Jonson's attitude towards the homoerotic environment of the Jacobean stage. See, for example, Richmond Barbour, '"When I Acted Young Antinous": Boy Actors and the Erotics of Jonsonian Theater', *PMLA* 110 (1995): 1006–22, and Mario DiGangi, *The Homoerotics of Early Modern Drama* (Cambridge: Cambridge University Press, 1997) 67–80. In my view neither Barbour nor DiGangi is sufficiently alert to the signs that Jonson found homoerotic attraction threatening, and inflected his representations of it with obvious distaste.
12. For a similar take on the tension between 'the ideal of aloof rationality' and Jonson's 'disorderly impulses', see David Riggs, *Ben Jonson: a Life* (Cambridge, MA: Harvard University Press, 1989) 44–5.
13. *Poems* 35.
14. *Poems* 41.
15. *Jonson* 1: 142.
16. *Poems* 99.
17. *Jonson* 1: 139, 140.
18. Thomas M. Greene, 'Ben Jonson and the Centred Self', *Studies in English Literature, 1500–1900* 10 (1970): 325–48.
19. *The Complete English Poems*, ed. A.J. Smith (Harmondsworth: Penguin, 1971) 85.
20. See Alexander Leggatt's discussion of Sejanus under the rubric of 'False Creations' in *Ben Jonson: his Vision and his Art* (London: Methuen, 1981) 1–5.

21. Richard S. Peterson, 'The Iconography of Jonson's *Pleasure Reconciled to Virtue*', *Journal of Medieval and Renaissance Studies* 5 (1975): 130–1.
22. *Jonson* 8: 607.
23. Quoted by Herford and Simpson in *Jonson* 11: 255.
24. *Jonson* 8: 585.
25. *Jonson* 8: 587–8.
26. *Jonson* 8: 623.
27. *Jonson* 8: 622.
28. *Jonson* 8: 620.
29. *Poems* 154.
30. Both Barbour, 'Boy Actors' 1012–13 and DiGangi, *Homoerotics* 75–6, are in my judgement too eager to accept this apparent invitation.
31. L.C. Knights, *Drama and Society in the Age of Jonson* (London: Chatto and Windus, 1937) 200–6.
32. R.B. Parker has shown how important these alternatives are by discussing the choices made by modern directors and actors in playing the scene; see '*Volpone* in Performance: 1921–1972', *Renaissance Drama* ns 9 (1978): 158–60.
33. See Parker, '*Volpone* in Performance' 159, and especially the comment quoted here by Frank Hauser, who directed the Oxford Playhouse production in 1966: 'The point I wanted to get across in the actual staging of it was that she *is* seduced, not wholly seduced, but tempted by it.'
34. See Edward B. Partridge, *The Broken Compass: a Study of the Major Comedies of Ben Jonson* (New York: Columbia University Press, 1958) 161–77; and Jonas Barish, *Ben Jonson and the Language of Prose Comedy* (Cambridge, MA: Harvard University Press, 1960) 147–86.
35. *Jonson* 8: 625.
36. See Laura Levine, *Men in Women's Clothing: Anti-Theatricality and Effeminization, 1579–1642* (Cambridge: Cambridge University Press, 1994) 83.
37. See Karen Newman, 'City Talk: Women and Commodification in Jonson's *Epicoene*', *ELH* 56 (1989): 507–10. William W.E. Slights takes this line of argument a step further, observing that 'what Jonson repeatedly registers in *Epicoene* is a deep concern that the theatre as an institution might be having a disastrously effeminizing effect on his entire city'. See *Ben Jonson and the Art of Secrecy* (Toronto: University of Toronto Press, 1994) 99.
38. For intelligent commentary on this gesture, and on what it implies about Jonson's take on the theatrical and the erotic, see Levine, *Men in Women's Clothing* 99–100, 105–6.
39. See Barish, *Prose Comedy* 212–15.
40. The review by Gillian Reynolds (in *Plays and Players* August 1978: 16–17) does not do justice to the vitality of the production, but it includes accurate information and two fine photographs.
41. See G.R. Hibbard, 'Ben Jonson and Human Nature', in *A Celebration of Ben Jonson*, ed. William Blissett et al. (Toronto: University of Toronto Press, 1973) 78–9.

4. The adverse body: John Marston

1. *The Essayes of Michael Lord of Montaigne*, trans. John Florio (London: Dent, 1910) 3: 166.
2. *Essais de Montaigne*, ed. Maurice Rat (Paris: Garnier, 1962) 2: 364.

3. See Adage 2302, 'suus cuique crepitus bene olet', in *Opera Omnia Desiderii Erasmi Roterodami*, ed. J.H. Waszink et al. (Amsterdam: North Holland Publishing Company/Elsevier, 1969–2001) 2.5: 242.
4. Alvin Kernan is right, I believe, when he draws a link between 'the vulgarity of [Marston's] vocabulary' and 'the sense of the innate foulness of man which results from the consistent use of this kind of language'; see *The Cankered Muse: Satire of the English Renaissance*, Yale Studies in English 142 (New Haven: Yale University Press, 1959) 100, 121.
5. *The Poems of John Marston*, ed. Arnold Davenport (Liverpool: Liverpool University Press, 1961) 53–4.
6. *Poems* 52, 54, 55, 59.
7. *Poems* 66.
8. Whether to read a given text of Marston's ironically or not has in fact been a recurrent problem for his readers and critics; see T.F. Wharton, *The Critical Fall and Rise of John Marston* (Columbia, SC: Camden House, 1994) 66–83.
9. See the discussion of authorship in Melchoiri's Introduction to *The Insatiate Countess* (9–16).
10. My biographical observations are based on Davenport's Introduction to the *Poems* (5–6) and on Philip J. Finkelpearl, *John Marston of the Middle Temple: an Elizabethan Dramatist in his Social Setting* (Cambridge, MA: Harvard University Press, 1969) 256–8.
11. *Poems* 165.
12. *Poems* 113.
13. *Poems* 112, 130, 132.
14. *Poems* 154.
15. Mikhail Bakhtin, *Rabelais and his World*, trans. Helene Iswolsky (Cambridge, MA: The MIT Press, 1968) 317. For discussion of a similar pattern in relation to many other Renaissance texts, including *Othello*, see Peter Stallybrass, 'Patriarchal Territories: the Body Enclosed', *Rewriting the Renaissance: the Discourses of Sexual Difference in Early Modern Europe*, ed. Margaret W. Ferguson, Maureen Quilligan, and Nancy J. Vickers (Chicago: University of Chicago Press, 1986) 123–42.
16. *Poems* 156–7.
17. See Finkelpearl, *Marston* 179–81.
18. See Kernan, *The Cankered Muse* 215–19, and T.F. Wharton, '*The Malcontent* and "Dreams, Visions, Fantasies" ', *Essays in Criticism* 24 (1974): 268–71.
19. *Essayes* 3: 94.
20. *Essayes* 3: 96.
21. *Essayes* 3: 80.
22. *Essayes* 3: 128.
23. *Essayes* 3: 347.
24. *Essayes* 3: 363.
25. *Essayes* 3: 123.
26. The principle of motion is ubiquitous in Montaigne; see for example 'Of the Inconstancie of our Actions' (*Essayes* 2: 7–15) or the epigrammatic statement, 'being consisteth in moving and action' (*Essayes* 2: 67). See also R.A. Sayce, *The Essays of Montaigne: a Critical Exploration* (Evanston, IL: Northwestern University Press, 1972) 99, and Jean Starobinski, *Montaigne en mouvement* (Paris: Gallimard, 1982) 257.
27. *Essayes* 3: 64.

28. *Essayes* 3: 72.
29. Jean Howard, in 'Mastering Difference in *The Dutch Courtesan*', *Shakespeare Studies* 24 (1996): 105–17, has proposed that the play is an exploration of what it means to live in a culture of hybridity, that is, in a cosmopolitan city where the marketplace increasingly promotes exposure to foreign products and people. Franceschina herself, on this reading, 'is cosmopolitanism rendered monstrous' (112).
30. My position here is similar to the one taken by Theodore Spencer: 'Montaigne accepts lust and its gratifications as a natural part of humanity; to Marston lust is unnatural and obscene...Montaigne's ideas must have come to him as a considerable shock. But as usual, he showed his repulsion by fervently embracing the object that caused it.' See 'John Marston', *The Criterion* 13 (1933–34): 596.
31. Lynda E. Boose, 'The 1599 Bishops' Ban, Elizabethan Pornography, and the Sexualization of the Jacobean Stage', in *Enclosure Acts: Sexuality, Property, and Culture in Early Modern England*, ed. Richard Burt and John Michael Archer (Ithaca, NY: Cornell University Press, 1994) 193.
32. Wharton, *The Critical Fall and Rise* 100.

5. One wench between them: Thomas Heywood, Francis Beaumont and John Fletcher

1. 'Rehearsal Logbook: John Dexter Directs *A Woman Killed with Kindness*', *Plays and Players* 18 (May 1971): 14.
2. Patricia Meyer Spacks, 'Honor and Perception in *A Woman Killed with Kindness*', *Modern Language Quarterly* 20 (1959): 325.
3. R.W. Van Fossen, 'Introduction', *A Woman Killed with Kindness* xxxi.
4. Robert Ornstein, 'Bourgeois Morality and Dramatic Convention in *A Woman Killed with Kindness*', in *English Renaissance Drama: Essays in Honor of Madeleine Doran and Mark Eccles*, ed. Standish Henning, Robert Kimbrough, and Richard Knowles (Carbondale: Southern Illinois University Press, 1976) 131.
5. Laura G. Bromley, 'Domestic Conduct in *A Woman Killed with Kindness*', *Studies in English Literature, 1500–1900* 26 (1986): 268.
6. Diana E. Henderson, 'Many Mansions: Reconstructing *A Woman Killed with Kindness*', *Studies in English Literature, 1500–1900* 26 (1986): 282.
7. David Atkinson, 'An Approach to the Main Plot of Thomas Heywood's *A Woman Killed with Kindness*', *English Studies* 70 (1989): 18.
8. *English Domestic Relations, 1487–1653: a Study of Matrimony and Family Life in Theory and Practice as Revealed by the Literature, Law, and History of the Period* (New York: Columbia University Press, 1917) 204.
9. 'The Puritans and Adultery: the Act of 1650 Reconsidered', in *Puritans and Revolutionaries: Essays in Seventeenth-Century History Presented to Christopher Hill*, ed. Donald Pennington and Keith Thomas (Oxford: Clarendon, 1978) 268.
10. Sir Frederick Pollock and Frederic William Maitland, *The History of English Law before the Time of Edward I*, 2nd edn (Cambridge: Cambridge University Press, 1898) 2: 484.
11. See F.G. Emmison, *Elizabethan Life: Disorder* (Chelmsford: Essex Historical Society, 1970) 154.

12. Gayle Rubin, 'The Traffic in Women: Notes on the "Political Economy" of Sex', in *Towards an Anthropology of Women*, ed. Rayna R. Reiter (New York: Monthly Review Press, 1975) 173.

13. Eve Kosofsky Sedgwick, *Between Men: English Literature and Male Homosocial Desire* (New York: Columbia University Press, 1985) 49.

14. See Rebecca Ann Bach, 'The Homosocial Imaginary of *A Woman Killed with Kindness*', *Textual Practice* 12 (1998): 503–24; and Lyn Bennett, 'The Homosocial Economies of *A Woman Killed with Kindness*', *Renaissance and Reformation/Renaissance et Réforme* 24.2 (Spring 2002): 135–61.

15. See Rick Bowers, '*A Woman Killed with Kindness*: Plausibility on a Smaller Scale', *Studies in English Literature, 1500–1900* 24 (1984): 304.

16. William Harrison, *The Description of England*, ed. Georges Edelen (Ithaca, NY: Cornell University Press, 1968) 189.

17. See G.R. Hibbard, 'Love, Marriage and Money in Shakespeare's Theatre and Shakespeare's England', *The Elizabethan Theatre* 6 (1975): 237.

18. William Perkins, *Of Christian Oeconomie: Or a Short Survey of the Right Manner of Erecting and Ordering a Familie, According to the Scriptures*, trans. Thomas Pickering (London, 1609) I3ᵛ.

19. David Cook, '*A Woman Killed with Kindness*: an Unshakespearian Tragedy', *English Studies* 45 (1964): 360; see also John Canuteson, 'The Theme of Forgiveness in the Plot and Subplot of *A Woman Killed with Kindness*', *Renaissance Drama* ns 2 (1969): 136–8.

20. See Freda L. Townsend, 'The Artistry of Thomas Heywood's Double Plots', *Philological Quarterly* 25 (1946): 100–2; Peter Ure, 'Marriage and Domestic Drama in Heywood and Ford', *English Studies* 32 (1951): 203–7; Spacks, 'Honor and Perception' 327–30; Canuteson, 'Theme of Forgiveness' 133–9; Bromley, 'Domestic Conduct' 269–71; Henderson, 'Many Mansions' 284–5.

21. John F. Danby, *Poets on Fortune's Hill: Studies in Sidney, Shakespeare, Beaumont & Fletcher* (London: Faber, 1952) 192.

22. See William Shullenberger, '"This For the Most Wrong'd of Women": a Reappraisal of *The Maid's Tragedy*', *Renaissance Drama* 13 (1982): 147–8, and Cristina León Alfar, 'Staging the Feminine Performance of Desire: Masochism in *The Maid's Tragedy*', *Papers on Language and Literature* 31 (1995): 319.

23. René Girard, *Deceit, Desire, and the Novel: Self and Other in Literary Structure*, trans. Yvonne Freccero (Baltimore: Johns Hopkins University Press, 1965) 50–1.

24. John Aubrey, *Brief Lives*, ed. Oliver Lawson Dick (1949; Harmondsworth: Penguin, 1972) 184.

25. See Sedgwick, *Between Men*: '"Homosocial" is a word occasionally used in history and the social sciences, where it describes social bonds between persons of the same sex; it is a neologism, obviously formed by analogy with "homosexual," and just as obviously meant to be distinguished from "homosexual"' (1).

26. Of these three positions the first is taken by Coleridge (see *Coleridge's Criticism of Shakespeare*, ed. R.A. Foakes [Detroit: Wayne State University Press, 1989] 133, 169), the second by Philip J. Finkelpearl in *Court and Country Politics in the Plays of Beaumont and Fletcher* (Princeton: Princeton University Press, 1990) 196–204. I am not aware of anyone having taken the third.

27. See Gerald Eades Bentley, *The Jacobean and Caroline Stage* (Oxford: Clarendon, 1941–68) 4: 555.

28. Jeffrey Masten, *Textual Intercourse: Collaboration, Authorship, and Sexualities in Renaissance Drama* (Cambridge: Cambridge University Press, 1997) 61–2.

6. Impossible desire: John Webster

1. William Blake, *The Marriage of Heaven and Hell*, in *Complete Writings*, ed. Geoffrey Keynes (1957; London: Oxford University Press, 1966) 152.
2. Henry Fitzjeffrey, *Satyres and Satyricall Epigrams* (London, 1617) F6ᵛ.
3. See R.W. Dent, *John Webster's Borrowing* (Berkeley: University of California Press, 1960) 10, who believes it 'extremely probable' that Webster's writing exhibits 'a density of borrowings unrivalled in English literature'.
4. Dena Goldberg '"By Report": the Spectator as Voyeur in Webster's *The White Devil*', *English Literary Renaissance* 17 (1987): 71.
5. See Geoffrey Chaucer, *The Knight's Tale* (l. 1761), *The Merchant's Tale* (l. 1986), *The Squire's Tale* (l. 479), and *The Legend of Good Women* (Prologue F, l. 503), in *The Works of Geoffrey Chaucer*, ed. F.N. Robinson, 2nd edn (Boston: Houghton Mifflin, 1957) 34, 122, 132, 494.
6. The spectators too are obliged to pass judgement on Vittoria; as Catherine Belsey remarks, 'The problem for the audience is not what Vittoria has done. That has been established in I.ii. The question is rather what she *is*.' See *The Subject of Tragedy: Identity and Difference in Renaissance Drama* (London: Methuen, 1985) 162.
7. Edmund Wilson, *Europe without Baedeker: Sketches among the Ruins of Italy, Greece and England* (Garden City, NY: Doubleday, 1947) 11–12.
8. '*The Duchess of Malfi* (Haymarket)', *Punch* 2 May 1945: 382.
9. '*The Duchess of Malfi*', *New Statesman* 28 April 1945: 271.
10. Frank Whigham has posed an ingenious answer to this question, based on the view that Ferdinand is, above all else, a 'threatened aristocrat'; what appears to be incestuous desire is therefore a form of endogamy, a desire for purity pushed far enough to express itself as 'hysterical compensation'. See 'Sexual and Social Mobility in *The Duchess of Malfi*', *PMLA* 100 (1985): 169–70. I agree with Richard A. McCabe, who finds this view 'unduly prescriptive'; it's more plausible, McCabe argues, that politics (aristocratic posturing) is repressed sexuality (incest fantasies) than the other way round: 'The point, I think, is that Ferdinand is not representative of any class or social outlook, but remains imprisoned within his own private melancholy.' See *Incest, Drama and Nature's Law: 1500–1700* (Cambridge: Cambridge University Press, 1993) 251–2. Lynn Enterline, in a sustained Lacanian reading of Ferdinand's narcissistic involvement with his sister, restores the sexual tension implicit in Ferdinand's language to its defining place in this relationship: 'The notoriously lurid and excessive quality of Webster's sexual imagery prevents it from being exhausted by explanations that turn to other areas of contemporary social conflict.' See '"Hairy on the In-side": *The Duchess of Malfi* and the Body of Lycanthropy', *Yale Journal of Criticism* 7 (Fall 1994): 92.
11. The Cheek by Jowl production (1996) was a case in point: according to John Peter, Scott Handy played Ferdinand with 'a hint...of greedy adolescent incest'; see 'Keep it in the Family', *Sunday Times* 7 January 1996: 10.19. Indeed, in my view there was more than just a hint of incest in their relationship; disconcertingly, the Duchess (played by Anastasia Hille) seemed fully aware of Ferdinand's erotic obsession, and at times used gestures or extra-textual whimpers to suggest that the sexual attraction was mutual and reciprocal.
12. The legal conventions governing marriages performed '*Per verba de presenti*' (1.1.479) are outlined by Ernest Schanzer in 'The Marriage Contracts in *Measure for Measure*', *Shakespeare Survey* 13 (1960): 81–9; the context of social attitudes is the subject of Frank W. Wadsworth's article, 'Webster's *Duchess of Malfi* in the

Light of Some Contemporary Ideas on Marriage and Remarriage', *Philological Quarterly* 35 (1956): 397–407; the critical issues raised by the unusual status of this marriage are intelligently reviewed by Charles R. Forker, *Skull beneath the Skin: the Achievement of John Webster* (Carbondale: Southern Illinois University Press, 1986) 297–302.

13. Linda Woodbridge admires this scene for its 'sane naturalness' as demonstrated by 'the easy banter and mutual teasing about sex'; see *Women and the English Renaissance: Literature and the Nature of Womankind* (Urbana: University of Illinois Press, 1984) 260. Christina Luckyj praises 'the playful intimacy of the bedroom scene' and describes some of the ways in which modern productions have simulated this mood in *A Winter's Snake: Dramatic Form in the Tragedies of John Webster* (Athens, GA: University of Georgia Press, 1989) 20, 24. Edward Pechter remarks on the 'quiet and relaxed intimacy' of the scene in *What Was Shakespeare? Renaissance Plays and Changing Critical Practice* (Ithaca: Cornell University Press, 1995) 100.

14. G. Wilson Knight, 'The Duchess of Malfi', *The Malahat Review* 4 (October 1967): 88–9.

7. An art that has no name: Thomas Middleton

1. The documents from which incidents in Middleton's early life must be inferred are carefully assembled, quoted from, and commented on by Mark Eccles in 'Thomas Middleton a Poett', *Studies in Philology* 54 (1957): 516–36; see esp. 520.

2. For the documents in question see Gerald Eades Bentley, *The Jacobean and Caroline Stage* (Oxford: Clarendon, 1941–68) 4: 871.

3. 'He has no message', Eliot wrote of Middleton; 'he is merely a great recorder'. See *Selected Essays*, 3rd edn (London: Faber, 1951) 169.

4. See Margot Heinemann, *Puritanism and Theatre: Thomas Middleton and Opposition Drama under the Early Stuarts* (Cambridge: Cambridge University Press, 1980). For a succinct review of 'Middleton's credentials as a moderate Puritan' see Gary Taylor, 'Forms of Opposition: Shakespeare and Middleton', *English Literary Renaissance* 24 (1994): 289–90; for a sceptical analysis of the putative connection between Middleton and puritanism, and a consideration of 'the substantial body of evidence which weighs against such an identification', see N.W. Bawcutt, 'Was Thomas Middleton a Puritan Dramatist?' *Modern Language Review* 94 (1999): 925–39.

5. T.S. Eliot, *For Lancelot Andrewes* (London: Faber, 1928) 7.

6. *Puritanism and Theatre* 77.

7. *The Works of Thomas Middleton*, ed. A.H. Bullen (London: John C. Nimmo, 1885–86) 7: 367.

8. Here and elsewhere my discussion is indebted to Richard Levin's exposition of the structure of *A Chaste Maid* in *The Multiple Plot in English Renaissance Drama* (Chicago: University of Chicago Press, 1971) 194–202.

9. Joanne Altieri argues that the 'cost' of the various acts of repression is 'resentment, epitomized in Allwit, who expresses it in asides that alternate with his servile public complacencies'. See 'Against Moralizing Jacobean Comedy: Middleton's *Chaste Maid*', *Criticism* 30 (1988): 179.

10. Gail Kern Paster has advanced a clever interpretation of the anti-feminist rhetoric of the play, including the images of women uncontrollably secreting

bodily fluids. I agree with Paster that such rhetoric helps to situate Allwit's anxiety about his role as a man, but I have serious doubts about her implicit claim that the play as a whole (and therefore its author) is endorsing patriarchal culture; see 'Leaky Vessels: the Incontinent Women of City Comedy', *Renaissance Drama* 18 (1987): 57, 63. My own reading is much closer to that of Coppélia Kahn, who argues that in *A Chaste Maid* and in the christening scene in particular 'Middleton celebrates the female body in Bakhtin's carnival mode: a body open, fertile, perpetually flowing and growing, consuming flesh and producing it in a limitless economy which transcends Lent'; see 'Whores and Wives in Jacobean Drama', in *In Another Country: Feminist Perspectives on Renaissance Drama*, ed. Dorothea Kehler and Susan Barker (Metuchen, NJ: Scarecrow Press, 1991) 254.

11. M.C. Bradbrook, *Themes and Conventions of Elizabethan Tragedy* (Cambridge: Cambridge University Press, 1935) 227.
12. Samuel Schoenbaum, *Middleton's Tragedies: a Critical Study* (New York: Columbia University Press, 1955) 119.
13. Nicholas Brooke, *Horrid Laughter in Jacobean Tragedy* (London: Open Books, 1979) 102.
14. Heinemann, *Puritanism and Theatre* 183–4.
15. Suzanne Gossett, '"Best Men are Molded out of Faults": Marrying the Rapist in Jacobean Drama', *English Literary Renaissance* 14 (1984): 319.
16. Anthony B. Dawson, '*Women Beware Women* and the Economy of Rape', *Studies in English Literature, 1500–1900* 27 (1987): 304.
17. Ingrid Hotz-Davies, '*A Chaste Maid in Cheapside* and *Women Beware Women*: Feminism, Anti-Feminism and the Limitations of Satire', *Cahiers Elisabéthains* 39 (April 1991): 35.
18. Murray Biggs, 'Does the Duke Rape Bianca in Middleton's *Women Beware Women*?', *Notes and Queries* 44 (1997): 100.
19. Celia R. Daileader, *Eroticism on the Renaissance Stage: Transcendence, Desire, and the Limits of the Visible* (Cambridge: Cambridge University Press, 1998) 25–6.
20. See Bentley, *Jacobean and Caroline Stage* 5: 1014–18.
21. Northrop Frye, *A Natural Perspective: the Development of Shakespearean Comedy and Romance* (New York: Columbia University Press, 1965) 38.
22. See Bentley, *Jacobean and Caroline Stage* 4: 863.
23. For comment on some of these qualities see, for example, Una Ellis-Fermor, *The Jacobean Drama: an Interpretation*, 4th edn (London: Methuen, 1958) 147–8; Christopher Ricks, 'The Moral and Poetic Structure of *The Changeling*', *Essays in Criticism* 10 (1960): 296–9; and Peter Morrison, 'A Cangoun in Zombieland: Middleton's Tetratological *Changeling*', in '*Accompaninge the Players*': *Essays Celebrating Thomas Middleton, 1580–1980*, ed. Kenneth Friedenreich (New York: AMS Press, 1983) 225–9.
24. Charlotte Brontë, *Jane Eyre*, ed. Q.D. Leavis (Harmondsworth: Penguin, 1966) 281.
25. Paula Johnson, 'Dissimulation Anatomized: *The Changeling*', *Philological Quarterly* 56 (1977): 335–6. See also Michael Neil's intelligently nuanced account of the trope of secrecy in this play in *Issues of Death: Mortality and Identity in English Renaissance Tragedy* (Oxford: Clarendon, 1997) 181–97.
26. M.C. Bradbrook makes this point in *Themes and Conventions* 219; see also Richard Levin's discussion in *The Multiple Plot* 41.
27. 'Dissimulation Anatomized' 334.

28. See T.B. Tomlinson, *A Study of Elizabethan and Jacobean Tragedy* (Cambridge: Cambridge University Press, 1964) 192–6, and Swapan Chakravorty, *Society and Politics in the Plays of Thomas Middleton* (Oxford: Clarendon, 1996) 145–7.

29. In Richard Eyre's National Theatre production (1988), the setting was transposed to a Spanish slave colony of the nineteenth century, and the part of De Flores was played by a black actor (George Harris). These strategic moves made the repressiveness of the social world, the otherness of De Flores, and the shocking energy of the relationship between Beatrice-Joanna (played by Miranda Richardson) and De Flores stand out as if printed in boldface. For comment on this production, including what appears to be reluctant praise for its unusual scenography, see Peter Porter, 'Pre-echoes and Paradoxes', *Times Literary Supplement* 8 July 1988: 756.

30. See Sara Eaton's advocacy of this position in 'Beatrice-Joanna and the Rhetoric of Love in *The Changeling*', *Theatre Journal* 36 (1984): 377.

31. L.G. Salingar, '*The Changeling* and the Drama of Domestic Life', *Essays and Studies* ns 32 (1979): 92. For concurring statements of this resemblance between Jacobean life and art, see also J.L. Simmons, 'Diabolical Realism in Middleton and Rowley's *The Changeling*', *Renaissance Drama* 11 (1980): 154–62; Heinemann, *Puritanism and Theatre* 178–9; and Chakravorty, *Society and Politics* 152–4.

32. '*The Changeling* and the Drama of Domestic Life' 95.

33. See William Empson, *Some Versions of Pastoral: a Study of the Pastoral Form in Literature* (1935; Harmondsworth: Penguin, 1966) 45–8.

34. Michel Foucault, *Madness and Civilization: a History of Insanity in the Age of Reason*, trans. Richard Howard (New York: Random House, 1965) 63–4.

35. *Madness and Civilization* 48, 50.

8. Endless dreams: John Ford

1. A.C. Swinburne, *Essays and Studies*, 3rd edn. (London: Chatto & Windus, 1888) 287–8.

2. See William Simon and John H. Gagnon, 'Sexual Scripts', *Society* 22.1 (November/December 1984): 53–60.

3. T.S. Eliot, *Selected Essays*, 3rd edn (London: Faber, 1951) 201.

4. *Love's Sacrifice* often gets perfunctory treatment even from critics who are deeply interested in the very questions it raises; see for example Alan Brissenden, 'Impediments to Love: a Theme in John Ford', *Renaissance Drama* 7 (1964): 96; Reid Barbour, 'John Ford and Resolve', *Studies in Philology* 86 (1989): 358; and Kathleen McLuskie, *Renaissance Dramatists* (London: Harvester Wheatsheaf, 1989) 252–3. There are notable exceptions, among them Juliet McMaster, who declares that '*Love's Sacrifice* is an explicit pronouncement on what is central to Ford's drama, the theme of frustration'; see 'John Ford, Dramatist of Frustration', *English Studies in Canada* 1 (1975): 268.

5. The dating of Ford's plays is necessarily provisional, since the evidence is incomplete. In general I am following the conjectural scheme proposed by Gerald Eades Bentley in *The Jacobean and Caroline Stage* (Oxford: Clarendon, 1941–68) 3: 436–7, 441–2. Bentley argues that, aside from works written in collaboration, Ford's plays fall into two groups: those written during Ford's association with the King's Men (*The Lover's Melancholy*, *The Broken Heart*, and *Beauty in a Trance* [lost]), and those written for Queen Henrietta Maria's Men (*Love's Sacrifice*, '*Tis Pity*, *Perkin Warbeck*, *The Fancies Chaste and Noble*, and *The Lady's Trial*). The meagre evidence available

would suggest that Ford left the King's company for Queen Henrietta Maria's in about 1630.

6. Richard Crashaw, *The Poems: English, Latin and Greek*, ed. L.C. Martin, 2nd edn (Oxford: Clarendon, 1957) 181.

7. See Ronald Huebert, *John Ford: Baroque English Dramatist* (Montreal: McGill-Queen's University Press, 1977) 97–101. See also R.J. Kaufmann, 'Ford's "Waste Land": *The Broken Heart*', *Renaissance Drama* ns 3 (1970): 175; Anne Barton, 'Oxymoron and the Structure of Ford's *The Broken Heart*', *Essays and Studies* ns 33 (1980): 85; and William D. Dyer, 'Holding/Withholding Environments: a Psychoanalytical Approach to Ford's *The Broken Heart*', *English Literary Renaissance* 21 (1991): 401–24.

8. For the poems by Suckling and Cowley, see *Ben Jonson and the Cavalier Poets*, ed. Hugh Maclean (New York: Norton, 1974) 261–2, 265, 340; for Behn's poem see *Kissing the Rod: an Anthology of Seventeenth-Century Women's Verse*, ed. Germaine Greer et al. (London: Virago, 1988) 258–9.

9. See, for example, Ernest Schanzer, 'The Marriage Contracts in *Measure for Measure*', *Shakespeare Survey* 13 (1960): 81–9, and Alan Macfarlane, *Marriage and Love in England: Modes of Reproduction 1300–1840* (Oxford: Blackwell, 1986) 299–301. For an early and intelligent application of this line of argument to *The Broken Heart*, see Glenn H. Blayney, 'Convention, Plot, and Structure in *The Broken Heart*', *Modern Philology* 56 (1958–59): 1–9.

10. Gerard Langbaine, the first critic of Ford's drama, remarked that *'Tis Pity* 'were to be commended, did not the Author paint the incestuous Love between *Giovanni*, and his Sister *Annabella*, in too beautiful Colours'; see *An Account of the English Dramatick Poets* (Oxford, 1691) 222.

11. Eliot's description of the incestuous lovers, though rhetorically enticing, is closer to caricature than to interpretation: 'Giovanni is merely selfish and self-willed, of a temperament to want a thing the more because it is forbidden; Annabella is pliant, vacillating and negative: the one almost a monster of egotism, the other virtually a moral defective' (*Selected Essays* 198). It would be possible for actors to play the lovers in this way, but that would surely reduce the tragedy to burlesque.

12. For a similar point, see R.J. Kaufmann, 'Ford's Tragic Perspective', *Texas Studies in Literature and Language* 1 (1959–60): 533–5.

13. Studies directed towards producing socio-political readings of the play seem to me unable to cope with the beauty (and hence the danger) of the relationship between Annabella and Giovanni. Terri Clerico, in 'The Politics of Blood: John Ford's *'Tis Pity She's a Whore*', *English Literary Renaissance* 22 (1992): 405–34, seeks to 'draw *'Tis Pity* into the mainstream of cultural materialist thought' (413). To accomplish this mission, Clerico demystifies Giovanni as follows: 'The result of his training at an Italian university, Giovanni's sophistical account of incest reflects a literalism that parodies mercantile pretensions to aristocratic manners and education' (421). Valerie L. Jephson and Bruce Thomas Boehrer, in 'Mythologizing the Middle Class: *'Tis Pity She's a Whore* and the Urban Bourgeoisie', *Renaissance and Reformation/Renaissance et Réforme* ns 18 (Summer 1994): 5–28, see Ford as an arch-conservative who reacts to emergent bourgeois values (as represented by Annabella and Giovanni, among others) with derision. 'It may seem ludicrous to claim that if you reject traditional absolutist social order you will end up sleeping with your brother or sister', they write. 'But that, put unceremoniously, is the moral of Ford's play' (15).

9. Conclusion

1. Lorenzo Valla, *On Pleasure*, trans. A. Kent Hieatt and Mariotella de Panizza Lorch (New York: Abaris Books, 1977) 59.
2. See Lawrence Stone, *The Family, Sex and Marriage in England 1500–1800* (New York: Harper, 1977) 190; Alan Macfarlane, *Marriage and Love in England: Modes of Reproduction 1300–1840* (Oxford: Blackwell, 1986) 132–4; and David Cressy, *Birth, Marriage, and Death: Ritual, Religion, and the Life-Cycle in Tudor and Stuart England* (Oxford: Oxford University Press, 1997) 256.
3. Linda Woodbridge, *Women and the English Renaissance: Literature and the Nature of Womankind, 1540–1620* (Urbana: University of Illinois Press, 1984) 249.

Bibliography

Drama texts

(This list identifies the editions used for all quotations from English Renaissance plays.)

Beaumont, Francis, and John Fletcher. *The Maid's Tragedy*. Ed. T.W. Craik. The Revels Plays. Manchester: Manchester University Press, 1988.

Ford, John. *The Broken Heart*. Ed. T.J.B. Spencer. The Revels Plays. Manchester: Manchester University Press, 1980.

——. *The Chronicle History of Perkin Warbeck: a Strange Truth*. Ed. Peter Ure. The Revels Plays. London: Methuen, 1968.

——. *Love's Sacrifice*. Ed. A.T. Moore. The Revels Plays. Manchester: Manchester University Press, 2002.

——. *'Tis Pity She's a Whore*. Ed. Derek Roper. The Revels Plays. London: Methuen, 1975.

Heywood, Thomas. *A Woman Killed with Kindness*. Ed. R.W. Van Fossen. The Revels Plays. London: Methuen, 1961.

Jonson, Ben. *The Alchemist*. Ed. Alvin B. Kernan. The Yale Ben Jonson. New Haven: Yale University Press, 1974.

——. *Bartholomew Fair*. Ed. Eugene M. Waith. The Yale Ben Jonson. New Haven: Yale University Press, 1963.

——. *The Complete Masques*. Ed. Stephen Orgel. The Yale Ben Jonson. New Haven: Yale University Press, 1969.

——. *Epicoene*. Ed. Edward Partridge. The Yale Ben Jonson. New Haven: Yale University Press, 1971.

——. *Every Man in his Humor*. Ed. Gabriele Bernhard Jackson. The Yale Ben Jonson. New Haven: Yale University Press, 1969.

——. *Sejanus*. Ed. Jonas A. Barish. The Yale Ben Jonson. New Haven: Yale University Press, 1965.

——. *Volpone*. Ed. Alvin B. Kernan. The Yale Ben Jonson. New Haven: Yale University Press, 1962.

Marlowe, Christopher. *Dido Queen of Carthage* and *The Massacre at Paris*. Ed. H.J. Oliver. The Revels Plays. London: Methuen, 1968.

——. *Doctor Faustus: a 1604-Version Edition*. Ed. Michael Keefer. Peterborough, ON: Broadview, 1991.

——. *Doctor Faustus: 1604–1616*. Ed. W.W. Greg. Oxford: Clarendon, 1950.

——. *Edward the Second*. Ed. Charles R. Forker. The Revels Plays. Manchester: Manchester University Press, 1994.

——. *The Jew of Malta*. Ed. N.W. Bawcutt. The Revels Plays. Manchester: Manchester University Press, 1978.

——. *Tamburlaine the Great*. Ed. J.S. Cunningham. The Revels Plays. Manchester: Manchester University Press, 1981.

Marston, John. *Antonio and Mellida*. Ed. G.K. Hunter. Regents Renaissance Drama Series. Lincoln: University of Nebraska Press, 1965.

——. *Antonio's Revenge: the Second Part of Antonio and Mellida*. Ed. G.K. Hunter. Regents Renaissance Drama Series. Lincoln: University of Nebraska Press, 1965.

——. *The Dutch Courtesan*. Ed. M.L. Wine. Regents Renaissance Drama Series. Lincoln: University of Nebraska Press, 1965.

——. *The Fawn*. Ed. Gerald A. Smith. Regents Renaissance Drama Series. Lincoln: University of Nebraska Press, 1964.

——. *The Malcontent*. Ed. G.K. Hunter. The Revels Plays. London: Methuen, 1975.

Marston, John, Lewis Machin and William Barksted. *The Insatiate Countess*. Ed. Giorgio Melchiori. The Revels Plays. Manchester: Manchester University Press, 1984.

Middleton, Thomas. *A Chaste Maid in Cheapside*. Ed. R.B. Parker. The Revels Plays. London: Methuen, 1969.

——. *A Game at Chess*. Ed. T.H. Howard-Hill. The Revels Plays. Manchester: Manchester University Press, 1993.

——. *Michaelmas Term*. Ed. Richard Levin. Regents Renaissance Drama Series. Loncoln: University of Nebraska Press, 1966.

——. *Women Beware Women*. Ed. J.R. Mulryne. The Revels Plays. London: Methuen, 1975.

Middleton, Thomas, and William Rowley. *The Changeling*. Ed. N.W. Bawcutt. The Revels Plays. London: Methuen, 1958.

Shakespeare, William. *Hamlet*. Ed. G.R. Hibbard. The Oxford Shakespeare. Oxford: Clarendon, 1987.

——. *Othello*. Ed. E.A.J. Honigmann. The Arden Shakespeare. Walton-on-Thames: Thomas Nelson, 1997.

——. *The Tempest*. Ed. Stephen Orgel. The Oxford Shakespeare. Oxford: Clarendon, 1987.

——. *The Tragedy of Anthony and Cleopatra*. Ed. Michael Neill. The Oxford Shakespeare. Oxford: Clarendon, 1994.

——. *Twelfth Night, or What You Will*. Ed. Roger Warren and Stanley Wells. The Oxford Shakespeare. Oxford: Clarendon, 1994.

The Three Parnassus Plays. Ed. J.B. Leishman. London: Nicholson and Watson, 1949.

Webster, John. *The Devil's Law-Case*. Ed. Elizabeth M. Brennan. The New Mermaids. London: Ernest Benn, 1975.

——. *The Duchess of Malfi*. Ed. John Russell Brown. The Revels Plays. London: Methuen, 1964.

——. *The White Devil*. Ed. John Russell Brown. 2nd edn. The Revels Plays. London: Methuen, 1966.

Literary and cultural texts

Aristotle, Horace, and Longinus. *Classical Literary Criticism*. Trans. T.S. Dorsch. Harmondsworth: Penguin, 1965.

Aubrey, John. *Brief Lives*. Ed. Oliver Lawson Dick. 1949. Harmondsworth: Penguin, 1972.

Blake, William. *Complete Writings*. Ed. Geoffrey Keynes. 1957. London: Oxford University Press, 1966.

Brontë, Charlotte. *Jane Eyre*. Ed. Q.D. Leavis. Harmondsworth: Penguin, 1966.

Cartwright, William. *The Plays and Poems of William Cartwright*. Ed. G. Blakemore Evans. Madison: University of Wisconsin Press, 1951.

Chaucer, Geoffrey. *The Works of Geoffrey Chaucer*. Ed. F.N. Robinson. 2nd edn. Boston: Houghton Mifflin, 1957.

Coleridge, Samuel Taylor. *Coleridge's Criticism of Shakepeare*. Ed. R.A. Foakes. Detroit: Wayne State University Press, 1989.

Crashaw, Richard. *The Poems: English, Latin and Greek*. Ed. L.C. Martin. 2nd edn. Oxford: Clarendon, 1957.

Donne, John. *The Complete English Poems*. Ed. A.J. Smith. Harmondsworth: Penguin, 1971.

Erasmus, Desiderius. *Opera Omnia Desiderii Erasmi Roterodami*. Ed. J.H. Waszink et al. 29 vols. and in 9 pts. Amsterdam: North Holland Publishing Company/Elsevier, 1969–2001.

Fitzjeffrey, Henry. *Satyres and Satyricall Epigrams*. London, 1617.

Ford, John. *A Line of Life: Pointing to the Immortalitie of a Vertuous Name*. London, 1620.

Freud, Sigmund. *The Standard Edition of the Complete Psychological Works of Sigmund Freud*. Trans. James Strachey and Anna Freud et al. 24 vols. London: Hogarth, 1953–74.

Greer, Germaine, Susan Hastings, Veslyn Medoff, and Melinda Sansone, eds. *Kissing the Rod: an Anthology of Seventeenth-Century Women's Verse*. London: Virago, 1988.

Harrison, William. *The Description of England*. Ed. Georges Edelen. Ithaca, NY: Cornell University Press, 1968.

Jonson, Ben. *Ben Jonson*. Ed. C.H. Herford, Percy Simpson, and Evelyn Simpson. 11 vols. Oxford: Clarendon, 1925–52.

——. *Poems*. Ed. Ian Donaldson. London: Oxford University Press, 1975.

Joyce, James. *A Portrait of the Artist as a Young Man*. New York: Viking, 1964.

Kant, Immanuel. *The Critique of Judgement*. Trans. James Creed Meredith. Oxford: Clarendon, 1952.

Langbaine, Gerard. *An Account of the English Dramatick Poets*. Oxford, 1691.

Maclean, Hugh, ed. *Ben Jonson and the Cavalier Poets*. New York: Norton, 1974.

Marston, John. *The Poems of John Marston*. Ed. Arnold Davenport. Liverpool: Liverpool University Press, 1961.

Middleton, Thomas. *The Works of Thomas Middleton*. Ed. A.H. Bullen. 8 vols. London: John C. Nimmo, 1885–86.

Montaigne, Michel de. *Essais de Montaigne*. Ed. Maurice Rat. 3 vols. Paris: Garnier, 1962.

——. *The Essayes of Michael Lord of Montaigne*. Trans. John Florio. 3 vols. London: Dent, 1910.

Perkins, William. *Of Christian Oeconomie: Or a Short Survey of the Right Manner of Erecting and Ordering a Familie, According to the Scriptures*. Trans. Thomas Pickering. London, 1609.

Plato. *The Collected Dialogues of Plato*. Ed. Edith Hamilton and Huntington Cairns. Bollingen Series 71. Princeton: Princeton University Press, 1963.

Pollock, Sir Frederick, and Frederic William Maitland. *The History of English Law before the Time of Edward I*. 2nd edn. 2 vols. Cambridge: Cambridge University Press, 1898.

Valla, Lorenzo. *On Pleasure*. Trans. A. Kent Hieatt and Mariotella de Panizza Lorch. New York: Abaris Books, 1977.

Critical and scholarly texts

Alfar, Cristina León. 'Staging the Feminine Performance of Desire: Masochism in *The Maid's Tragedy*'. *Papers on Language and Literature* 31 (1995): 313–33.

Altieri, Joanne. 'Against Moralizing Jacobean Comedy: Middleton's *Chaste Maid*'. *Criticism* 30 (1988): 171–87.

Atkinson, David. 'An Approach to the Main Plot of Thomas Heywood's *A Woman Killed with Kindness*'. *English Studies* 70 (1989): 15–27.

Bach, Rebecca Ann. 'The Homosocial Imaginary of *A Woman Killed with Kindness*'. *Textual Practice* 12 (1998): 503–24.

Bakhtin, Mikhail. *Rabelais and his World*. Trans. Helene Iswolsky. Cambridge, MA: MIT Press, 1968.

Barbour, Reid. 'John Ford and Resolve'. *Studies in Philology* 86 (1989): 341–66.

Barbour, Richmond. '"When I Acted Young Antinous": Boy Actors and the Erotics of Jonsonian Theater'. *PMLA* 110 (1995): 1006–22.

Barish, Jonas. *The Antitheatrical Prejudice*. Berkeley: University of California Press, 1981.

——. *Ben Jonson and the Language of Prose Comedy*. Cambridge, MA: Harvard University Press, 1960.

——. 'Jonson and the Loathèd Stage'. In *A Celebration of Ben Jonson*. Ed. William Blissett, Julian Patrick, and R.W. Van Fossen. Toronto: University of Toronto Press, 1973. 27–53.

Bartels, Emily C. *Spectacles of Strangeness: Imperialism, Alienation, and Marlowe*. Philadelphia: University of Pennsylvania Press, 1993.

Barthes, Roland. 'The Death of the Author'. In *Image/Music/Text*. Trans. Stephen Heath. New York: Farrar, Straus and Giroux, 1977. 142–8.

——. *The Pleasure of the Text*. Trans. Richard Miller. New York: Hill and Wang, 1975.

Barton, Anne. 'Oxymoron and the Structure of Ford's *The Broken Heart*'. *Essays and Studies* ns 33 (1980): 70–94.

Bawcutt, N.W. 'Was Thomas Middleton a Puritan Dramatist?' *Modern Language Review* 94 (1999): 925–39.

Belsey, Catherine. *Desire: Love Stories in Western Culture*. Oxford: Blackwell, 1994.

——. 'Desire's Excess and the English Renaissance Theatre: *Edward II, Troilus and Cressida, Othello*'. In *Erotic Politics: Desire on the Renaissance Stage*. Ed. Susan Zimmerman. London: Routledge, 1992. 84–102.

——. *Shakespeare and the Loss of Eden: the Construction of Family Values in Early Modern Culture*. Basingstoke: Macmillan Press – now Palgrave Macmillan, 1999.

——. *The Subject of Tragedy: Identity and Difference in Renaissance Drama*. London: Methuen, 1985.

Bennett, Lyn. 'The Homosocial Economics of *A Woman Killed with Kindness*'. *Renaissance and Reformation/Renaissance et Réforme* 24.2 (Spring 2002): 136–61.

Bentley, Gerald Eades. *The Jacobean and Caroline Stage*. 7 vols. Oxford: Clarendon, 1941–68.

Biggs, Murray. 'Does the Duke Rape Bianca in Middleton's *Women Beware Women*?' *Notes and Queries* 44 (1997): 97–100.

Blayney, Glenn H. 'Convention, Plot, and Structure in *The Broken Heart*'. *Modern Philology* 56 (1958–59): 1–9.

Boose, Lynda E. 'The 1599 Bishops' Ban, Elizabethan Pornography, and the Sexualization of the Jacobean Stage'. In *Enclosure Acts: Sexuality, Property, and Culture in Early Modern England*. Ed. Richard Burt and John Michael Archer. Ithaca, NY: Cornell University Press, 1994. 185–200.

Bowers, Rick. '*A Woman Killed with Kindness*: Plausibility on a Smaller Scale'. *Studies in English Literature, 1500–1900* 24 (1984): 293–306.

Boyette, Purvis E. 'Wanton Humour and Wanton Poets: Homosexuality in Marlowe's *Edward II*'. *Tulane Studies in English* 22 (1977): 33–50.

Bradbrook, M.C. *Themes and Conventions of Elizabethan Tragedy*. Cambridge: Cambridge University Press, 1935.

Brady, Jennifer. '"Beware the Poet": Authority and Judgment in Jonson's *Epigrammes*'. *Studies in English Literature, 1500–1900* 23 (1983): 95–112.

——. 'Fear and Loathing in Marlowe's *Edward II*'. In *Sexuality and Politics in Renaissance Drama*. Ed. Carole Levin and Karen Robertson. Studies in Renaissance Literature 10. Lewiston, NY: Edwin Mellen, 1991. 175–91.

Bray, Alan. 'Homosexuality and Signs of Male Friendship in Elizabethan England'. *History Workshop Journal* 29 (1990): 1–19.
——. *Homosexuality in Renaissance England*. London: Gay Men's Press, 1982.
Bredbeck, Gregory W. *Sodomy and Interpretation: Marlowe to Milton*. Ithaca, NY: Cornell University Press, 1991.
Brissenden, Alan. 'Impediments to Love: a Theme in John Ford'. *Renaissance Drama* 7 (1964): 95–102.
Brodwin, Leonora Leet. '*Edward II*: Marlowe's Culminating Treatment of Love'. *ELH* 31 (1964): 139–55.
Bromley, Laura G. 'Domestic Conduct in *A Woman Killed with Kindness*'. *Studies in English Literature, 1500–1900* 26 (1986): 259–76.
Brooke, C.F. Tucker. *The Life of Marlowe and the Tragedy of Dido Queen of Carthage*. London: Methuen, 1930.
Brooke, Nicholas. *Horrid Laughter in Jacobean Tragedy*. London: Open Books, 1979.
——. 'Marlowe the Dramatist'. In *Elizabethan Theatre*. Ed. John Russell Brown and Bernard Harris. Stratford-upon-Avon Studies 9. London: Edward Arnold, 1966. 87–105.
Cady, Joseph. '"Masculine Love," Renaissance Writing, and the "New Invention" of Homosexuality'. In *Homosexuality in Renaissance and Enlightenment England: Literary Representations in Historical Context*. Ed. Claude J. Summers. New York: Haworth, 1992. 9–40.
Canuteson, John. 'The Theme of Forgiveness in the Plot and Subplot of *A Woman Killed with Kindness*'. *Renaissance Drama* ns 2 (1969): 123–41.
Cartelli, Thomas. *Marlowe, Shakespeare, and the Economy of Theatrical Experience*. Philadelphia: University of Pennsylvania Press, 1991.
——. 'Queer Edward II: Postmodern Sexualities and the Early Modern Subject'. In *Marlowe, History, and Sexuality: New Critical Essays on Christopher Marlowe*. Ed. Paul Whitefield White. New York: AMS Press, 1998. 213–23.
Chakravorty, Swapan. *Society and Politics in the Plays of Thomas Middleton*. Oxford: Clarendon, 1996.
Clerico, Terri. 'The Politics of Blood: John Ford's *'Tis Pity She's a Whore*'. *English Literary Renaissance* 22 (1992): 405–34.
Comensoli, Viviana. 'Homophobia and the Regulation of Desire: a Psychoanalytic Reading of Marlowe's *Edward II*'. *Journal of the History of Sexuality* 4 (1993–94): 175–200.
Connor, Steven. 'Aesthetics, Pleasure and Value'. In *The Politics of Pleasure: Aesthetics and Cultural Theory*. Ed. Stephen Regan. Buckingham: Open University Press, 1992. 203–20.
Cook, David. '*A Woman Killed with Kindness*: an Unshakespearian Tragedy'. *English Studies* 45 (1964): 353–72.
Corngold, Stanley. *Complex Pleasure: Forms of Feeling in German Literature*. Stanford: Stanford University Press, 1998.
Cressy, David. *Birth, Marriage, and Death: Ritual, Religion, and the Life-Cycle in Tudor and Stuart England*. Oxford: Oxford University Press, 1997.
Daileader, Celia R. *Eroticism on the Renaissance Stage: Transcendence, Desire, and the Limits of the Visible*. Cambridge: Cambridge University Press, 1998.
Danby, John F. *Poets on Fortune's Hill: Studies in Sidney, Shakespeare, Beaumont & Fletcher*. London: Faber, 1952.
Dawson, Anthony B. '*Women Beware Women* and the Economy of Rape'. *Studies in English Literature, 1500–1900* 27 (1987): 303–20.
Dent, R.W. *John Webster's Borrowing*. Berkeley: University of California Press, 1960.

DiGangi, Mario. *The Homoerotics of Early Modern Drama*. Cambridge: Cambridge University Press, 1997.

——. 'Marlowe, Queer Studies, and Renaissance Homoeroticism'. In *Marlowe, History, and Sexuality: New Critical Essays on Christopher Marlowe*. Ed. Paul Whitefield White. New York: AMS Press, 1998.

Dyer, William D. 'Holding/Withholding Environments: a Psychoanalytic Approach to Ford's *The Broken Heart'. English Literary Renaissance* 21 (1991): 401–24.

Eaton, Sara. 'Beatrice-Joanna and the Rhetoric of Love in *The Changeling'. Theatre Journal* 36 (1984): 371–82.

Eccles, Mark. 'Thomas Middleton a Poett'. *Studies in Philology* 54 (1957): 516–36.

Eliot, T.S. *For Lancelot Andrewes*. London: Faber, 1928.

——. *Selected Essays*. 3rd edn. London: Faber, 1951.

Ellis, Havelock. *Sexual Inversion. Studies in the Psychology of Sex* 2. 3rd edn. 1901. Philadelphia: F.A. Davis, 1928.

Ellis-Fermor, Una. *The Jacobean Drama: an Interpretation*. 4th edn. London: Methuen, 1958.

Emmison, F.G. *Elizabethan Life: Disorder*. Chelmsford: Essex Historical Society, 1970.

——. *Elizabethan Life: Morals and the Church Courts*. Chelmsford: Essex County Council, 1973.

Empson, William. *Some Versions of Pastoral: a Study of the Pastoral Form in Literature*. 1935. Harmondsworth: Penguin, 1966.

Enterline, Lynn. '"Hairy on the In-side": *The Duchess of Malfi* and the Body of Lycanthropy'. *The Yale Journal of Criticism* 7 (Fall 1994): 85–129.

Finkelpearl, Philip J. *Court and Country Politics in the Plays of Beaumont and Fletcher*. Princeton: Princeton University Press, 1990.

——. *John Marston of the Middle Temple: an Elizabethan Dramatist in his Social Setting*. Cambridge, MA: Harvard University Press, 1969.

Forker, Charles R. *Skull beneath the Skin: the Achievement of John Webster*. Carbondale: Southern Illinois University Press, 1986.

Foucault, Michel. *The History of Sexuality*, vol. 1: Introduction. Trans. Robert Hurley. New York: Random House, 1978.

——. *Madness and Civilization: a History of Insanity in the Age of Reason*. Trans. Richard Howard. New York: Random House, 1965.

——. 'What Is an Author?' Trans. Josué V. Harari. *The Foucault Reader*. Ed. Paul Rainbow. New York: Pantheon, 1984. 101–20.

Frye, Northrop. *A Natural Perspective: the Development of Shakespearean Comedy and Romance*. New York: Columbia University Press, 1965.

Gearhart, Suzanne. 'The Taming of Michel Foucault: New Historicism, Psychoanalysis, and the Subversion of Power'. *New Literary History* 28 (1997): 457–80.

Girard, René. *Deceit, Desire, and the Novel: Self and Other in Literary Structure*. Trans. Yvonne Freccero. Baltimore: Johns Hopkins University Press, 1965.

Goldberg, Dena. '"By Report": the Spectator as Voyeur in Webster's *The White Devil'. English Literary Renaissance* 17 (1987): 67–84.

Goldberg, Jonathan. *Sodometries: Renaissance Texts, Modern Sexualities*. Stanford: Stanford University Press, 1992.

——. 'Sodomy and Society: the Case of Christopher Marlowe'. *Southwest Review* 69 (1984): 371–8.

Gordon, D.J. 'Poet and Architect: the Intellectual Setting of the Quarrel between Ben Jonson and Inigo Jones'. *Journal of the Warburg and Courtauld Institutes* 12 (1949): 152–72.

Gosling, J.C.B. and C.C.W. Taylor. *The Greeks on Pleasure*. Oxford: Clarendon, 1982.

Gossett, Suzanne. '"Best Men are Molded out of Faults": Marrying the Rapist in Jacobean Drama'. *English Literary Renaissance* 14 (1984): 305–27.

Greenblatt, Stephen. *Learning to Curse: Essays in Early Modern Culture*. New York: Routledge, 1990.

——. *Renaissance Self-Fashioning: from More to Shakespeare*. Chicago: University of Chicago Press, 1980.

——. *Shakespearean Negotiations: the Circulation of Social Energy in Renaissance England*. Oxford: Clarendon, 1988.

Greene, Thomas M. 'Ben Jonson and the Centered Self'. *Studies in English Literature, 1500–1900* 10 (1970): 325–48.

Greer, Germaine. *The Female Eunuch*. New York: McGraw-Hill, 1971.

Guy-Bray, Stephen. 'Homophobia and the Depoliticising of *Edward II*'. *English Studies in Canada* 17 (1991): 125–33.

Hansen, Elizabeth. 'Against a Synechdochic Shakespeare'. In *Discontinuities: New Essays on Renaissance Literature and Criticism*. Ed. Viviana Comensoli and Paul Stevens. Toronto: University of Toronto Press, 1998. 75–95.

Hattaway, Michael. 'Christopher Marlowe: Ideology and Subversion'. In *Christopher Marlowe and English Renaissance Culture*. Ed. Daryll Grantley and Peter Roberts. Aldershot: Scolar Press, 1996. 198–228.

Heinemann, Margot. *Puritanism and Theatre: Thomas Middleton and Opposition Drama under the Early Stuarts*. Cambridge: Cambridge University Press, 1980.

Helgerson, Richard. *Self-Crowned Laureates: Spenser, Jonson, Milton, and the Literary System*. Berkeley: University of California Press, 1983.

Henderson, Diana E. 'Many Mansions: Reconstructing *A Woman Killed with Kindness*'. *Studies in English Literature, 1500–1900* 26 (1986): 277–94.

Hibbard, G.R. 'Ben Jonson and Human Nature'. In *A Celebration of Ben Jonson*. Ed. William Blissett, Julian Patrick, and R.W. Van Fossen. Toronto: University of Toronto Press, 1973. 55–81.

——. 'Love, Marriage and Money in Shakespeare's Theatre and Shakespeare's England'. *The Elizabethan Theatre* 6 (1975): 134–55.

Hotz-Davies, Ingrid. '*A Chaste Maid in Cheapside* and *Women Beware Women*: Feminism, Anti-feminism and the Limitations of Satire'. *Cahiers Elizabéthains* 39 (April 1991): 29–39.

Howard, Jean. 'Mastering Difference in *The Dutch Courtesan*'. *Shakespeare Studies* 24 (1996): 105–17.

——. *The Stage and Social Struggle in Early Modern England*. London: Routledge, 1994.

Huebert, Ronald. *John Ford: Baroque English Dramatist*. Montreal: McGill-Queen's University Press, 1977.

Jameson, Fredric. 'Pleasure: a Political Issue'. In *the Ideologies of Theory: Essays 1971–1986*. Minneapolis: University of Minnesota Press, 1988. 2: 61–74.

Jarman, Derek. *Queer Edward II*. London: British Film Institute, 1991.

Jephson, Valerie L., and Bruce Thomas Boehrer. 'Mythologizing the Middle Class: *'Tis Pity She's a Whore* and the Urban Bourgeoisie'. *Renaissance and Reformation/Renaissance et Réforme* ns 18 (Summer 1994): 5–28.

Johnson, Paula. 'Dissimulation Anatomized: *The Changeling*'. *Philological Quarterly* 56 (1977): 329–38.

Kahn, Coppélia. 'Whores and Wives in Jacobean Drama'. In *In Another Country: Feminist Perspectives on Renaissance Drama*. Ed. Dorothea Kehler and Susan Barker. Metuchen, NJ: Scarecrow Press, 1991. 246–60.

Kaufmann, R.J. 'Ford's Tragic Perspective'. *Texas Studies in Literature and Language* 1 (1959–60): 522–37.

——. 'Ford's "Waste Land": *The Broken Heart'*. *Renaissance Drama* ns 3 (1970): 167–87.

Kay, W. David. *Ben Jonson: a Literary Life*. Basingstoke: Macmillan Press – now Palgrave Macmillan, 1995.

Kelly-Gadol, Joan. 'Did Women Have a Renaissance?' In *Becoming Visible: Women in European History*. Ed. Renate Bridenthal and Claudia Koonz. Boston: Houghton Mifflin, 1977. 137–64.

Kernan, Alvin. *The Cankered Muse: Satire of the English Renaissance*. Yale Studies in English 142. New Haven: Yale University Press, 1959.

Knight, G. Wilson. '*The Duchess of Malfi'*. *The Malahat Review* 4 (October 1967): 88–113.

Knights, L.C. *Drama and Society in the Age of Jonson*. London: Chatto and Windus, 1937.

——. 'The Strange Case of Christopher Marlowe'. In *Further Explorations*. Stanford: Stanford University Press, 1965. 75–98.

Kuin, Roger. *Chamber Music: Elizabethan Sonnet Sequences and the Pleasure of Criticism*. Toronto: University of Toronto Press, 1998.

Kuriyama, Constance Brown. *Hammer or Anvil: Psychological Patterns in Christopher Marlowe's Plays*. New Brunswick, NJ: Rutgers University Press, 1980.

Lacan, Jacques. *The Four Fundamental Concepts of Psycho-Analysis*. Ed. Jacques-Alain Miller. Trans. Alan Sheridan. Harmondsworth: Penguin, 1994.

Leggatt, Alexander. *Ben Jonson: his Vision and his Art*. London: Methuen, 1981.

Levin, Harry. 'Marlowe Today'. *Tulane Drama Review* 8 (Summer 1964): 22–31.

——. *The Overreacher: a Study of Christopher Marlowe*. Cambridge, MA: Harvard University Press, 1952.

Levin, Richard. *The Multiple Plot in English Renaissance Drama*. Chicago: University of Chicago Press, 1971.

Levine, Laura. *Men in Women's Clothing: Anti-Theatricality and Effeminization, 1579–1642*. Cambridge: Cambridge University Press, 1996.

Luckyj, Christina. *A Winter's Snake: Dramatic Form in the Tragedies of John Webster*. Athens, GA: University of Georgia Press, 1989.

Macfarlane, Alan. *Marriage and Love in England: Modes of Reproduction 1300–1840*. Oxford: Blackwell, 1986.

Marcus, Leah. *Unediting the Renaissance: Shakespeare, Marlowe, Milton*. London: Routledge, 1996.

Masten, Jeffrey. *Textual Intercourse: Collaboration, Authorship, and Sexualities in Renaissance Drama*. Cambridge: Cambridge University Press, 1997.

Maus, Katharine Eisaman. *Inwardness and Theater in the English Renaissance*. Chicago: University of Chicago Press, 1995.

McAdam, Ian. *The Irony of Identity: Self and Imagination in the Drama of Christopher Marlowe*. Newark: University of Delaware Press, 1999.

McCabe, Richard A. *Incest, Drama and Nature's Law: 1500–1700*. Cambridge: Cambridge University Press, 1993.

McLuskie, Kathleen. *Renaissance Dramatists*. London: Harvester Wheatsheaf, 1989.

McMaster, Juliet. 'John Ford, Dramatist of Frustration'. *English Studies in Canada* 1 (1975): 266–79.

McMillin, Scott, and Sally-Beth MacLean. *The Queen's Men and their Plays*. Cambridge: Cambridge University Press, 1998.

Mills, L.G. 'The Meaning of *Edward II'*. *Modern Philology* 32 (1934–35): 11–31.

Morris, Brian. 'Comic Method in Marlowe's *Hero and Leander*'. In *Christopher Marlowe: Mermaid Critical Commentaries*. Ed. Brian Morris. London: Ernest Benn, 1968. 115–31.

Morrison, Peter. 'A Cangoun in Zombieland: Middleton's Tetratological *Changeling*'. In *'Accompaninge the Players': Essays Celebrating Thomas Middleton, 1580–1980*. Ed. Kenneth Friedenreich. New York: AMS Press, 1983. 219–41.

Mortimer, Raymond. '*The Duchess of Malfi*'. Review of Haymarket Production. *The New Statesman* 28 April 1945: 271.

Neely, Carol Thomas. 'Constructing the Subject: Feminist Practice and the New Renaissance Discourses'. *English Literary Renaissance* 18 (1988): 5–18.

Neill, Michael. *Issues of Death: Mortality and Identity in English Renaissance Tragedy*. Oxford: Clarendon, 1997.

Newman, Karen. 'City Talk: Women and Commodification in Jonson's *Epicoene*'. *ELH* 56 (1989): 503–18.

Nuttal, A.D. *Why Does Tragedy Give Pleasure?* Oxford: Clarendon, 1996.

Orgel, Stephen. *Impersonations: the Performance of Gender in Shakespeare's England*. Cambridge: Cambridge University Press, 1996.

Ornstein, Robert. 'Bourgeois Morality and Dramatic Convention in *A Woman Killed with Kindness*'. In *English Renaissance Drama: Essays in Honor of Madeleine Doran and Mark Eccles*. Ed. Standish Henning, Robert Kimbrough, and Richard Knowles. Carbondale: Southern Illinois University Press, 1976. 128–41.

Parker, R.B. '*Volpone* in Performance: 1921–1972'. *Renaissance Drama* ns 9 (1978): 147–73.

Partridge, Edward B. *The Broken Compass: a Study of the Major Comedies of Ben Jonson*. New York: Columbia University Press, 1958.

——. 'Jonson's Large and Unique View of Life'. *The Elizabethan Theatre* 4 (1972): 143–67.

Paster, Gail Kern. 'Leaky Vessels: the Incontinent Women of City Comedy'. *Renaissance Drama* 18 (1987): 43–65.

Pechter, Edward. 'The New Historicism and Its Discontents: Politicizing Renaissance Drama'. *PMLA* 102 (1987): 292–303.

——. *What Was Shakespeare? Renaissance Plays and Changing Critical Practice*. Ithaca, NY: Cornell University Press, 1995.

Peter, John. 'Keep it in the Family'. Review of the Cheek by Jowl Production of *The Duchess of Malfi*. *Sunday Times* 7 January 1996: 10.19.

Peterson, Richard S. 'The Iconography of Jonson's *Pleasure Reconciled to Virtue*'. *Journal of Medieval and Renaissance Studies* 5 (1975): 123–62.

Porter, Joseph A. 'Marlowe, Shakespeare, and the Canonization of Heterosexuality'. *South Atlantic Quarterly* 88 (1989): 127–47.

Porter, Peter. 'Pre-echoes and Paradoxes'. Review of the National Theatre Production of *The Changeling*. *Times Literary Supplement* 8 July 1988: 756.

Powell, Chilton Latham. *English Domestic Relations, 1487–1653: a Study of Matrimony and Family Life in Theory and Practice as Revealed by the Literature, Law, and History of the Period*. New York: Columbia University Press, 1917.

Praz, Mario. 'Christopher Marlowe'. *English Studies* 13 (1931): 209–23.

Rasmussen, Eric. *A Textual Companion to Doctor Faustus*. Manchester: Manchester University Press, 1993.

'Rehearsal Logbook: John Dexter Directs *A Woman Killed with Kindness*'. *Plays and Players* May 1971: 14–18.

Reynolds, Gillian. '*Bartholomew Fair*'. Review of the Young Vic Production. *Plays and Players* August 1978: 16–17.

Ricks, Christopher. 'The Moral and Poetic Structure of *The Changeling*'. *Essays in Criticism* 10 (1960): 290–306.

Riggs, David. *Ben Jonson: a Life*. Cambridge, MA: Harvard University Press, 1989.

Robertson, Toby (interviewed by John Russell Brown). 'Directing *Edward II*'. *Tulane Drama Review* 8 (Summer 1964): 174–83.

Rose, Mary Beth. *The Expense of Spirit: Love and Sexuality in English Renaissance Drama*. Ithaca, NY: Cornell University Press, 1988.

Rubin, Gayle. 'The Traffic in Women'. In *Towards an Anthropology of Women*. Ed. Rayna R. Reiter. New York: Monthly Review Press, 1975. 157–210.

Salingar, L.G. '*The Changeling* and the Drama of Domestic Life'. *Essays and Studies* ns 32 (1979): 80–96.

Sayce, R.A. *The Essays of Montaigne: a Critical Exploration*. Evanston, IL: Northwestern University Press, 1972.

Schanzer, Ernest. 'The Marriage Contracts in *Measure for Measure*'. *Shakespeare Survey* 13 (1960): 81–9.

Schoenbaum, Samuel. *Middleton's Tragedies: a Critical Study*. New York: Columbia University Press, 1955.

Sedgwick, Eve Kosofsky. *Between Men: English Literature and Male Homosocial Desire*. New York: Columbia University Press, 1985.

Shapiro, James. 'Recent Studies in Tudor and Stuart Drama'. *Studies in English Literature, 1500–1900* 36 (1996): 481–518.

Shklovsky, Victor. 'Art as Technique'. In *Russian Formalist Criticism: Four Essays*. Ed. and trans. Lee T. Lemon and Marion J. Reis. Lincoln: University of Nebraska Press, 1965. 3–24.

Shullenberger, William. '"This For the Most Wrong'd of Women": a Reappraisal of *The Maid's Tragedy*'. *Renaissance Drama* 13 (1982): 131–56.

Simmons, J.L. 'Diabolical Realism in Middleton and Rowley's *The Changeling*'. *Renaissance Drama* 11 (1980): 135–70.

Simon, William, and John H. Gagnon. 'Sexual Scripts'. *Society* November-December 1984: 53–60.

Slights, William W.E. *Ben Jonson and the Art of Secrecy*. Toronto: University of Toronto Press, 1994.

Smith, Bruce R. *Homosexual Desire in Shakespeare's England: a Cultural Poetics*. Chicago: University of Chicago Press, 1991.

Snow, Edward A. 'Marlowe's *Doctor Faustus* and the Ends of Desire'. In *Two Renaissance Mythmakers: Christopher Marlowe and Ben Jonson*. Ed. Alvin Kernan. Selected Papers from the English Institute ns 1. Baltimore: Johns Hopkins University Press, 1977. 70–110.

Spacks, Patricia Meyer. 'Honor and Perception in *A Woman Killed with Kindness*'. *Modern Language Quarterly* 20 (1959): 321–32.

Spencer, Theodore. 'John Marston'. *The Criterion* 13 (1933–34): 581–99.

Stallybrass, Peter. 'Patriarchal Territories: the Body Enclosed'. In *Rewriting the Renaissance: the Discourses of Sexual Difference in Early Modern Europe*. Ed. Margaret W. Ferguson, Maureen Quilligan, and Nancy J. Vickers. Chicago: University of Chicago Press, 1986. 123–42.

Starobinski, Jean. *Montaigne en mouvement*. Paris: Gallimard, 1982.

Steiner, Wendy. *The Scandal of Pleasure: Art in an Age of Fundamentalism*. Chicago: University of Chicago Press, 1995.

Stone, Lawrence. *The Family, Sex and Marriage in England, 1500–1800*. New York: Harper, 1977.

Summers, Claude J. 'Sex, Politics, and Self-Realization in *Edward II*'. In *'A Poet and a Filthy Play-Maker': New Essays on Christopher Marlowe*. Ed. Kenneth Friedenreich, Roma Gill, and Constance B. Kuriyama. New York: AMS Press, 1988. 221–40.

Swinburne, A.C. *Essays and Studies*. 3rd edn. London: Chatto and Windus, 1888.

Taylor, Gary. 'Forms of Opposition: Shakespeare and Middleton'. *English Literary Renaissance* 24 (1994): 283–314.

Thomas, Keith. 'The Puritans and Adultery: the Act of 1650 Reconsidered'. In *Puritans and Revolutionaries: Essays in Seventeenth-Century History Presented to Christopher Hill*. Ed. Donald Pennington and Keith Thomas. Oxford: Clarendon, 1978. 257–82.

Tomlinson, T.B. *A Study of Elizabethan and Jacobean Tragedy*. Cambridge: Cambridge University Press, 1964.

Townsend, Freda L. 'The Artistry of Thomas Heywood's Double Plots'. *Philological Quarterly* 25 (1946): 97–119.

Traub, Valerie. *Desire and Anxiety: Circulations of Sexuality in Shakespearean Drama*. London: Routledge, 1992.

Trewin, J.C. '*The Duchess of Malfi* (Haymarket)'. *Punch* 2 May 1945: 382.

Tromly, Fred B. *Playing with Desire: Christopher Marlowe and the Art of Tantalization*. Toronto: University of Toronto Press, 1998.

Ure, Peter. 'Marriage and Domestic Drama in Heywood and Ford'. *English Studies* 32 (1951): 200–16.

Wadsworth, Frank W. 'Webster's *Duchess of Malfi* in the Light of Some Contemporary Ideas on Marriage and Remarriage'. *Philological Quarterly* 35 (1956): 394–407.

Wernham, R.B. 'Christopher Marlowe at Flushing in 1592'. *English Historical Review* 91 (1976): 344–5.

Wharton, T.F. *The Critical Fall and Rise of John Marston*. Columbia, SC: Camden House, 1994.

——. '*The Malcontent* and "Dreams, Visions, Fantasies"'. *Essays in Criticism* 24 (1974): 261–74.

Whigham, Frank. 'Sexual and Social Mobility in *The Duchess of Malfi*'. *PMLA* 100 (1985): 167–86.

Wilson, Edmund. *Europe without Baedeker: Sketches among the Ruins of Italy, Greece, and England*. Garden City, NY: Doubleday, 1947.

Woodbridge, Linda. *Women and the English Renaissance: Literature and the Nature of Womankind, 1540–1620*. Urbana: University of Illinois Press, 1984.

Woods, Gregory. 'Body, Costume, and Desire in Christopher Marlowe'. In *Homosexuality in Renaissance and Enlightenment England: Literary Representations in Historical Context*. Ed. Claude J. Summers. New York: Haworth, 1992. 69–84.

Young, Michael B. *James VI and I and the History of Homosexuality*. Basingstoke: Macmillan Press – now Palgrave Macmillan, 2000.

Index

Printed in the United States
28319LVS00003B/20